AUSCHWITZ IN ENGLAND

A Record of a Libel Action

BY *Mavis M. Hill,* BARRISTER-AT-LAW

AND *L. Norman Williams,* BARRISTER-AT-LAW

FOREWORD BY THE RIGHT HONORABLE LORD DENNING,
Master of the Rolls

INTRODUCTION BY ALAN U. SCHWARTZ

AUSCHWITZ IN ENGLAND

A Record of a Libel Action

STEIN AND DAY / *Publishers* / New York

First published in the United States of America by Stein and Day, 1965
First published in England by MacGibbon & Kee Ltd, 1965
Library of Congress Catalog Card No. 65-16307

Printed in the United States of America

Stein and Day / Publishers / 7 East 48 Street, New York, N. Y. 10017

TO

THREE WOMEN DOCTORS

Prisoners in Block 10

Auschwitz 1943

ACKNOWLEDGEMENTS

The authors gratefully acknowledge and thank the following: The Times Publishing Company Limited for allowing them to make use of the reports which appeared in *The Times*; The Incorporated Council of Law Reporting for England and Wales for allowing them to reproduce the Report of *Dering v. Uris and Others* [*1964*] 2 W.L.R. 1298; and the Editor of the Law Reports for advising and assisting.

INTRODUCTION

THIS book is an account of a libel case which took place in England in April and May of 1964. Lawyers know that libel cases can set off sparks which turn into conflagrations. In that sense, surely this was the libel case to end them all. I doubt very much whether its significance could be overstated. It resulted in a quiet and stately English courtroom becoming the stage upon which were re-enacted atrocities perhaps among the most hideous men have ever committed.

It began with the precipitous action of one man who had served as a prisoner-doctor at Auschwitz during the Second World War and, when he began the action, was comfortably ensconced in a profitable medical practice in London. His case was technically a suit against Leon Uris, the author of *Exodus,* and his English publishers. Dr. Dering came out of obscurity to claim he had been libeled because he was referred to in the book as having performed experimental sexual surgery, without benefit of anesthetic, upon young Jewish prisoners at Auschwitz. Before the trial was over, the specter of Auschwitz descended upon that courtroom and affected everyone in it. In castrating men and removing the ovaries from women, Dr. Dering thought he did no wrong. As each victim of the Nazi horror stood up to bear witness to his shame, the legal issues in the case became entwined inexorably in the overriding moral question of whether his position was justified. It is this theme which is central also to the Eichman case and to so many of the trials of Nazis since the war.

No book, no play, no motion picture I know approaches this factual account of a libel case in communicating the extent and meaning of this unspeakable blot on our past. Beside its muted and unadorned prose, the rich colors of books like *Exodus* grow pale and fade rapidly from memory—an irony, no doubt, but only one of many with which one wrestles before one has completed the experience of this book.

Although this book is addressed to the layman, even to the lawyer as a layman, American lawyers will learn much from the manner in which the case was tried and the points of law which were raised. They will also be impressed by the skill and techniques of opposing counsel, one of whom, Lord Gardiner, is now Lord Chancellor of England. Reading this account, I was once again reminded that nowhere is human dignity more evident than in an English court of law. It is a heritage of which we can be proud, and could do better to emulate. At one point in the trial, a Polish doctor who spoke no English misunderstood a question asked him and answered in a way which brought laughter to the courtroom. The authors tell us "The Judge said that there must be no laughter while this witness was in the box, for he could not understand what we were laughing at and it might embarrass him." Clearly, in this country we have a long way to go.

More important than the process of the trial, or its outcome and the assessment of costs (which will surprise you), is the basic legal and moral issue of guilt. Although, again ironically, the question of criminal responsibility was technically not at issue, it nevertheless became the pivotal point of the case. Should a man be held responsible for criminal acts, even murder, where his refusal would result in his own death? The judges at Nuremberg, sitting amidst the rubble of Western Europe (and perhaps influenced by it), decided in the affirmative. English law says otherwise, except where murder is involved. But, as the judge in this case pointed out, the question is not new. It has haunted men through history.

Of course, in the world of men, the question never arises in a pristine state. There are always complications. There were complications in the Dering case also, and you will find much testimony and much discussion as to whether, even in Auschwitz, death was in fact the only alternative to disobedience. Most of the witnesses (many brought to England to testify, few able to testify in English) insisted that there were other alternatives. Some had actually refused to do what Dr. Dering did and had lived to tell about it. Their conclusion seems persuasive. But as they speak to us of the unspeakable, it is perhaps easy for us to try to shut out all complexity, to reduce good and evil to black and white and to let our emotions rather than our reason govern.

And yet, as this case shows, a simple answer may well be the wrong one. Justice, even with regard to basic matters, is never simple because human motives are complicated, and empathy is a less than adequate substitute for complex reality. In one sense, we can never pass judgment fairly on events we were not a party to because, being removed, we can never appreciate fully the particular circumstances which surrounded those events. But we must, and do, pass judgment, though we are given pause by other questions: Who of us shall judge? What standards can we use?

Nor, I suggest, does an appeal to "law" supply the answer. For law, despite the mysterious jargon with which it has disguised itself over the centuries, is made by men and interpreted by men and enforced by men. It is thus the creature and not the cause of man's morality. Nowhere is this more evident than in the pages of this book.

ALAN U. SCHWARTZ
New York
January, 1965

FOREWORD

IT IS strange that in the year 1964 a Judge and jury in England should have to decide the truth of what happened in a prison in Poland over twenty-one years before. Did a doctor in that prison perform operations on Jewish men and women for the purpose of experiments in sterilization?

While the trial was in progress, many thought: 'All this is too horrible. Let us turn over this page of history and forget it'. Yet the truth should be made known, if only to show how at one time a civilized country reverted to barbarism, and thus remind us of the perils that are not far away.

This book is by two of the regular Law Reporters in the Royal Courts of Justice. They are qualified members of the Bar. Much of their skill is used in reporting points of law for the regular series of *Law Reports* for the use of lawyers. But when a case of historic and social import arises, they turn their skill to a wider public. Many will know how well they perform their task. They keep to what matters, and reject what is irrelevant. They are alert to notice the interjections by the Judge, the quips of counsel, the gestures of the witness. All these touches make the proceedings come alive.

The very essence of a Law Report is to give a 'fair and accurate report' of what goes on in Court, so that people outside can know what those inside can see and hear. It can be done well, or it can be done badly. In the hands of these two, it is a work of literature equal to that of the historian or the dramatist.

Lawyers, too, will find much to profit from in this book. It is written, not by academic lawyers unfamiliar with the Courts, but by trained practitioners, familiar with all the procedure of the Courts. Many a lesson can be learnt here which cannot be found in a text book, as to pleadings in libel actions, taking money out of Court, particulars of justification, cross-examination, and the like. It might almost be headed: 'How to conduct a libel action'.

Surely a tribute must be made to the Press. As the proceedings were in open Court (save for one witness *in camera*), the newspapers were entitled to report the names and addresses of the witnesses who had suffered these grievous operations. The British Press representatives willingly agreed to keep them anonymous, and did so. We must always adhere to the principle that 'Every Court of Justice is open to every subject of the Queen', including the newspaper reporters. We have nothing to fear from open and public courts—and much to gain—so long as the Press act with such responsibility as they showed in this case.

Many are the reports of State Trials or Famous Trials. None will have greater interest or importance than this trial of the libel action of *Dering* v. *Uris and Others*.

3 August 1964 DENNING

CONTENTS

PART I: INTRODUCTORY

PART II: CASE FOR DR DERING

PART III: DEFENCE BEGINS

PART I: INTRODUCTORY

CHAPTER I

Preliminaries

SCOPE OF THE RECORD

THIS book is a record of the trial of a libel action.

The action was a civil claim for damages for defamation, brought by a sixty-one-year-old surgeon of Polish origin, Dr Wladislaw Alexander Dering, O.B.E., practising in London, against the American author, and the publishers in the United Kingdom, of *Exodus*, a very long novel about the tribulations and triumphs of the Jews in Europe and the Middle East in the twentieth century. In the novel a few pages are devoted to the appalling concentration camp set up by the Germans under Hitler at Auschwitz (Oswiecim) in Poland, where Dr Dering had been a prisoner from August 1940 to January 1944. One paragraph, consisting of a solitary sentence, described 'human guinea-pig' experiments having as their object the mass sterilization of people of Jewish blood; and in that sentence was a single reference to a doctor whose name was spelt 'Dehring'. That single reference, Dr Dering claimed, was a libel on him, and that claim led to an eighteen-day trial in the Royal Courts of Justice in the Strand, London, with a judge, a jury and five counsel.

The issues raised by the trial went far beyond the right of a man to claim compensation for damage done to his reputation by the publication of a defamatory statement; they pose for everybody basic questions of morals and ethics and human behaviour in adversity. The essence of this record is what the witnesses, counsel and the Judge said in court. From that, those issues appear.

In setting down the essentials of their own notes and observations throughout the hearing, the authors have summarized and eliminated much repetitive evidence and other material having no direct bearing on the main issues to which the trial was directed. A detailed summary of the many striking and incidental features of this unusual action forms the first part of this book, which is not a mere verbatim transcript of the evidence, and is not based on one. Some formal matters appear in the appendix.

ISSUES ON THE PLEADINGS

On 22 June 1962, Dr Dering issued a writ claiming 'damages for libel contained in page 155 of a book entitled *Exodus*', written by Mr Leon Uris, published by William Kimber & Co., Ltd., and printed by Purnell & Sons Ltd. It was followed by his Statement of Claim dated 21 December 1962. In it he stated that he was a registered medical practitioner in partnership as a general practitioner in England; that *Exodus* which was first published in 1959 had had a wide circulation throughout the United Kingdom; and that the defendants had 'falsely and maliciously written, published and printed' the following words:

> 'Here in Block X, Dr Wirthe' (*sic*) 'used women as guinea-pigs and Dr Schumann sterilized by castration and X-ray and Caluberg' (*sic*) 'removed ovaries and Dr Dehring performed seventeen thousand "experiments" in surgery without anaesthetic'.

Dr Dering claimed that the words in relation to 'Dr Dehring' referred to him, since, at the time, he was a prisoner-doctor at Auschwitz, and Dr Wirths, Dr Schumann and Clauberg were 'among his associates'. He claimed that by reason of the publication he had been gravely injured in his character, credit and reputation and in the way of his profession, and had been brought into public scandal, odium and contempt. He claimed damages against each of the defendants.

Because libel actions are costly and because it is very often possible to arrive at a sensible settlement, many such actions never come to trial; and in every legal term, the Law Reports columns of *The Times* print 'Statements in Open Court' which are in effect satisfactory settlements of libel actions. Counsel for both parties come to Court, an agreed statement is read to the Judge which indicates the substance of the libel, expresses regret by the libellers for having made an unwarranted attack on the plaintiff, and, in most cases, states that the defendants have agreed to pay a sum by way of damages and agreed costs to the plaintiff. The Judge then allows the record to be withdrawn, and the action is at an end. The plaintiff has had his name cleared in public.

There was such a statement in open court in Dr Dering's action; and on 3 May 1963 *The Times*[1] published a retraction and apology by the printers, Purnell & Sons Ltd., for printing in *Exodus* the statement that 'during the last war Dr Dering "performed seventeen thousand 'experiments' in surgery without anaesthetic" at a German concentration camp'. The printers stated that, at the time *Exodus* was first published, they were unaware of Dr Dering's existence; and that they had agreed to pay him 'a substantial sum by way of damages and an agreed sum in respect of the expense to which he had been put in this matter'. The 'sum' referred to was £500.

The printers were out of the action; but the author and publishers were not. At one time such a settlement would have brought all the proceedings against all the defendants to an end; but changes in the law, reflected in revisions of the Rules of the Supreme Court (which regulate the conduct of all proceedings in the High Court of Justice) now provide for the situation in which one defendant may withdraw,[2] as best he may, and the others may continue to defend if they wish. The author and publishers in this case chose to continue to defend.

Having stated his claim against the author and publishers, the plaintiff—Dr Dering—would have to show three things: that the words were published (that is usually not difficult where, as here, the words were in print); that they referred to him (that is sometimes more difficult); and that they were defamatory of him. Only when he has done all that does the defence have to begin to prove anything. In this case, however, when the defences of the author and publishers were delivered in December 1962 and early in 1963, those three matters were all admitted; and each defendant pleaded in identical terms one only of the various available defences to an action for libel—'justification'—that is, that the words were true or substantially true. The legal effect of that was immediately to shift to the defence the burden of proving that the words were true, and the first move was made in the pleadings by providing 'Particulars of Justification', that is, details of the facts which the defence intended to prove and rely on at the trial.

[1] See Appendix, pages 279–80. [2] See Appendix, pages 282–3 n.

The defence, having made the three admissions, went on to state that the words were true in substance and in fact, subject to exceptions; and 'Particulars of Exceptions' were set out, which in effect meant that the defence was conceding that the paragraph in *Exodus* was wrong in three respects: the defence did not seek to support the precise figure of 17,000 but still alleged that Dr Dering 'performed a very large number of "experimental" operations on both men and women'; did not allege that the operations were performed entirely without anaesthetic, but did allege that they were performed only under a painfully administered spinal anaesthetic so that the subject was conscious throughout; and 'Block 21'[1] was substituted for 'Block X'.[2] It was stated further that the defendants would, if necessary, rely on section 5 of the Defamation Act, 1952;[3] and, finally, any injury to Dr Dering's reputation was formally denied.

From the particulars then provided and from what counsel said during the trial it may be inferred that the defence at that stage was based only on information from two prisoners in Auschwitz in 1943—Dr Alina Brewda, a qualified woman doctor, and Dr Stanislaw Klodzinski, then a medical student. After that defence, with its particulars of exceptions and the first set of particulars of justification had been delivered, it would appear that the defendants and their legal advisers obtained more information, the most important source being a register of surgical operations in Block 21 at Auschwitz, which had survived and was to play a special part at the trial. As a result of legal moves and countermoves on both sides, both sets of particulars were amended in various respects.

Early on, the defence, when pressed to state the number of operations on which they relied, answered, 'A figure between one hundred and two hundred'. But what the defendants alleged by way of particulars of justification and particulars of exceptions in their final pre-trial form were in summary as follows:

There was a list of 130 numbered lines, each having a date between 5 March 1943 and 10 November 1943; an individual prisoner's number and name; and the nature of an operation in Latin, such as

[1] The prisoners' hospital Block at Auschwitz.

[2] I.e. Block 10, the 'experimental' Block.

[3] See page 249 n.

castratio, *sterilisatio*, *amputatio testis sin.*, *amputatio testis dex.*, *amputatio testis utriusque*, *ovariectomia sin.*, and *ovariectomia dex.* It included ten ovariectomies on '10.11.43'. Details were provided of ovariectomy operations on 'some ten to twelve Greek girls', all inmates of Block 10, performed 'in or about October 1943' by Dr Dering, without 'medical, physiological or other legitimate reason' and when, 'to his knowledge', some of the girls had on their backs or abdomens, or both, irradiation burns such as were likely to render any wound inflicted on them difficult or impossible to heal, and one girl had already undergone previous ovariectomy.

The mode of performing each operation was that Dr Dering, 'in the annexe of the operating theatre', injected the girl with a spinal anaesthetic while she was forcibly held down by two orderlies; that the administration of the anaesthetic, effected without any previous relatively painless injection in the proposed track of the main injection, caused great pain so that many of the girls screamed; that the girl was then carried forcibly into the theatre by the orderlies and strapped down on the operating table, tilted at an angle of about thirty degrees with the girl's head downwards; that Dr Dering 'made abdominal incisions, cut the peritoneum, inserted a forceps to lift up the uterus, placed a forceps between the tube and the ovary and cut off the ovary', which he then placed in a specimen basin beside the table; then he inserted stitches, but 'in rough and ready manner', failing to secure them properly and 'without covering the pedicle with the peritoneal flap'. Each operation lasted no more than ten minutes; a normal and proper time would have been considerably longer. There was no washing or sterilization of either instruments or appliances, nor did Dr Dering wash his hands, between each operation. During the operations he referred to notes beside him, from which he appeared to decide whether to remove a right or a left ovary. Each girl was fully conscious, though anaesthetized from the waist downwards, and was acutely distressed throughout each operation.

Dr Alina Brewda was ordered to attend and was present throughout the operations for the purpose of attempting to calm the girls. During the first operation she asked Dr Dering, 'Do you realize these girls have had irradiation quite recently, what are you doing?', and he replied that he knew all about it and was doing an ovariectomy; she said, 'The wound will never heal because of this irradiation', and he did not reply. Just before the incisions Dr Brewda asked him, 'What do you think you are doing? This is a young girl; she has already had a radiation on the ovary, so why do you operate?', and he did not reply. During the second operation she said, 'You know you are really operating on these girls as if they were corpses', and he said nothing; during a later operation on a girl with previous irradiation burns Dr Brewda said, 'Leave them alone. They are suffering enough already from the burns', and he said, 'Shut up. I have my orders. They will kill me. I have to do it'; and when she asked, 'What am I to do with these girls if they develop an internal haemorrhage?', he replied, 'Don't worry. Nothing will happen'. When a girl with a scar from a previous ovariectomy was about to be operated on, and Dr Brewda said, 'I suppose you have already removed one ovary here. You are not going to make this girl a female eunuch, are you?' he said, 'That's not your business'.

During the operations some of the girls waited within earshot of, and one or two in the annexe to, the theatre.

After the operations the girls were taken back to Block 10; one girl, aged about sixteen, died of internal haemorrhage within a few hours, a second within twenty-four hours, and a third some three days later. All were in acute pain, and there were insufficient supplies, or none, of morphia or drugs, and inadequate dressings and only paper bandages in Block 10; by the fifth day every wound in the surviving girls was wide open, necrotic, and smelling noxiously.

Dr Dering did not visit Block 10 for the first four days after the operation, despite frequent messages sent by Dr Brewda urging him to come. He visited the Block for a short period on the fifth day, when Dr Brewda showed him the girls' condition, described to him the deaths, and asked what she was to do with the other girls then, and whether he could not give her something for them; but he said nothing, and left. He never sent any medical supplies or drugs at any time, and never again visited the girls; and, 'by a date in the autumn of 1944', six surviving girls were still in bed with only partial and abnormal healing of their wounds.

On a date in 1943 in Block 21 Dr Dering performed operations on some twelve young Jews for the removal of one or both testicles, one operation being performed in the presence of a medical student prisoner Klodzinski, in less than ten minutes, the subject being conscious, though apparently anaesthetized from the waist downwards; and the testicle, after removal, was placed in a kidney-shaped bowl. Again, there was no 'medical, physiological or other legitimate reason' for the operations.

The Court was invited to infer from the conversations set out, and from 'the speed, facility and expertise' with which Dr Dering performed the operations of ovariectomy and the operation for the removal of a testicle, that the operations were experimental and that he had previously performed other similar experimental operations up to a number 'not exceeding 116 on men and up to a number not exceeding three on women'. The operations were experimental, additionally, because of their nature; because Dr Dering had made numerous admissions to Dr Brewda that they were experimental; and because on numerous occasions they were performed successively on groups of prisoners on the same day.

'HE WHO ASSERTS MUST PROVE'

Because of the admissions in the defence, that they published the words defamatory of Dr Dering, he had in effect shown all that was necessary on his part to establish a case which the defendants had to answer. He had technically no need to do more than go into court and sit back, leaving it to them, within the limits of their written defences and the two sets of particulars, and 'on the balance of probabilities', to prove their assertion that the words were true.

But that course of action has a grave disadvantage. The Court would first see the case from the point of view of the defence witnesses and first impressions may be important. Further, in any libel action where the defence is justification, the rôle of the parties may, curiously, appear to be reversed. The aggrieved citizen claiming damages for an attack on his personal and professional reputation may seem to be standing his trial, almost like the accused on a criminal charge, with the 'prosecution' (represented by the defence) seeking to prove that he is guilty. This was not 'The Trial of Dr Dering'. It was Dr Dering's own action for damages against the author and publishers on whom the burden of proving their allegations lay. Dr Dering did not have to prove that they were untrue.

However illogical it may seem, therefore, it is now the practice, particularly where grave charges are pleaded by way of justification, for the plaintiff to go into the witness box after his counsel has opened the case, so that the jury see it first through the eyes of the plaintiff, who sets up the defence allegations only for the purpose of knocking them down.

The 'charges' in this case were certainly grave. The 'experiments' referred to in the offending paragraph of *Exodus* were in the context of experiments carried out by the Germans having as their object the sterilization *en masse* of people of Jewish blood—the genocidal Nazi 'final solution of the Jewish problem'.

In 1947, similar charges had been made against Dr Dering when he was placed on the United Nations list of war criminals on the complaints of the Polish, French, and Czechoslovak Governments. An application was made for his extradition from England, and the British Government (curiously using deportation instead of extradition procedure) held him in Brixton Prison for over nineteen months while an investigation was being made into the charges. Then he was released, receiving a letter dated 30 August 1948, from the Home Office stating that the Home Secretary had 'now decided that there is not sufficient evidence to support a *prima facie* case for the surrender of Dr Dering to the Polish Government as a war criminal'. Since that time Dr Dering had spent ten years in the Colonial Medical Service, had been awarded the O.B.E., and was practising under the National Health Service in North London.

Now, in this case, similar 'charges' were being levelled at him by the defence.

There being no need for Dr Dering to file any further pleading in the action, it was clear to those who knew the state of the pleadings that his case would be opened, and he and his witnesses would be called to give evidence before the defence case was opened and their witnesses called. That is what, in fact, happened.

A PAYMENT INTO COURT

Before the action came on for hearing many steps had to be taken by the legal advisers on both sides. One step taken by the publishers was to cause complications[1] later, because the author, for whatever reason, did not take the same step. The publishers, no doubt advised by their legal representatives, estimated forty shillings as a sufficient compensation for Dr Dering, and on 19 March 1964 paid that sum into court.

[1] See Appendix, pages 282–5.

It was not always possible for the defendant to a libel action to make a payment into court before trial; but now that he is able to do so, he may to some extent guard against being ordered to pay costs by making a good guess at what a judge or jury will award to the plaintiff, and paying that estimated sum into court. That gives the plaintiff the opportunity of accepting the sum in court as sufficient, calling a halt to the action, and being sure of getting his costs up to that date. If the plaintiff goes on with the action and is awarded damages not exceeding the sum in court, he is most unlikely to be awarded any of his costs incurred 'after the date of payment in'.

The author in this case paid nothing into court. Dr Dering did not accept the forty shillings as sufficient compensation, but continued his action.

He also chose to exercise the right, now very limited in civil actions, but still available in actions for libel, of requiring his action to be tried with a jury.

The preliminaries being complete, witnesses from three continents were marshalled, documents and lists of relevant documents ('affidavits of documents') were assembled and exchanged, briefs were delivered to counsel, and *Dering* v. *Uris and Others* was printed in the Daily Cause List of actions for hearing in Queen's Bench Court II before Mr Justice Lawton and a jury on Monday 13 April 1964.

CHAPTER II

The Trial

SYNOPSIS OF THE ACTION

THE beginning of the trial was temporarily delayed. Ten men and two women were in the jury box, the court officials, the parties, counsel, solicitors, law reporters and shorthand writer were in their places, briefs and documents and books of reference were piled on the ledges and spread over the benches, the Press box was unusually full, and the court was crowded. The Judge was seated, the Associate called on the case for hearing, and Mr Colin Duncan, Q.C. for Dr Dering, rose to his feet. Then the Judge, after a short discussion with counsel, offered the jurors two grounds on which to apply for release from service on this case—'exceptional hardship' and 'if any of you lost a relative in a concentration camp'. No juror made application on either ground. The trial began.

The evidence presented on behalf of Dr Dering was given by seven witnesses: Dr Dering himself; Dr Christopher Hewer, an expert on anaesthesia; three Polish men who had been prisoners at Auschwitz; Dr Jan Grabczynski, a surgeon from Poland; and Dr Josep Mezyk, a medical practioner from Chicago, who had both been fellow prisoners with Dr Dering at Auschwitz. Dr Dering, Dr Hewer, Dr Mezyk, and one other Polish witness living in London spoke English; his other witnesses gave evidence in Polish, which was interpreted.

The evidence presented on behalf of the defendants was given by twenty-two witnesses; eight of ten women on whom ovariectomies were performed on 10 November 1943, and six men who had had testicles removed at Auschwitz in 1943; Herr Hermann Langbein, from Vienna, a political prisoner at Auschwitz; Dr Stanislaw Klodzinski, a third-year medical student when sent to Auschwitz; Dr John David Ebsworth, of London, an expert on anaesthesia; Dr Dorota Lorska, of Warsaw, a 'guinea-pig' and later prisoner-doctor at Auschwitz; Dr Alina Brewda, of London, a prisoner-doctor at Auschwitz; Professor William Charles Wallace Nixon, an expert on gynaecological surgery; Sir Brian Wellingham Windeyer, of London, an expert on radiology; and Dr Adelaide Hautval, of Paris, a prisoner-doctor at Auschwitz. Dr Ebsworth, Professor Nixon, Sir Brian Windeyer, a male witness *in camera*, and Dr Brewda gave evidence in English. The other defence witnesses gave evidence in Hebrew, Judeo-Spanish, Polish, German and French, which were interpreted.

On the calendar, twenty-three days after the trial started, eighteen continuous court sitting days, on 6 May 1964, the jury, having been in retirement for 155 minutes, returned to court and awarded Dr Dering one halfpenny damages.

Actions for libel are outside the scope of legal aid, so that a plaintiff who brings such an action, however limited his means, has to bear the costs which fall on even a successful plaintiff, and run the greater risk of costs if he loses, or wins a Pyrrhic victory, with a verdict in his favour but an award of one halfpenny damages (at present 'the smallest coin of the realm'). Dr Dering won a Pyrrhic victory. The Judge ordered him to pay the costs incurred by the author and publishers after the date when the publishers paid the forty shillings into court, leaving the parties to bear the costs each had incurred before the date.

THE REGISTER

The listed witnesses do not include the mute witness. Seldom, perhaps never, in any recorded trial of a civil action in England can a theatre register of surgical operations have been a more important witness than the Auschwitz Prison Hospital Operations Register, now preserved in the national Museum at Oswiecim in Poland. The Judge, when he entrusted it to the care of the jury as they retired to consider their verdict, described it as an historic document of the greatest value and importance, a part of Polish history which would be remembered for ever; and he adjured them to treat it with the greatest respect. 'What an awful thing it would be', he said, 'if, in pointing out one of these *casus explorativus*, some guide in Auschwitz pointed to a tea stain which had been inflicted on this register in London!'

The first such register, Dr Dering told the court, had been

started by him when he began operating in Block 21 at Auschwitz in 1941; and he said that he kept, in whole or in part, three or four. The surviving register was a folio book in a blue and green binder; and part of it was meticulously written up in a fine Italian hand which Dr Dering said was his handwriting, in neat tabulated columns, recording the operation serial number, the date, the tattooed number of the prisoner, the prisoner's surname and first name, the diagnosis in Latin medical terminology, the name of the surgeon, the name of his assistant or anaesthetist, if any, the nature of the anaesthetic administered, and, finally, the nature of the operation performed. Dr Dering also told the court that he used to write it up every evening from notes of his day's work made on pieces of paper.

The number of the first operation entered in the surviving register, in Dr Dering's handwriting, was 14,139, on 22 February 1943; the last in his hand was 18,064, on 28 August 1943; and the last entry in the book with which the court was concerned was 19,521, on 10 November 1943. After 28 August the handwriting changed, but there was the same meticulous care in the recording. No one in court identified the later handwriting. At one time Dr Dering appeared to be suggesting that that part had been fabricated at a later date because the ink was of a different colour, 'black, fresh'.

The majority of the entries, Dr Dering told the Judge in answer to specific questions with the register before him, were of minor operations—the lancing of boils and abscesses, the treatment of bruises and abrasions, the typical day-to-day surgery which must have given great relief, and was needed for patients who, as German slave workers, were suffering constant savage beatings, doing hard manual labour on a starvation diet, and living like animals in conditions of filth and overcrowding.

Among the entries, however, were the 130 operations, where he was recorded as either the surgeon or the assistant, on which the defence relied to justify the sting of the libel that Dr Dering had performed 'experiments' in surgery. Of those 130 entries forty-six were in Dr Dering's own handwriting.

The register had never been and was not, even during the trial, in the possession and control of the defendants or their legal advisers. It remained at all times in the custody and control of the Polish Government. An official from the Polish Embassy in London attended with the register daily at 10.30 a.m. and took it back to the Embassy each night. It was first put in evidence at noon on the second day of the trial, and was handled only when the evidence made it essential; for other purposes photographic copies of the relevant pages were used.

Within the four walls of the court it was the most speaking of dumb mouths. The jury were told of Dr Dering's lament, when he was held in Brixton Prison in 1947 and 1948 facing deportation as an alleged war criminal, that 'the best documents would be the surgical diary for which I cared so very much, thinking of its usefulness in the future. Alas! it disappeared.' Where the entries were in his own handwriting Dr Dering accepted them as accurate and at one point explained an 'inaccuracy'.

The register was also the basis of an intervention by the Judge. At the end of Dr Dering's re-examination, the Judge told Dr Dering to take the original register in his hands, stand up so that everyone could see him, put it on the ledge of the witness box, open it at random between the beginning and the point flagged by the Judge, and read out the English equivalents of the entries of a typical day's work in the prison operating theatre. He opened it at page 112, recording many minor operations—but towards the bottom of the page were three of the operations by Dr Dering on men with which the defence was concerned.

An entry in the register was also to his witness, Dr Grabczynski, proof beyond reasonable doubt; his attitude was 'now that I have seen the register I accept that it was so'; and he gave a brief electrifying account of seeing the register once after his 'release' by the Germans from Auschwitz early in 1944, when he said, 'Three days after the liberation of the camp in 1945 I returned to the camp and there I saw the book in the same place where it used to be'. He added that he had never seen it again until it was produced to him in court.

The defendants were not only *not* under any duty to disclose the existence of the register to Dr Dering or his advisers before the trial, but they were not in a position to produce it. They could have used it as a surprise confrontation in court. But they gave Dr Dering and his advisers the benefit of having, in advance, photographic copies of the relevant pages, so that he could know what he would or might have to meet at the trial. Dr Dering, therefore, knew that the register would be evidence, and that what he had written in it would be the subject of keen investigation and inquiry. Whether he knew that in the wake of the register would come the actual individuals identified and traced through it we do not know.

The relevance of this mute witness can hardly be over-estimated. As Lord Gardiner, Q.C. for the defence, told the jury in his opening speech, if it had not been for the register and the searches which it made possible, the trial of Dr Dering's action might have been little more than his evidence against that of Dr Brewda.

ANONYMITY

Efforts were made at all times and on all sides to respect the requests for anonymity made by the victims of the experiments at Auschwitz who had been willing to come to the court to give evidence. All the middle-aged men and women who had been the young men and girls of 1943 identified themselves not only by giving their names and present addresses but also by the silent gesture of pulling up the left sleeve and exposing the forearm, bearing the number tattooed by the Nazis, which the interpreter then read out to the court, for checking in the register and with the 130 listed operations.

The request for anonymity first arose on the second day, 14 April, when Mr Duncan was questioning Dr Dering, and a case was referred to by name. Lord Gardiner intervened to say that there were three ways of identifying the witnesses by number: by the register operation number; by the tattooed number; and by the numbers running from 1 to 130 in the particulars. It might, he said, be a great shock for the victims, if still alive, or the parent of a victim who was dead, to have to read in a newspaper that one or both sex glands had been removed. The Press always took note of any observations from the Bench on this kind of point. Mr Duncan 'entirely agreed'; and the Judge said that in his experience, once a matter of this kind had been brought to the attention of the Press, they could be relied on to use their discretion.

The subject was mentioned again on the fifth day, 17 April, when some of the witnesses were in court; and again on the sixth day, 20 April, when the first woman called by the defence went into the witness box. Lord Gardiner told the Judge that some of those whom he wished to call had said throughout that they were not prepared to go into the witness box if their names or photographs were to be in the newspapers. Of course, as the witnesses were in London, subpoenas could be served; but that would be tantamount to tricking them, and the defence could not do that.

The Judge said that he could not tell the Press what they were to do. It put Judge and Press in a very difficult position if a judge, with one breath, said that he could not give directions to the Press but that they were not to do it. 'All I can say—I have said it before, and I'll say it again—is that I, as one of Her Majesty's judges, would be appalled if any photograph or other method of identification of a witness who has been the victim of one of these appalling operations should appear in the Press which would in any way enable anybody in any part of the world to point a finger at them and say, "That is one of the people who had these awful things done to them". I cannot help thinking that, after I have expressed this view, it would be a very rash editor who published any such thing. At the same time I have got to leave it entirely to the discretion of the Press; and, from my knowledge of them, I am satisfied that I shall not be disappointed in what they do.'

A message was conveyed from the Press box to the defence solicitors and communicated to Lord Gardiner and the court, that the British Press representatives in court would preserve the witnesses' anonymity. The Judge said that the court was not in any way discouraging the Press from reporting the sufferings of the witnesses and he hoped that reporters from other countries present in court would follow the course proposed by the British Press.

Again on the ninth day, 23 April, the subject was raised—this time by the Judge, who, as soon as he sat, took the unusual course of addressing the 'Gentlemen of the Press' directly 'about the reporting of this case'. He said that the case had proceeded on the assumption that no details would be printed which could lead to identification of the witnesses; but, that morning, he had received a letter from a member of the public, calling attention to a report in a well-known newspaper, which he would not name because he had not yet had an opportunity to check whether the letter was well-founded or not. The letter said that a passage in the report gave the country, town, sex, colour of eyes, build and hair characteristics of a witness, said that she was a certain age when sent to Auschwitz, was now twenty-one years older, and referred to a child. The letter suggested that these details might be enough to enable people in the town where she lived to identify her.

'I call attention to reporting in that sort of way', said the Judge, 'because it may very well do the kind of harm which everybody in court is most anxious to avoid. Now that I have drawn attention to the dangers I am sure they will be borne in mind.'

In this record appropriate reticence has been observed, and a fictitious name, 'Marta', has been given to 'the seventh woman'.

The matter arose again, in a somewhat different way, on 27 April, when Lord Gardiner, then in the middle of questioning Dr Brewda, made a successful application for a man to give his evidence *in camera*—an unusual occurrence in a libel action. The man, he said, had read about the trial; he was employed in a quasi-professional capacity in London and had volunteered to give evidence; but he had said that, whatever might or might not appear in the newspapers, it would be 'all round London in no time' if he were to give evidence in public. The Judge said that the circumstances were so special that he would allow the evidence to be given *in camera*, but he hoped that that would not get into the practice books, since it was not at all typical.

DR GRABCZYNSKI AND THE SUPPLEMENTARY PARTICULARS

Another facet of the trial was the concern of the Judge that Dr Dering's important witness, Dr Jan Grabczynski, from Poland, should be available to give evidence on recall at the end of the defence case, should Dr Dering require his presence; and that was linked with another occurrence, very unusual in a libel action, which was that the defendants were permitted, in effect, to enlarge their case during its hearing by adding to the particulars and to deliver 'Supplementary Particulars of Justification'.

Dr Grabczynski had come to London specifically for the purpose of giving his evidence, and he had a limited visa. He gave evidence which was highly relevant to the issues raised for the jury's decision, for he had actually been present and taken part in many of the operations under inquiry. When he had given that evidence and had been cross-examined on the fifth day, 17 April, the Judge, with foresight or prescience, said that the court would like him to remain in London until the end of the hearing. Mr Duncan explained about the limited visa; and the Judge said that, though he would not order Dr Grabczynski to remain, he hoped that he would stay as long as possible. On 20 April, Mr Duncan told the Judge that, although Dr Grabczynski did not wish to appear discourteous to the court, he would be in serious trouble if he did not return; and he returned to Poland.

In any action, if there is, or is likely to be, dispute about what happened on a particular occasion, and where the defence propose to call witnesses to give evidence about what happened, it is the duty of defence counsel to give any witness for the plaintiff the opportunity of stating his version of the occasion—to 'put it to the witness' in cross-examination. If, however, through oversight or for some other reason, the defence version is not put while the plaintiff or the appropriate witness is in the witness box and the defence case has begun, the difficulty is often resolved by the Judge allowing the defence witness to give his version and then, after the defence case is closed, allowing the plaintiff or his witness to be recalled for examination and cross-examination on the particular matter. In a libel action, where the defence is justification, this is most unlikely to happen, for the particulars have set out the facts on which the defendants will rely and normally the defence is bound by those particulars.

The defendants in Dr Dering's action, however, found themselves in a most unusual situation. Many of the defence witnesses had come from overseas; statements about the evidence which they would be able to give had been taken in their own countries in their native languages by local lawyers, and had been forwarded to the defendants' legal advisers in London. The witnesses themselves arrived in England only a short time before they were to give evidence. When they were interviewed by the English solicitors, it was discovered that they could give much more detail than had originally been thought. The defendants' legal advisers considered some of that detail important and relevant, and the witnesses were asked about it at the trial; but, of course, it had not appeared in the pre-trial particulars.

The first piece of such evidence was given by 'the first man', and it was to the effect that Dr Dering had taken an active part in what were referred to as 'the semen tests' after irradiation and before surgical removal of testicles.

Mr Duncan immediately objected that not only did that allegation not appear in the particulars but that it had not been put to Dr Dering. (In fact it had been 'put to' Dr Dering in cross-examination, but he had denied any knowledge of the tests.)

The Judge thought that this evidence could have a bearing on the extent to which Dr Dering might be morally and legally responsible for what he had done, and a discussion followed. The upshot was that that allegation and any others of a similar character on which the defence wished to rely, should be put into writing in the form of supplementary particulars of justification, and it was agreed that afterwards there would be further legal argument in the absence of the jury, and that the Judge would decide whether or not the defendants should be permitted to 'deliver' the new particulars and so make them part of their case. On 23 April, legal argument took place for well over an hour.

Only one incident in the new matter directly involved Dr Grabczynski—an incident alleging an exchange of words in Polish at an operation for the removal of the remaining testicle of 'the third man', the register showing Dr Grabczynski to have been present. Of course, because it had not been known, when Dr Dering was giving evidence and being cross-examined, that this piece of evidence would be given, it had not been put to him by Lord Gardiner and for the same reason he had not put it to Dr Grabczynski.

To recall Dr Dering presented no difficulty; but Dr Grabczynski was in Poland, and to bring him back would be expensive and might be difficult. In answer to an inquiry from the Judge, Lord Gardiner said that the defendants would bear the cost of bringing Dr Grabczynski back to London if Mr Duncan should require it. The Judge then gave his ruling[1] which, he said with judicial caution, was 'somewhat unusual' in a libel action, allowing the supplementary particulars to be delivered, and Mr Duncan at once said that he would desire to bring Dr Grabczynski back.

The third man gave his evidence about the incident on 24 April.

[1] See Appendix, pages 281–2.

He stated that when he had asked Dr Dering at the moment before the operation, why he was to be operated on again, Dr Dering had said, in their common language, Polish, 'Stop barking like a dog. You will die anyway'.

The Judge then told the jury the effect of his ruling on the previous day. (The jury were never, in fact, provided with copies of the supplementary particulars, although they had the other pleadings.)

The Judge then added, with all the weight of his judicial authority that, quite conscious of what he was doing, he desired to say that, if Dr Grabczynski were willing to come back—and it was essentially a matter for him—the court would regard it as 'deplorable' if any obstacle were put in his way by the Polish authorities. He added that it was clear that the Polish authorities would want the truth to be known; and he hoped that everything possible would be done to get Dr Grabczynski here. The Judge was, in other words, if not actually warning a sovereign government against doing anything to make the doctor's return difficult or impossible, at least expressing a strong view.

The return of Dr Grabczynski was next mentioned on 28 April, when Mr Duncan told the court that his solicitors had been in communication with the doctor, who had said that, speaking for himself, he was prepared to return, but that it might take a little time to get a passport and visa. The Judge immediately offered to help; and his clerk was dispatched to inform the Foreign Office by telephone that a letter from the Judge to the Foreign Secretary would be on the way, inquiring whether the matter could be expedited with the help of the British Embassy in Warsaw.

Dr Grabczynski's possible return was mentioned on the three succeeding days; and, after Dr Dering had been recalled, had denied all recollection of the incident of the exchange of words in Polish, and had concluded his evidence on Friday, 1 May, Mr Duncan told the Judge that Dr Dering's stepdaughter, perhaps somewhat optimistically, had gone to London Airport the day before to meet such planes as had arrived from Poland; but Dr Grabczynski had not arrived. The Judge, stretching time to the limit, gave Mr Duncan until 10.30 a.m. on Monday morning, 4 May, when final speeches were to begin. They began, and the trial ended, without Dr Grabczynski having given evidence again.

'ENGLISH IS NOT YOUR MOTHER-TONGUE'

Another striking aspect of the trial was that, apart from the four independent expert witnesses, not a single witness spoke English as his or her own language. Dr Dering's command of English. save in his own specialized field of medical and surgical terms, seemed only fair: idiomatic refinements tended to escape him at first hearing; and perhaps some of the unhappy phrases he used—such as 'silly experiments'—are attributable to a limited command of English. He had the habit, common to most Slavs speaking English, of frequently omitting the definite and indefinite article, and using tenses incorrectly.

Dr Brewda, of Polish origin, also spoke English as a foreigner, though she had a good command of her adopted language and its idiom, and was little hampered in giving evidence or being cross-examined in English.

As for the rest, all but Dr Mezyk, one Pole, and the London witness *in camera*, spoke through interpreters. Yet, in retrospect and even at the time, one was not conscious of that as a disadvantage or handicap. It may be that the interpreters, who were also foreign, used words which conveyed the essence of the witnesses' answers, so that the hearer had the illusion of reality. Also the simple phrases, 'This I can never forget'; 'How could I be cheerful? I had strong pain'; 'When I look at myself I am destroyed—my whole life'; 'She was taken away in the middle of the night and I never saw her again', made a lasting mental and emotional impact.

The most arduous task fell on the interpreter from Hebrew, a kindly man, the eternal grandfather figure, who sat with his arm half round the back of the chair on which the witness was sitting, as if supporting the men or women who were having to speak of the most terrible experiences of their young days. When the luncheon adjournment arrived during cross-examination of the first woman and the Judge asked the Hebrew interpreter to see that she did not talk to anyone or allow anyone to talk to her during the adjournment, and suggested that the interpreter should 'look after her during lunch', one might have had a brief mental picture of the interpreter taking her down to the cafeteria in the crypt of the Law Courts, and advising her which, among the strange English dishes available, it would be wise for her to choose. It was he who, when 'Marta', after becoming distressed, spoke a tumble of words, interpreted what she had said by the monosyllable, 'Yes'; and who, when asked what else she had said, seemed almost regretfully to admit that she had added, 'I want vengeance'—in just the way that a loving grandfather seeks to excuse the indiscretions of his grandchild.

Another kindly grandfather figure, with an obvious delight in scholarship, was the interpreter from the native language of the Sephardi Jewesses from Greece—a language variously called in court 'Spanish-Catalan', 'Spanioli', 'Catalan', and 'Judeo-Spanish'. The interpreter was visibly pleased when the Judge showed interest in this *lingua franca* and seized the chance to explain its linguistic make-up. He, too, tended to use in translation the simple words which expressed, in a way strangely more effective than perfect English would have done, the events and emotions being interpreted.

There were two Polish interpreters, both women, one for Dr Dering's witnesses and the other for the defence. Both were efficient, as was also the interpreter from German, who was required only for the evidence of Herr Langbein.

The most frustrated of the interpreters, who had the opportunity to say only a few words, was the interpreter provided for modern Greek, sworn in to translate the evidence of 'the second woman', born in Salonika and living in the United States. He was magnificently tall, with a clear ringing voice to echo finely round the heights above the theatre at Delphi. But, first, the woman understood some English and began by answering counsel's earliest questions in English. Then, when the Judge called attention to the 'ridiculous situation' and the witness again elected to give her evidence in her native tongue (which had been understood to be 'Greek'), the interpreter was stopped dead in his tracks at her first reply; and then he told the court that the witness was speaking in a language which was not Greek and which he did not understand (it was in fact Judeo-Spanish); and he had to retire.

Then to the rescue came the amateur interpreter—the woman's husband, who had flown from California with her, was sitting in the body of the court and knew and understood both English and Judeo-Spanish. He was sworn in as an interpreter, instructed by the Judge that he should not summarize the witness' answers but give them in direct speech according to the rules of interpreting in English legal proceedings, and made an excellent job of his unexpected task—though he slipped up once, for, to the question addressed to his wife through him, 'When were you married?' he himself answered with the date, without conveying the question to his wife.

An unofficial interpreter was a Polish-speaking journalist in the Press box who helpfully translated medical phrases over which the interpreter hesitated during Dr Grabczynski's evidence in chief. The Judge said that though he was delighted to have the international Press in his court, the gentleman who, no doubt with the best will in the world, was trying to help, should observe the rules of court as to evidence being given through a sworn interpreter.

The interpreter from French, required only for the evidence of Dr Hautval, had the hardest task of all. She was youthful, small, and seemed timid, and her range of English appeared limited. Also, of course, many of those in court, and particularly the Judge, followed the evidence in French.

Anyone would have been at a disadvantage beside the calm dignity of that woman of courage and faith. Yet even through the halting phrases shone the fearless spirit of a woman who believed herself to be destined for an early and horrible death, but had resolved that 'in the short time that is left to us we should behave as human beings'.

SWEARING THE WITNESSES

Dr Dering, the first witness to be sworn, took the book from the usher and repeated the oath administered by the court associate. Then the Judge asked Dr Dering whether he was satisfied that he had taken the oath in a manner binding on him. He said that he did not mind how he took the oath; he was a Christian and a Roman Catholic—whereupon he was firmly told by the Judge that he should take the oath in the proper manner; and he was sworn again on the Douai version.

Dr Grabczynski, living and working in modern Poland, having no religious beliefs, affirmed—as also, for the same reason, did Dr Lorska, a Communist of long standing; and so did Herr Langbein.

The second woman—from California—caused consternation among the defendants' legal representatives by saying that she did not care whether she was sworn on the Old or the New Testament; but when the Judge said that would not do, and asked her religion, she took the oath on the Old Testament, as did all the other Jewish 'victims'. The English experts took the oath in the conventional Anglican manner on the New Testament.

Dr Hautval, however, was unique. As a devout Protestant, she asked to be sworn 'on the Bible'; and a large black Bible was produced for her to hold up while she undertook—perhaps superfluously—to tell nothing but the truth.

ORIGIN OF THE LIBEL

One matter which was made quite clear at an early stage of the trial, was that the substance of the reference of which Dr Dering complained at page 155 of *Exodus* had previously appeared in an earlier publication—*Underground, The Story of a People*, by Joseph Tenenbaum, published by the Philosophical Library Inc., New York, in 1952—a book which that author described in his preface as being the result of 'much research' and based to a large extent on the study of hitherto unpublished documents and individual affidavits of Jewish survivors of the anti-Nazi struggle. At pages 272–273, Mr Tenenbaum's book had a description of the camp at Auschwitz as serving also as an experimental station, with human beings used as guinea-pigs; and in referring to the experiments he, too, had a single reference to 'Dr Dehring, Professor Clauberg's assistant and one of the surgeons of the camp', and stating that 'he was a Pole'. Dr Dering said in cross-examination that he had not read Tenenbaum's *Underground* when it was published, but had seen it during the preparation of his action, and that the passage in *Exodus* had been brought to his attention some time after his return to England from Somaliland.

THE MISSING DEFENDANTS

Another unusual facet of this case was that after the printers had gone out of the action, the remaining defendants—the author and publishers—played no part in the trial itself; they did not give evidence. Having admitted the libel, they could prove nothing in regard to the issues before the jury. Of course, if substantial damages had been awarded they would have been responsible for them. They were directly interested in the verdict and in any order which the Judge in his discretion might make as to costs—in a case where the costs must have run into tens of thousands of pounds. They were present in court every day of the hearing.

MYSTERIES

There were some matters arising during the hearing which remained closed books to the end. On the ninth day of the trial the Judge mentioned that he had received 'two telegrams from Poland'; he showed them to counsel for both sides, and said that he would refrain from comment and would put their contents out of his mind. A photographed document was handed to both Dr Dering and Dr Grabczynski by Lord Gardiner; Dr Dering said that it was in German (it was dated '17 December 1943') and that he had never seen it before; and Dr Grabczynski said the same. There was the statement that the second man wanted but was not allowed to make about something which happened after his second testicle had been amputated on German orders by Dr Dering.

THE DEAD

To those who could not help but see beyond the walls of the court the larger human setting of these events, there were ghosts too—the girl Bella who died of an internal haemorrhage the night after the operation, and the other girl, Buena, who 'was screaming and crying all the time' until she, too, died a day or two later. There was the sad haunting figure of Dr Samuel, a Jewish surgeon, who had performed operations on women and girls in Block 10 for Dr Schumann's experimental purposes and on the Nazi doctors' orders; who reported Dr Hautval to the Nazi Dr Wirths for refusing to assist in such operations; who was said by all three women doctors who gave evidence to have become mentally confused and senile because of his experiences; who was, according to Dr Dering's letter, 'old and useless and covered with eczema'; and who was eventually sent to the gas chambers. Yet he, when he removed an ovary from 'Marta', had her anaesthetized with chloroform during the long operation, and as she told the court, assured her that when it was all over she would be 'like the others', meaning that she would have children like the others. There was the first family of the second man—the family which 'disappeared when he was taken to a Jewish prisoner-of-war camp after the Germans invaded Poland in 1939; Ernst Burger, Austrian resistance leader, hanged at Auschwitz on 30 December 1944; and Dr Lorska's first husband, the Czech Dr Klein, who perished in a concentration camp after the Spanish Civil War ended and the Second World War began. There were the millions who perished in the gas chambers . . .

SHADOWS

There were shadows too: the sinister shadow of Dr Horst Schumann, the doctor in *Luftwaffe* uniform, looking on, unmasked, in the 'aseptic' operating theatre, with a sign on his face 'as if after an operation', who was said to have escaped trial as a war criminal and to be now living in Ghana. There was Dr Josef Mengele, whom Dr Hautval refused to help in his experiments on Jewish twins 'conducted with unheard-of cruelty'. There was Krystyna Dering (born Ossowska), the young woman who had been a fellow student of Dr Brewda in Warsaw in the late 1920s, who married Dr Dering in the early 'thirties, who was in prison in Warsaw when her husband was 'released' from the camp to work at an outside hospital in January 1944, and who appeared again for a moment, during the cross-examination of Dr Klodzinski as a woman still living in Poland and asking questions about her former husband in a restaurant in Cracow in 1962. There was the first 'Mr G' who did not come to give evidence of identity at the Bow Street hearing on the extradition inquiry in 1948. All these are outside the scope of the record, but they were on the periphery of the action. And finally, always, there was the Goya canvas of the victims—the cluster of terrified young girls, torn from their families in the sun-bleached plains of Salonika and transported like animals to the bleak plains of Northern Europe, waiting their turn to have an ovary excised for Nazi 'experiments' without benefit of general anaesthesia; the queues of indignant and anxious young men in the corridor waiting for their turn to have a testicle removed; and behind each of the men who gave their evidence 'fifteen shadows' (operated on by Dr Dering and Dr Grabczynski) of whom nothing was heard in court save the sum totals of 'the operations on that day'.

PUBLIC AND PRESS

The action aroused widespread public interest throughout the long hearing. Every day the limited seating space was crammed and all the available standing room filled. Queues formed all day in the corridor outside the court in the hope that if someone came out someone else could be let in, the doors being kept locked under the supervision of ushers who admitted only those having some duty in court.

The Press box, too, was filled to capacity. There were the regular law service agency representatives, a body of skilled reporters who cover every case in the High Court from the news rather than the legal angle, and send out accurate and succinct reports not only 'on the tape' for the national daily newspapers, but also for regional and local newspapers and hundreds of professional and trade journals. There were also 'special' reporters and correspondents from the national and London evening papers, the weeklies and Sunday papers, as well as many foreign Press representatives.

An overall review of the day-to-day reports of this trial in the national Press illustrates the difficulty of really giving a fair and accurate contemporaneous report of legal proceedings if they last more than a day or two, in light of the generally accepted view that most news stories are 'dead' in twenty-four hours. This trial was (not surprisingly in view of its unusual interest) well covered in the national Press. On the first day it was given banner headline treatment in all the popular papers, and again for the result; on the intervening days the reports tended to be of only episodic interest on inside pages. It is possible that the urgent and repeated requests for anonymity for the victims, which the Press respected, were also a slight curb on journalists whose specialty is the personal interview (with photograph); but most of the national dailies covered the trial adequately. *The Times* Law Reports have for at least the last eighty years been in a special category in that they are prepared by barristers and edited by a legal editor, and therefore have the quasi-authoritative status of being citable to the court. The action of *Dering* v. *Uris and Others* was fully reported each day, the total space given to it amounting to well over one thousand column-inches of fine print.

The *Guardian*, which began its own series of Law Reports a year or so ago, was represented by 'Our Legal Correspondent' and the trial was intelligently treated: but the first day's report had the somewhat startling sub-head: ' "War Crimes Trial" in Britain', which illustrates how easy it is to fall into the error of regarding this action as the trial of Dr Dering. The *Daily Telegraph*, by 'Daily Telegraph Reporter', and the *Daily Worker*, had a report every day. The *Daily Express*, by its special correspondent Frank Goldsworthy, and 'Express Staff Reporter', reported the opening of the case fully and every day of evidence, and, of course, the result was well displayed. The *Daily Herald* coverage was balanced between the parties; the *Daily Mail* was generous to the opening week of the case, with many pictures of the personalities involved, but gave less space as the hearing went into a second, third, and fourth week, though it followed up the story during the week after the result. The *Daily Mirror*, which also treated the evidence for each side fairly, had the perspicacity to pick out Dr Adelaide Hautval's evidence in bold print in a prominent position on 30 April. The *Daily Sketch* started off with a full story, but had large gaps later on, as did the *Evening Standard*.

The *Evening News* on May 5 misreported Mr Duncan's 'pink herrings' (a forensic diminution of Lord Gardiner's 'red herring'), as 'pickled herrings'.

After the result, when the Press felt free to comment, almost every newspaper and every weekly and Sunday paper had special articles by way of comment and analysis. The *Sunday Times* in particular published two impressive articles, one analytical of the moral issues, and the other an account by Michael Hamlyn of 'How the Dering Dossier was Built Up'—after an interview with Mr Solomon Kaufman, the senior partner in the firm of Kaufman and Seigal who acted for Mr Uris, and who had played the most active part in the world-wide search for evidence for the defence—a story which must in itself be the material for a book; but that, like comment, is outside the scope of this record.

CHAPTER III

The Court

THE JUDGE

THE Honourable Mr Justice Lawton (Sir Frederick Horace Lawton, Kt) was raised to the Bench in 1961, having been called to the bar by Inner Temple in 1935. His conduct of the trial from start to finish was considerate and firm, but quite distinct from the aloof detachment which the judicial office connotes in some minds. He did not at any time descend into the dust of the arena, but he took part in the trial as a judge of humanity, who regarded it as his duty not only to direct the jury on questions of law but also to assist them to appreciate the dilemma of a professional man imprisoned in the 'indescribable hell of Auschwitz', whose relevant acts were to be judged by the standards, not of the saint, but of the ordinary man and woman, and according to the law of England.

He showed consideration for everyone involved in the case: for the jury, in giving them the opportunity to withdraw on exceptional grounds at the beginning, in asking counsel to state how they were putting their cases so that the jury might understand, and in explaining to the jury the relevance or irrelevance of some of the questions being put to witnesses; for the Press under unusual restraint; and for the situation with regard to Dr Grabczynski. He made sensible arrangements for a witness with an interpreter to sit at a side table on the level of the Bench while giving evidence which is always slow. He was solicitous for the comfort and convenience of everyone involved and especially those who had been subjected to what he repeatedly referred to as appalling experiences. He was inquisitorial of some of the witnesses, testing their knowledge of the languages in which they said statements had been made at the relevant time. He obviously listened to their evidence, not only as interpreted, but also as they gave it in their own languages, saying that he had understood the gist of evidence in Hebrew and Judeo-Spanish; and he actively assisted in the translation from French. He showed a human interest in the day-to-day living conditions of the prisoners, how they kept warm in Block 10 in November, what they did, how they survived.

The Judge used his judicial authority (when, on the second day Mr Duncan told him that Dr Dering had been subjected, over the telephone, to threats of physical violence) by warning anyone who attempted to prejudge this case or to interfere with the administration of justice that they would be prosecuted with the full vigour of the law; and no further threats were reported to the court.

He told the jury that he was relieved that not he but they had to judge the moral issues of blame or no blame. Yet as a person he must have formed his own view, and certainly he posed the question which everyone must have asked, 'How would I have come through such an ordeal?'

Was he surprised at the verdict?

THE JURY

The jury, ten men and two women, are shrouded in the customary anonymity of jurors. They were mostly middle aged so that one may assume that the men had done their stint of National Service or active service in the Second World War and that the women might be housewives. We know positively that none sought to be excused on grounds of exceptional hardship or because they might be unduly distressed by the subject matter for their consideration. We do not know whether any of them knew any of the foreign languages in which the evidence was given. We do not know their religion or lack of it. We do not know the details of their findings of fact, whom they believed and whom they disbelieved or discounted. We do not know the basis on which they reached their verdict. We know only the result.

During the long trial they appeared almost stolidly impassive in listening to evidence as evocative of pity and terror as any jury in a civil action must ever have had to hear in an English court of law. None were detected in any furtive wiping of the eyes with a hand or a handkerchief. They arrived on time each morning and sat cramped in their two narrow benches from 10.30 a.m. to 1 p.m. and again from 2 p.m. to 4.15 p.m. or later, having to cope with a growing pile of documents. It is not improbable that they were well aware that they were the judges of fact in an action of historic interest.

COUNSEL

Gerald Austin Gardiner was created a life baron on 23 December 1963, taking the title Lord Gardiner of Kittisford in the County of Somerset. He was 'called within the Bar' in 1948, having been called to the Bar by Inner Temple in 1925. He practised as Lord Gardiner, Q.C. (He has since become Lord Chancellor.)

Tall, thin, pale and austere, he has no histrionic tricks. He speaks quietly and quickly, his voice scarcely seeming to alter in tone or inflection, but it is a delicate and skilful instrument, and his art is that of understatement, not of declamation. He stands upright and looks directly at the person he is addressing. His only idiosyncrasy is the slow rolling up and unrolling of the 'fee-bag' string which hangs down the front of his gown. His speech in this trial was both quiet and effective, but he also resorted to colloquial expressions such as 'That was anti-Semitism, that was', and 'Hoicking out their ovaries', which caught the attention in a case of such grave import.

Peter Colin Duncan, Q.C., was called within the Bar in 1963, having been called to the Bar by Inner Temple in 1928. Shortish and neither pale nor austere, he takes the jury into his confidence, speaking rapidly, the words almost tumbling over one another. He was described by the Judge in this case as 'the Homer of that section of the English Bar concerning itself with libel'. He leans against the back of leading counsel's row and, whether making a speech or examining or cross-examining a witness, is as likely to address his remarks to the people on either side of him or behind counsel's row as the person for whom they are intended. He, too, like Lord Gardiner, has a habit of playing with his gown; he bunches it up into a bundle at his back until it begins to slip off his shoulders, and then hitches it up again and re-starts the whole process.

Mr Brian Thomas Neill, junior counsel for Dr Dering, was called to the Bar by Inner Temple in November 1949.

Mr David Couzens-Hardy Hirst, first junior counsel for the defence, was called to the Bar by Inner Temple in June 1951.

Mr Louis Jacques Blom-Cooper, second junior counsel for the defence, was called to the Bar by Middle Temple in July 1952.

'THE JURY MUST DECIDE ON THE EVIDENCE'

What the jury had to decide was whether on the evidence the defence had proved that the libel that Dr Dering performed 'seventeen thousand "experiments" in surgery without anaesthetic' was sufficiently justified by establishing what they had established of the particulars relied on in the pleadings.

Inevitably a substantial part of the evidence was directed to the mode of performance (by a Polish surgeon, assisted by another Polish surgeon, both prisoners in Auschwitz and both under the arbitrary orders of the Nazi controllers of the camp) of ten operations for ovariectomy—the excision of part of the female reproductive organ—under a local anaesthetic on an afternoon, 10 November 1943, after the subjects for operation had been submitted to irradiation for the purpose of experiments in sterilization.

Juries often have to make decisions on facts relating to matters of which the representative citizen can have little special knowledge, and it is customary for a jury—and also for a Judge sitting alone—to have assistance on such technical matters from 'expert' witnesses, whose function it is to give objective and informed opinions which the Judge or jury can then apply. In this case the expert evidence was directed to assisting the jury to determine, if necessary, whether in the state of knowledge in the early 1940s it was reasonable to fear that irradiation of the sexual organs might result in some form of cancer; whether the surgery at the operations, as spoken to by witnesses on both sides, was efficient; and whether a spinal anaesthetic was, in the circumstances of the cases, proper.

Whether the jury ever determined any of those issues is, of course, not known, for their findings are never made public.

The direct evidence about the happenings in the period of a couple of hours in the Auschwitz Prison Hospital in Block 21 was given, on the one hand, by the two Polish surgeons (Dr Dering and Dr Grabczynski) and on the other by Dr Alina Brewda (whose presence was denied by Dr Dering and admitted with qualifications by Dr Grabczynski, but who said herself that she was present throughout), and by the eight surviving victims of the experiments in irradiation and operation, all of whom testified that Dr Brewda was there, in touching phrases—'she was like a mother'; 'she consoled me'; 'she patted my cheek'.

The subject matter was to many people unbearable and shocking. It was the stuff of classic tragedy—but happening in our own time.

THE ISSUE THAT WAS NEVER DECIDED

On the fifth day of the hearing, during the evidence of Dr Grabczynski, the Judge asked Lord Gardiner whether it was his case that the mere fact that Dr Dering physically performed the operations which he had admitted performing justified the libel, 'even though he felt under duress—and justifiably so'. Lord Gardiner replied that everything done by the Germans in the last war was done by an individual, and that the International Military Tribunal at Nuremburg which had tried the war criminals had rejected the defence, 'I was told to do it by my superior German officers'.

The Judge then said, 'But these happen to be the Royal Courts of Justice, and this case is going to be dealt with by the common law of England'.

To the official law reporters that interchange bore the hallmark of a potential leading case, for whatever the jury might decide on specific questions about the facts, the Judge might overrule their effect by his decision on the law as to the extent to which duress or coercion under threat might be an answer.

On the fifteenth day, when the defence witnesses had completed their evidence (the evidence of Dr Dering on recall had been adjourned to the following day, and the jury had been told that they need not attend) the Judge and counsel considered together the way in which the issues should be put to the jury.

Lord Gardiner said that he was very anxious that nothing now submitted by him should tempt the Judge to give any direction which might be open to question on appeal, for the long-term interest of both parties was that this case should finish at this trial —a retrial would be a tragedy on both sides.[1]

When the practical questions had been agreed, Lord Gardiner

[1] If an appeal from the verdict of a jury is allowed on the ground that the Judge misdirected the jury on law or fact, neither the Court of Appeal nor the House of Lords has power to do more than order a retrial.

asked whether he might make some submissions on the question of coercion.

The Judge had already made up his mind. He said that he had read every case on coercion in English law, and supposed that Lord Gardiner had done the same; and he had the impression that the law on this subject was 'astonishingly vague'. He did not understand why treason had been deemed to be an offence to which 'duress' was not an answer. He had decided that he would do no more than point out to the jury that the law of England was vague, but that the one thing which English law had always said was that duress was no answer to murder: and that was what he told them in his summing-up, so that question of law did not arise and was not decided, and *Dering* v. *Uris and Others*, therefore, appears in the official Law Reports as a decision on two other questions.[1]

[1] See Appendix, pages 282–5.

PART II: CASE FOR DR DERING

1962.—D.—No. 1281

IN THE HIGH COURT OF JUSTICE
QUEEN'S BENCH DIVISION

Before: MR JUSTICE LAWTON and a jury

Between

WLADYSLAW ALEXANDER DERING	Plaintiff
and	
LEON URIS	First Defendant
WILLIAM KIMBER AND COMPANY LIMITED	Second Defendants

Counsel for the plaintiff:	Mr Colin Duncan Q.C. and Mr Brian Neill.
Counsel for the defendants:	Lord Gardiner Q.C., Mr David Hirst, and Mr Louis Blom-Cooper.
Solicitors for the plaintiff:	Messrs Wright & Bull.
Solicitors for the first defendant:	Messrs Kaufman & Seigal.
Solicitors for the second defendants:	Messrs Rubinstein Nash and Company.

CHAPTER IV

Opening the Case to the Jury

As Mr Colin Duncan, Q.C., leading counsel for Dr Dering, rose to open his case to the jury, Mr Justice Lawton asked Mr Duncan and Lord Gardiner how long they thought the case would last. They agreed that it must be at least three weeks.

The Judge: One other matter. I have read the pleadings. Do you think it might be advisable for me to ask the jury whether any member has lost a relative in any German concentration camp?

Mr Duncan thought Yes. Lord Gardiner demurred. 'A jury in this country', he said, 'is chosen completely at random so as to provide a cross-section of the whole community. I would not object to the question being asked, if your Lordship thinks it right. But once one starts seeking to exclude people who have feelings one way, one might include people who have feelings the other way.'

The Judge: Then I don't propose to ask it.

Mr Duncan said that he was only concerned lest the jury's feelings should be embarrassed.

Lord Gardiner: I have no objection to the jury being told the nature of the action and asked if they have any feelings about it.

The Judge then turned to the jury, and told them that jury service sometimes lay lightly on the public; but they would have to bear the burden of a case likely to last two or three weeks. If any of them thought that that would impose exceptional hardship he would listen to an application to be excused. 'Exceptional hardship', he explained, 'I regard as a man who is running a one-man business which literally has to close down if he is summoned to serve on a jury, and also a lady who is looking after young children or sick or elderly relatives, where absence from home may cause a very large measure of inconvenience. Do any of you wish to be excused on the ground of exceptional hardship?'

No member of the jury made application.

The Judge then told them that this case concerned happenings during the war in Auschwitz concentration camp. 'If any of you lost a relative in those camps and feel you might be unduly distressed by having to listen to detail', he said, 'will you please say so?'

No member of the jury said anything.

Mr Duncan rose to his feet again and addressed the jury. This action, he told them, for damages for libel, was as grave a case as had ever come before the courts in this country. There had originally been three separate defendants, but the jury were concerned with only two of them. The first was Mr Leon Uris, the author of a successful book called *Exodus*, which some of the jury might have read or heard about; and the second were the publishers of the book, Messrs William Kimber & Company Ltd.

'The third defendants', he said 'were Purnell & Sons Ltd., the printers of the book. But they have paid £500 and made an apology in court,[1] and so they can be dismissed from your minds.'

The case they had to try, Mr Duncan continued, was long, serious and bitter, and would inevitably tax their passions and harrow their feelings. The events to be investigated were not the everyday events of London in 1964 but the indescribable hell of the Nazi camp at Auschwitz some twenty years ago—one of the most nauseating chapters in human history. It was impossible to bring a proper judgment to bear on the conduct of people at that time without importing some of the atmosphere of that inferno in which innocent persons were tortured by thousands and murdered by millions, and where the last vestige of the dignity of man was drowned in squalor and bestiality. That was the background against which the jury had to form their opinion of the behaviour of the principal characters in this tragedy. This case did not fall into the category of the amusing or the fascinating. They were all there to discharge a painful duty. They must, so far as possible, put personal feelings and anything which they might have heard or read about the case out of their minds.

Dr Dering, the plaintiff, had since 1960 been a partner in a general medical practice in Finsbury Park. The book *Exodus* had been published in 1959. Dr Dering was abroad when it was pub-

[1] Strictly, the jury should not have been told this.

lished, and it only came to his notice some time later. When he did read it, he could hardly believe his eyes. Dr Dering then made his claim, which unlike that of the defence, was short and simple.

Mr Duncan read the words complained of.

> 'Here in Block X, Dr Wirthe used women as guinea-pigs and Dr Schumann sterilized by castration and X-ray and Clauberg removed ovaries and Dr Dehring performed seventeen thousand "experiments" in surgery without anaesthetic.'

The jury's first duty was to decide the ordinary meaning of the words. What *was* the ordinary and natural meaning of these words to the citizens of Finsbury Park where Dr Dering practised, or to his brother doctors up and down the country? Would not they think: 'God, How appalling: *Our* Dr Dering is one of those Nazi fiends who did such diabolical things at Auschwitz, and carried out 17,000 operations without anaesthetic on helpless victims! He must be a monster'. That should be well in the jury's mind before they heard the defence.

The defence, justification, was a complete defence, no matter how defamatory the words or what the motive for publication. The time-honoured plea was that the words were true in substance and in fact. But it was no defence to say that something *else* was true. A defendant could not wriggle out by saying, for example: 'I admit I called the plaintiff a murderer. The words are true in substance and in fact with this exception, that I need only prove that he was once involved in a brawl'. That might sound like *Alice in Wonderland*; but that, or something like it, was what the defendants were trying to say in this case.

'I am telling you', said Mr Duncan, 'that there is no defence whatever to Dr Dering's claim; and the only question is: What is the proper sum to award as damages?'

The defences of both the defendants left in the fight were the same. The defence could not rely on anything other than the 'particulars of justification' except with leave of the court. There were also 'particulars of exceptions'. The particulars of justification and the particulars of exceptions, meant, Mr Duncan supposed, particulars of words that were true and particulars of words that were not true.

The exceptions were, first: while alleging a very large number of operations, the defendants did not seek to support the precise figure of 17,000. Comment on that would be reserved for the moment. Secondly: while alleging that Dr Dering performed the operations under only a spinal anaesthetic so that the subject was conscious throughout, they did not allege that the operations were performed entirely without anaesthetic. That was, presumably, to give the impression that the anaesthesia was in some way improper. Thirdly: the defence said that the operations took place in the operating theatre in Block 21 and not in Block 10.

'I do not wish to appear cynical or facetious', said Mr Duncan, 'but it is no defence to plead that the words are true and then give particulars saying that the words are not true.'

The words complained of were '17,000', and the defence said: 'Well, that is true, except that we don't rely on the precise figure of 17,000'; and when Dr Dering wanted to know what they were talking about, they said: 'Between 100 and 200'.

Then they had been ordered to give particulars about the allegation that the operations were 'experimental' and the nature of the operation on each patient. Of course, there was nothing defamatory in saying that a surgeon had carried out 100 operations, for that was his job. What made it defamatory was to say that he had carried out 'experimental' operations, and in the context of 'guinea-pigs'. That was the sting. The answers had been given in the further and better particulars of the defence.[1]

'You will see, members of the jury', said Mr Duncan, 'that we have now arrived at a figure of 130 as a "gloss" on the 17,000 originally stated.' Dr Dering would say that many of the particulars were untrue.

From the libel alone, the ordinary reader of these words would never guess the first important fact, which was that Dr Dering was not and never had been a Nazi or a German. The company in which he appeared in the paragraph—the other names mentioned—were German doctors at the camp. But there was nothing to tell the casual reader that Dr Dering, whom they might know as a doctor practising in Finsbury Park, had himself come to Auschwitz as a prisoner, and was subjected to all its indignities and horrors, and was not an 'experimental' surgeon.

Dr Dering was a Pole. He had received his medical education at

[1] See pages 18–21.

Warsaw University, qualifying in 1928, and practised as a surgeon specializing in gynaecology and obstetrics until the war started in 1939. When Warsaw was occupied by the Germans, he became a member of the underground army. In July 1940 he was arrested by the Gestapo, and on 15 August was transferred to Auschwitz, the scene of all this misery. At first he was put to work as a labourer, and shortly afterwards was admitted to hospital with dysentery.

When it was discovered that he was a doctor and a surgeon he was made to work as an orderly—and the jury would hear what beastliness that involved—for the best part of a year. In July or August 1941, he had been made a prisoner-doctor and put in charge of the operating theatre in Block 21.

He welcomed that appointment, because at the time there were no qualified surgeons at all; and while he held it he did perform or assist at an almost astronomical number of operations—17,000 to 20,000. But they were proper, necessary, operations on his suffering fellow-prisoners. By his skill and courage thousands had been relieved from worse agonies than death. And now, in 1964, the jury were concerned only with something like 130 operations which were said to be not ordinary proper operations.

In that camp, if prisoners did not obey, they were 'punished'. That word was a gross understatement; for persons who did not obey even trivial orders were 'liquidated' or murdered. 'With the spring trickling through the windows of this court in 1964' Mr Duncan continued, 'it is difficult but necessary for us to put ourselves into the horror and stench of that prison where the prisoners did what they were told—or else. . . .'

A very significant feature of this case was that proper operation registers had been kept—as in a properly conducted hospital—and happily, though surprisingly, some of these registers had survived to the present day. The jury would see them in due course. Many of the entries in them were in Dr Dering's own hand; but *he* did not have the registers. It was the defence which had produced them, as they were bound to do.

Lord Gardiner intervened to say that the registers had come from Poland.

'Anyway', Mr Duncan retorted, 'they are available now; and when you see them, you will understand the nature of each operation described in the register, and judge for yourselves whether the

17,000 operations were "experimental" or not. I say to you that not one single operation was performed other than with a perfectly proper anaesthetic properly administered.'

In August 1943, Dr Dering had been put in charge of the whole camp hospital. After that date he performed operations only rarely, and then only major operations. In January 1944, he was removed from Auschwitz to a hospital outside the camp. That move had not been initiated by him. He had been sent as a prisoner, under orders.

While Dr Dering was at Auschwitz he had been second-in-command of the underground movement in the camp—the national resistance movement—and had managed to get extra medical supplies and food for his fellow prisoners, irrespective of their race or creed. At appalling risk to himself and under these ghastly conditions he used to hide his patients to avoid their being sent to the gas chambers. He saved no one knew how many lives. And this was the man now depicted as a monster and stood up in a rogues' gallery with the German doctors in that short paragraph, as though he were in league with them!

Dr Dering's history after the end of the war was also not uninteresting. He had first been captured by the Russians and imprisoned for eight days, and then released. He came to England in August 1946, and worked at the Polish General Hospital in Huntingdon.

Then in 1947 there had been a grim episode. His extradition to Poland as a war criminal was demanded. He was arrested and put into Brixton Prison where he remained for nineteen and a half months while an investigation was made into charges—false charges, the jury might think—against him. At the end, the responsible authorities held that there was no *prima facie* case against him, and he was released, and received a letter of apology from the Home Secretary.

Maybe he thought that that was the end of the disgraceful suggestions. At any rate he went on with his professional career and later obtained a post as medical officer in the Colonial Service and worked for ten years in Somaliland, finishing up as Senior Medical Officer (Surgical). He returned to England in 1960 and was awarded the O.B.E. for his services—a somewhat strange decoration for a 'war criminal'! There seemed no reason why he should not continue to enjoy the reputation he had earned and the good name to which he was clearly entitled. But it was not to be. It could only have been with the gravest distaste that Dr Dering had caused to be raised again the horrible memories of the past. But what was he to do? What could he do other than come before an English jury and say: 'This is untrue', and ask them to clear his name for him in the only way a jury could clear his name?

Mr Duncan then took the jury paragraph by paragraph through the particulars of justification.[1]

Dr Dering would say that no doubt he assisted in the ovariectomy operations on ten to twelve Greek girls aged between fifteen and nineteen years; and there was the register to show which he performed. But he would tell them two things: first, that he never carried out any 'experimental' operations whatever. If that were true, the jury might think that was an end of the case. And second, that he never carried out any single operation without an anaesthetic. If that were correct, the jury might think *that* was an end of the case.

That did not mean, however, that experiments were not being carried out by the Germans. There was no doubt that at one period the Germans decided to carry out experiments on both male and female persons by the use of X-rays on their genital organs, to find out the dose which would produce sterility. That having been done without, of course, consulting Dr Dering, they were sent to the operating theatre in Block 21 to have the defiled organs removed for further experiments.

On the medical aspect, opinions about the effect of X-rays were different in 1943 and 1963; and in 1943 it was clearly in Dr Dering's mind that to leave irradiated organs unremoved would mean grave risk to the health and even the life of the person so treated. He would say that, if he had been back in Warsaw in 1938 or 1939 and had found patients so irradiated, he would have advised removal. He was correcting the evil effects of other people's experiments.

There was also the factual aspect. In Auschwitz, if you were ordered to carry out an operation, either you did it or you were bumped off. What was the right thing for anybody in his position to do?

[1] See pages 18–21.

The particulars said that there was no medical, physiological or other legitimate reason for the operations. There *was* no such reason for the irradiation—but the moment they came to him, there was every reason for the operations.

On the allegation that 'to the plaintiff's knowledge' a number of the girls had irradiation burns at the time of the operation likely to render any wound inflicted on them difficult or impossible to heal, if the words 'irradiation burns' meant marks indicating that the victims had been subjected to X-rays, that was quite true. But it was quite untrue to say that Dr Dering performed any single operation where irradiation had rendered the operation dangerous. One girl *had* been brought in with severe burns; and, at imminent risk to his life and safety, he had refused to perform the operation. He had survived; but the girl did not. She was immediately dispatched.

It was also untrue that any operation was ever performed on any girl who had had a previous ovariectomy. As to the anaesthetic, a general anaesthetic could have been used, for there was no shortage of supplies. But there was a school of thought which considered that a spinal anaesthetic was the only type of anaesthetic which should be used for this sort of operation.

The allegation that the girls had been 'forcibly held down' was tendentious. It was universal practice to hold a patient while a spinal anaesthetic was being given, because a sudden reaction might be disastrous. It was untrue that the girls screamed; and if the word 'forcibly' was used to suggest struggling victims, that was untrue. Every patient had been heavily drugged with morphia. Again, strapping down was not a piece of horrible brutality, but universal practice.

The description of the operation in the particulars was substantially correct; but as to the stitches, Dr Dering, would, so far as his modesty would allow, tell the jury that he did them skilfully, that each operation lasted not much more than ten minutes, and that the quicker it was done the better for the patient. It was flatly untrue that there was no washing or sterilization of instruments between each operation and that he 'did not wash his hands between each operation'.

On the particulars about the conversations which Dr Alina Brewda was alleged to have had with him during the operations

Dr Dering would say that Dr Brewda was not there, and that he had never had those conversations with her, either during the operations or at all, from the beginning to the end of the time that he was at Auschwitz. He also denied any knowledge of any girl dying after the operations. Had any girl died, he would have been told. It was untrue that there was a shortage of drugs, or that paper bandages were used, or to say other than that when he visited the girls after the operations they were making normal progress. On the last allegation about the girls, Dr Dering was not at Auschwitz 'in the autumn of 1944' to see whether or not they were still confined to their beds.

As for the male patients, Dr Dering had been faced with the same problem. He removed the radiated organ before gangrene, cancer, or death intervened.

The final paragraph invited the court to infer from the alleged conversations with Dr Brewda and 'from the speed, facility and expertise with which he performed' the operations detailed in the particulars that they were 'experimental' and that he had previously performed other similar experimental operations up to the numbers set out in the particulars.

Would the jury hang a dog on the inferences they were asked to draw? Not a single operation was experimental, although some were merciful improvements of previous irradiation. The defendants sought to blazon this man as a monster. The jury were about to see him. Was he?

Dr Dering was then called to give evidence, after Mr Duncan had been opening the case for about four hours.

CHAPTER V

'I was Prisoner-doctor'

DR Wladyslaw Alexander Dering, O.B.E., accepted the book from the usher and repeated the oath administered by the court associate.

The Judge: Dr Dering, are you satisfied that you have taken the oath in a manner binding on you?

Dr Dering: Yes.

The Judge: On what Testament?

Dr Dering: It does not matter. I am a Christian and Roman Catholic.

The Judge: You had better be sworn properly. Take the Douai version.

Dr Dering again repeated the oath as administered by the associate.

Giving his evidence in chief in answers to Mr Duncan, he said that he was a general medical practitioner under the National Health Service, and was in partnership with another doctor, a friend, at 145 Seven Sisters Road, London, N.7. He had been born in Poland, qualified as a doctor in Warsaw in 1928, and later specialized in gynaecology and obstetrics.

On 10 November 1939, he joined the Polish underground army in German-occupied Warsaw. 'I had six-roomed flat which was used for the underground movement and our task was to prepare medical services in the case of a rising.' Meanwhile he had carried on his professional work unmolested. But on 3 July 1940, he had been arrested by the Gestapo, interrogated, and 'they beat me with fists and clubs'. On 15 August 1940, he had been taken to Auschwitz with 1,500 others. 'It was advisable to keep secret that I was a qualified doctor because German policy was to destroy intellectuals and professional people.'

He, like other prisoners, had suffered indignities and violence 'for no known reasons'. On his thirty-eighth birthday in March 1941, he had been beaten on the buttocks thirty-eight times, for no other reason than that it was his birthday. That had had a permanent effect on his health.

At first he had worked as a general labourer. Later, as a male nurse, he was ordered to organize a surgical out-patient department where he did minor operations. In 1941 the Germans decided to build a proper operating theatre and surgical ward, and he was made prison doctor. A system of aseptic operations was established; and it was his duty to perform such operations. Conditions were 'possible', if not favourable, for such work.

In mid-1941 there was a great improvement in the supply of equipment, instruments and drugs. The theatre was in Block 21; and as soon as it was ready German doctors started to operate there. He and his fellow-prisoners had had to work from 6 a.m. to 6 p.m. with unqualified assistants, much of the time being spent in treating the results of punishments inflicted by the Germans. He had kept a record of all the operations which took place in the theatre, both those which he performed and those at which he assisted, from June 1941 to the end of August 1943.

Mr Duncan: When you were given this appointment in Block 21, were there any other qualified surgeons available?

Dr Dering: There were physicians but not surgeons other than myself. They were mostly Polish fellow-prisoners.

He had now seen one of the registers, and noted that after the end of August a number of operations were ascribed to him. He did not accept that those had been performed by him. They were not in his handwriting.

Mr Duncan: What happened to you in August 1943 which resulted in your not keeping these registers any longer?

Dr Dering said that, at that date, he had been put in charge of the prison hospital as *Lagerälteste Krankenartz*, and 'after that my duties were quite different'. He had performed only a few major operations. 'Lesser operations' were done by three or four younger surgeons, 'always prisoners'. At all times he was under the orders of German doctors, and an S.S. corporal who assisted them was 'practically the whole day' in the hospital. The man who had for most of the two years given him his orders from day to day was Dr Entress.

Mr Duncan: You have heard me say more than once to the jury that throughout the time you were there a number of unfortunates were sent to the gas chambers. Pause before you answer. I want you to tell the jury what was under your personal supervision?

Dr Dering: Each ten days or fortnight Germans used to select people who were ill longer than six weeks and had not much chance of recovering quickly and so useless for the Germans; and a German doctor or his assistant went through the wards and just simply looked at various patients and, without explanation or cause, chose a hundred to a hundred and fifty people to be sent to the gas chambers outside the main gate at Birkenau.

Mr Duncan: You were all this time a prisoner in the camp. Did you ever get outside?

Dr Dering: Yes, occasionally.

He added that he had been sent once to organize an infectious department elsewhere. He had been able to improve conditions, building water pipes, latrines, and so on.

Mr Duncan: The doctor who performed this horrible task of selecting patients for the gas chambers—would that be Dr Entress?

Dr Dering: Entress and any other S.S. doctor.

Mr Duncan: Did you throughout the time do everything you could to save your patients from being victimized in this way?

Dr Dering: Each time.

At first, he said, prisoners were described only by numbers which the Germans used to write on their chests. They were easily washed off; and he had instructed his dressers to wash them off and substitute the numbers of those already dead. Thirty or forty lives might have been saved in that way. Then the Germans found out this form of 'cheating', and used to send lists of those intended for the gas chambers to be typed in the office; but members of the underground who worked in the office, on his instructions, substituted the cards of the dead for the cards left on the designated patients' beds.

His position in the hospital was officially that of doctor, but in practice it was that of 'prisoner-doctor'. The routine was that, at 6 a.m. when people started to go to the factories they gathered in front of the hospital block and prisoner-doctors examined them and 'put everything on individual out-patient cards'. About 9 a.m. the S.S. doctor appeared, and the prisoner-doctors had to present him with a list of those who should be admitted to hospital. 'Usually German doctor simply approved what we suggested, and according to the number of available beds the prisoners were admitted.' It had been his task each day to select as in-patients, from as many as six hundred patients needing treatment, the twenty to forty for whom alone beds were available.

At first his clothing had been blue striped canvas shirt, trousers and overall; but in 1942 or 1943 he had been ordered to wear a distinctive medical uniform.

He and his staff used to hide old people, or people needing more than the permitted six weeks to recover, in the infectious diseases room, where the Germans were unwilling to go. Later the Germans had brought in the system of tattooing a number on the prisoner's left forearm. He himself had had 'such a number'.

The Judge: Have you still got it?

Dr Dering: I excised it, my Lord. There is still a scar. I had it excised in 1945 when I was being persecuted in Poland and threatened with hanging.

He had seen people being killed by many methods. Executions were carried out between Blocks 10 and 11, where there was a high wall; prisoners were shot in the back of the neck. Another method was by phenol injection—at first intravenously, but later, as that required skill, the Germans elaborated the method of injection with long-needled syringes straight into the heart. Four victims would be seated in pairs, naked, back to back on chairs, and an S.S. corporal, assisted by a prisoner, would then inject quickly—and it was all over 'in a short moment'.

Mr Duncan: Do you remember an occasion when you were asked to give an injection of a particular kind?

Dr Dering: Yes. I was reporting to German doctor accompanied by deputy Block leading prisoner and was told a prisoner needed an injection of glucose. It was strange to me that the German doctor or leading prisoner should not do it themselves. But it was ordered. I took the syringe and noticed that the fluid was heavy and a special colour unlike glucose; and the smell was that of phenol. I put the syringe back and said I was sorry but I would not do that injection. The doctor ordered the leading prisoner to do it and I did then for the first time in my life watch how quickly people die after an injection of phenol.

Mr Duncan asked about the other names in the paragraph in *Exodus*. Dr Dering said there were two named 'Wirths'—one the S.S. chief medical officer and the other his younger brother, who, he had heard, was 'experimenting in Block 10'. That was all he could tell about 'Dr Wirths'.

'Dr Schumann' had appeared in the theatre one day in *Luftwaffe* uniform and had been told that Dr Dering was 'our surgeon and at your disposal'. Dr Schumann then told him, 'very politely' that he was carrying out experiments on the sexual glands of men and women by X-ray and wanted him to remove the X-rayed testicles and ovaries. 'My first reply was: "It is not essential indication if they are not suffering from anything, and I don't think we as doctors could do these things." He said: "Don't you think I can do with prisoners what I like?" and left the theatre.'

Mr Duncan: Did you have anything further personally to do with Dr Schumann?

Dr Dering: No. It was the beginning. I was very much upset at my punishment for refusing. I asked my colleagues . . .

Mr Duncan: What do you mean by your punishment?

Dr Dering said that he had been threatened, and punished for refusing to give the phenol injection by not being allowed to leave the camp for two weeks. After the proposal from Dr Schumann he had discussed it with his colleagues.

Lord Gardiner said he would like to know the colleagues' names. Dr Dering named Dr Grabczynski and Dr Diem, who were Poles; Dr Steinberg—'of Jewish nationality'; Professor Olbrycht—an old man; and 'maybe someone else'. 'The common opinion was that there was no sense in refusing, for if we refused we would not save the people because it would be done either by other doctors or by some unskilled person, or—as Schumann threatened—he could send victims to gas chambers and get surgical help to remove X-rayed testicles which he needed for his purpose.' His friends had agreed that it would be 'stupidity' to refuse, because the X-rayed glands were dead or could be presumed to be dead and would be no further use as genital organs. 'We concluded that if we did not help, not only would we not save them but we ourselves would be in danger.'

Mr Duncan: I want your help about the medical side, and the views you formed in 1941 and 1942 about the effects of radiation on the genital organs of both men and women and the desirability or otherwise of leaving such organs in the human frame.

Dr Dering said that the tissue of the sex glands was very sensitive to X-rays. They could be destroyed entirely and never regenerate; or the doses could be partial so that the gland was rendered inactive for a year or six months; or, if the dose was very small, it 'could produce some harm to the gland tissue' by exciting the growth of 'something undesirable, like a seminoma—one of the worst kinds of carcinoma of the testicle'. 'From this point of view it was common sense not to make too much harm of people losing their destroyed gland but winning their lives, and our lives as well.'

Mr Duncan: If you had been under no pressure—in peace time when you were a free agent—would you, in the then state of medical knowledge, have left these irradiated organs in, or would you have advised their removal?

Dr Dering: If I had today a private patient who had X-rayed testicle I would examine him and, if finding no changes, probably I would advise him to wait a couple of months and see me frequently. Bearing in mind theoretically what would happen to X-rayed people, I think I was quite justified from medical point of view to remove the small part of the body which had no meaning for the man but could eventually have endangered him.

He was asked about the third name mentioned in the paragraph —'Clauberg'. Dr Dering said that Dr Wirths had introduced him to Clauberg in the autumn of 1943, in Block 10. Professor Clauberg was already known to him by repute as a professor of gynaecology and also from medical literature. Clauberg had asked him whether he was 'pure surgeon' or whether he knew something of gynaecology. He had replied that gynaecology was his specialty. Clauberg had then turned to Dr Wirths and said: 'This is the man I am looking for', and asked Dr Dering why he was in the camp. He said he did not know. Clauberg said: 'You Poles never know'; and he and Dr Wirths left. Half an hour later Clauberg returned to the theatre by himself and told Dr Dering that 'my case was serious and there was no chance of my leaving the camp'; but that he (Clauberg) was in charge of a private hospital at Koenigshuette which needed trained doctors. 'He said he would do everything he could to take me from the camp. My feelings were very strange. I did not know what to think.'

During the next two months, he had seen Professor Clauberg entering Block 10 once or twice. 'At the end of 1943, Professor Clauberg again appeared in the theatre and told me he is very sure he can do very much. Again it was nothing for me. Then one day at the beginning of January 1944, Dr Wirths came to the theatre and told me: "Unfortunately Professor Clauberg is much more powerful than we believed. He went to Berlin. I think he is gynaecologist to Mrs Himmler, and he brought the order that 'Prisoner 1723 Dr Dering will be given on loan to Professor Clauberg for one year'." '

Mr Duncan: Were you given any choice in the matter?

Dr Dering: No. It was ordered.

He was then given civilian clothes and went to the hospital in Silesia under Clauberg, who warned him that if he did anything stupid like trying to escape, his wife, who was in prison in Warsaw, would be executed; and, of course, if they captured him, he, too, would be executed. He had had to sign 'such an engagement'. He had still been a prisoner. His case was not exceptional. Several doctors from Auschwitz had been taken from the camp and put into civilian hospitals.

As a leader of the underground, he had been kept fully informed of what was going on and was able to keep in touch with the Warsaw underground; and he had been able to make many improvements in the camp, building showers, getting hot water supplies and anti-typhus vaccine and medicines from Cracow. At the beginning only his underground organization had existed, but after he was removed from the camp, many 'pretended to do the job' which he and his friends had done from the beginning, and there had been some hostility from 'communistic prisoners'.

Mr Duncan: Throughout the whole time that you were in Auschwitz, did you carry out any experimental operations?

Dr Dering: No.

Mr Duncan: Throughout the whole time, did you ever carry out an operation, properly so called, without an anaesthetic?

Dr Dering: No, except it could have happened in the beginning when we had no anaesthetics at all and something called for immediate surgical intervention—an abscess or a septic leg.

Dr Dering agreed that for most of the cases with which the court would be concerned he had used a single spinal injection as the anaesthetic. It was simple, because it needed only one prick, and produced full anaesthesia; it did not need an anaesthetist, and anyway none was available. Had he been free to choose, he would at that date have chosen a spinal rather than a general anaesthetic. He had deliberately chosen to use them for 15,000 operations in Somaliland—1,500 a year for ten years. The position was quite different now, when surgeons were not responsible for anaesthesia.

The Register was produced to the court by a representative of the Polish Embassy and was passed to Dr Dering.

Mr Duncan: Do you recognize that as one of the registers kept at Auschwitz?

Dr Dering: I do.

Mr Duncan: What is the first date in the book?

Dr Dering: February 22, 1943.

Mr Duncan: What is the last date?

Dr Dering: I would like to explain that my handwriting . . .

The Judge: Just answer the question.

Dr Dering turned the pages of the register, and then said: 23 February, possibly, 1944. It is not clear. There is no year.

Mr Duncan: Are some of the entries actually made in your handwriting, by you?

Dr Dering: Yes.

He agreed that all the entries up to 28 August 1943, were by him and he accepted them as accurate, but, though the entries after August purported to record the same sort of detail, none were in his handwriting, and he was not prepared to accept as accurate any which were not in his handwriting.

A bundle of the pleadings was passed to Dr Dering.

Mr Duncan: Do you remember when you first began to keep a register of operations at Auschwitz?

Dr Dering: I do not remember the exact date—we wanted to have documents for use against the Germans. Probably early in 1941.

He thought he had kept, in whole or in part, three, 'probably four', registers. All the registers looked like the one produced, which was the last during his stay at the camp.

He was then taken through the Particulars of Justification.

He said that, 'in October 1943', he performed five ovariectomy operations. He doubted whether he had assisted at others. So far as he knew they were on young Jewesses from Greece or Epirus, aged about nineteen or twenty, and inmates of Block 10. All the girls had been irradiated.

'I carried out the operations because the cases belonged to Dr Schumann who had experimented on them by X-ray and needed their ovaries for further exploration. That was the research. Dr Schumann sent the girls to me in the theatre, and I could not refuse. To refuse would be sabotage. That meant only one thing in the camp.'

He denied that there had been bad irradiation burns, save in one case. It was not true that to his knowledge at least one of the girls had, at the time of the operation, undergone a previous ovariectomy operation. He would have seen the scar, and there was no such case. The injections were not given in the annexe to the operating theatre but on the table of the theatre. They had been given properly, with the patient in a sitting position, bent forward. Had the patient not been held by his orderly, the needle might have broken. It was normal practice to have the patient held. The injection caused much less pain than any other subcutaneous injection. None of the girls had screamed. He had given only one injection rather than two injections to each patient: that was the method in which he had been trained before the war. Surgeons dealing with private, well-paying patients, might give two injections, but that did not prevent pain. Logically that was 'a nonsense'. What he did was perfectly proper.

Each patient was strapped on to the operating table; that was the normal and universal practice at any hospital.

The table was not tilted as much as 30 degrees, but there was a surgical reason for tilting the table.

Mr Duncan: In the particulars, a paragraph sets out details of the operation. In a general way does that describe an ovariectomy properly done or not?

Dr Dering agreed that it did. But it was not true that he had inserted stitches 'in rough and ready manner'. They were properly inserted after the operations, which lasted ten or twelve minutes. Nobody except the assistant could have seen whether he had covered the pedicle.

It was routine that a set of instruments should be permanently in the sterilizer. It was untrue that he did not wash his hands between each operation. He always washed his hands before and after each operation, and used rubber gloves and cotton gloves.

He did not refer to any notes, for he had none. Each patient had been injected with morphia before coming into the theatre and most of them were asleep. 'I don't remember the girls being distressed', he added, 'but I do not think that they were happy.' The girls could not have seen what was going on, for there was a screen between their faces and the lower parts of their bodies.

Mr Duncan: Was any operation carried out by you in any sense an experiment?

Dr Dering: No. I was not interested in experiment.

Mr Duncan: Were these operations properly performed?

Dr Dering: In normal, surgical way according to surgical principles.

Mr Duncan: Although it was in Auschwitz?

Dr Dering: Yes.

Mr Duncan: You know who is referred to as 'Dr Brewda'?

He did. He had first met Dr Brewda in Warsaw in 1926 when she was a medical student, and later at the University Clinic. She had come to the camp in September 1943, shortly after he had become the senior in the hospital. She was put in charge of the female experimental block—Block 10. It was no part of his duty to go to Block 10 at all; but he had gone there to see 'a good new X-ray apparatus' and also to see patients after ovariectomies. So far as he could recall, Dr Brewda had appeared in Block 21 with nurses and a German sentry in September 1943, bringing some swabs and material to be sterilized. She had been surprised to meet him there and had asked him what he was doing. 'There on the desk in the theatre room was exposed a register; and I just presented her with the register. She looked at it and expressed her surprise that already seventeen thousand operations had been performed.'

Mr Duncan: Was Dr Brewda present throughout one or any of the operations on the five girls we are talking about?

Dr Dering: Never.

Mr Duncan read the particulars alleging the first of the five conversations between Dr Brewda and Dr Dering during the ovariectomy operations and asked: 'Did any conversation resembling that ever take place between you and Dr Brewda anywhere?'

Dr Dering: Never.

He then denied one after the other each of the conversations alleged. He also denied that during each operation some of the girls waiting in the corridor were within earshot of the theatre. There was no room in the theatre proper for people or visitors. It was undesirable to have 'outside people'.

Mr Duncan: It is said that one girl aged about sixteen died of internal haemorrhage within a few hours; and another within twenty-four hours; and another within three days of the operation, each in acute pain. What means had you, other than visits after the operations, of knowing for certain whether the patients on whom you had operated were alive or dead?

Dr Dering said that he would have been told immediately by the staff under his supervision if anything had gone wrong or if anyone had died. It was not true that there had been only paper bandages. No such thing had been brought to his notice. Normal cotton bandages were used for abdominal operations; and if supplies were short they used to paint a sort of blue stuff round the dressing and stick on a piece of gauze. That was suitable for the purpose; and those were the dressings used for the girls.

He had visited Block 10 to see the girls on the fourth or fifth day after the operations—a proper period where patients had been left by him in the care of qualified women doctors—Dr Brewda and 'Dr Dora Klein' [Dr Lorska]. He had had no message from Dr Brewda urging him to come and 'do something' for the patients. Dr Brewda had gone round with him on his normal post-operational visit.

Mr Duncan: Were any of the girls not there because they had died?

Dr Dering: No. They were all there.

The post-operational condition of the girls, he said, was satisfactory. The wounds were not, and could not, from the pathological point of view, have been in the condition described in the particulars, for even a wound going septic would not have opened in five days. There had been no talk about the death of any girl, nor had Dr Brewda asked him for something more for the girls. It had been no part of his duty to send drugs or medical supplies to Block 10. He had not visited the girls again. That was in accordance with proper professional practice, for this kind of 'minor operation' usually healed within seven or eight days.

Mr Duncan: Until this case, has it ever been suggested to you that in fact these surviving girls were still in bed when you left in January 1944?

Dr Dering: No.

He also denied that he had ever performed a testicle operation in the presence of a prisoner student named Klodzinski. Patients undergoing that operation were anaesthetized in the same way as the girls—by spinal injection—and premedicated by morphia before they reached the theatre. The time taken was ample for simple operations done with skill. The less time they took the less risk there was of post-operative shock.

Mr Duncan referred Dr Dering to the particulars alleging that the operations were 'by inference experimental', and asked:

'Have you given us your evidence of what in fact happened at each of these operations and the circumstances in which you performed them?'

Dr Dering: Yes.

Mr Duncan: Then it is for the jury to make up their minds whether they think that constitutes an experimental operation.

Photograph copies of pages of the register and the list of 130 operations in the particulars were handed to Dr Dering, and copies were also supplied to the jury. He said that he had checked that each case in the list was in the register produced in court. Though he did not in 1964 remember much about the actual operation, he could, by looking at the last column, tell its nature, and also which of the patients had had irradiation before coming to him. There were two in the first forty-six which had not been previously X-rayed. Two or three cases in the list had been sentenced by a German court to have testicles removed. An entry of *amputatio testis sin.* in the register indicated to him a patient sent to him by Schumann after X-ray for the removal of the left testicle. Schumann also sent a list showing which testicle, left or right, was to be removed.

Mr Duncan: Do you remember, of your own recollection—because this is very important—whether, with the exception of two or three cases we are going to discuss, they were all patients who had had radiation?

Dr Dering: Yes, all.

Of the two 'exceptions', one was a simple hernia and the testicle was not removed; the other was a hernia and tumor where it was surgically necessary to remove the testicle.

He remembered one case as that of a person sentenced by a German court to have his testicles removed. That operation, being a sentence, was reserved for S.S. doctors; but on a number of occasions the S.S. doctor began the operation and left Dr Dering to finish it.

He was referred to the original register and 'No. 10' in the list—an operation on 20 May 1943, described as *casus explorativus, castratio*. That, he said, was a castration after X-ray. Another—'No. 40', *sterilisatio*—had been a German woman sentenced by a German court for some crime against morality. Case 'No. 2' on 12 April 1943, was a German gypsy sentenced to be sterilized because of some hereditary disease. The German court usually ordered 'exactly what was to be done'. He did not remember why he, rather than the German doctors, had done it. He had assisted at another operation following a court sentence—*vita sexualis anormalis*. 'Assisting' meant preparing the patient and helping during the procedure. Some of the Germans were 'not very advanced surgeons', and he had had to watch in order to prevent their making mistakes—'as in a teaching hospital'. Three entries, Nos. 47, 48 and 49, on 16 September—not in his handwriting—indicated Germans who had not been X-rayed. Though he was recorded as the surgeon, he thought it unlikely that he had been, and did not remember them; and there were two on 30 September. He did not accept them as accurate.

He agreed that despite the removal of one testicle a man would still have sexual desire and be able to have children.

About October 1943 he said a female patient had been brought to him with very bad radiation burns. He reported to the Germans that the operation could not be carried out because the tissue had been destroyed. 'I think I convinced the Germans that the operation could not be performed.'

Mr Duncan: What was the immediate result of that decision?

Dr Dering: The girl was sent to the gas chamber.

Mr Duncan: So your efforts to save her were not successful?

Dr Dering: Not successful.

For the first few weeks after the Gestapo had taken him from Auschwitz to Clauberg's hospital in January 1944, he had not been allowed to go anywhere. Later he was allowed to go to church and the cinema. He had remained there as a prisoner. On 19 January 1945, Clauberg had left, with some of the patients, and he himself continued to look after the Silesian people. On 19 April, the Russians arrived. They had arrested him and put him in gaol; but he was released eight days later, on Easter Sunday, and went to Warsaw where he 'learned something' about himself. The underground gave him false documents, and he got a job as an agricultural worker. He left Poland because his life was in danger, and joined the 2nd Corps under General Anders in Italy; and in August 1946 he came to England as a surgeon in an army hospital.

In January 1947 he had been 'invited to London for interview'. He had been taken to Brixton Prison and was there for nineteen and a half months while an investigation was held to see whether he should be extradited to Poland. Then he was released and worked at the St John and St Elizabeth Hospital in London for fifteen months as a gynaecologist and obstetrician; and later obtained an appointment with the Colonial medical service, in British Somaliland where he stayed for ten years. He had been awarded the O.B.E.

As a result of his experiences at Auschwitz and earlier, he had developed a right side hernia and large varicose veins; he had lost some teeth because of the beatings he received; and he suffered from insomnia and anxiety. He was sixty-one.

Mr Duncan: Looking back from 1964 into the horrible past, do you feel that you did all you could for your suffering fellow creatures at Auschwitz?

Dr Dering: Yes. I did my best.

Mr Duncan: So far as you and your conscience are concerned, would you do the same today?

Dr Dering: I would do just the same today. Maybe it would be done better, due to my experience.

CHAPTER VI

Dr Dering Cross-examined

THE REGISTER

LORD GARDINER began cross-examining Dr Dering after he had been giving evidence for over five hours. The first questions were directed to the Register.

Dr Dering said that the head of a hospital did not himself have to keep a register of operations but ought to advise that the surgeon should keep one, and could not order the surgeon to keep it. The surgeon ought to keep it.

All the entries in the register in court up to 'September' 1943 were made by him, whether or not he performed the operation. His practice had been to enter up the register each evening from notes made on pieces of paper.

As far as he remembered, when he became head of the hospital, he had been succeeded in his duties as prison surgeon by Dr Grabczynski, and thought that the register had been kept up. All the entries from the beginning of September were in the same handwriting, but it was not Dr Grabczynski's handwriting, and not necessarily that of a doctor. Many boys learned Latin at school and could write. So far as he could recollect, during 'this short time I still stayed in the camp', each doctor performing an operation personally entered it in the register, 'and signed with his name', so that different handwritings should appear.

Lord Gardiner referred him to a photograph of page 90, and asked: In the column headed 'Note' you see, about tenth from the bottom, *casus explorativus*? Is the ordinary meaning of that an operation done in order to find out what is the matter with the patient?

Dr Dering: It was embarrassing question to ask German . . .

The Judge: Dr Dering, I appreciate that English is not your mother tongue, but I would be grateful, and so would the jury, if you would follow the question carefully, and answer the question you have been asked. All you have been asked at the moment is, 'What is the ordinary meaning of *casus explorativus*?' or, 'What is the ordinary medical meaning of *casus explorativus*?'

Lord Gardiner: Ordinarily *casus explorativus* means an operation, does it not, in order to arrive at a diagnosis?

Dr Dering: This diagnosis was put just to notify . . .

The Judge: Dr Dering, this illustrates what I asked you to do. I want you to be careful about it. You see, you are now trying to tell us why, in the register, it was put down in a certain way. That is not what Lord Gardiner is asking you. Would you ask it again, Lord Gardiner?

Lord Gardiner: Is the ordinary meaning, to a doctor, of the words *casus explorativus* an operation done in order to assist in a diagnosis?

Dr Dering: Yes.

Lord Gardiner: That was not the nature of any of the operations in the last ten lines of this page, was it?

Dr Dering: Not of this kind.

Lord Gardiner: It was a false description?

Dr Dering: False?

Lord Gardiner: That is right, is it not?

Dr Dering: It was false in your meaning, but we had to put some diagnosis. Proper diagnosis would be 'X-rayed testicle'.

Lord Gardiner: The proper diagnosis would have been 'for one of Dr Schumann's experiments', would it not?

Dr Dering: Dr Schumann's experiments. But we could not use these things because we could be in trouble with Dr Schumann.

Lord Gardiner: Then *amputatio testis*, you told us, is the removal of a testicle, and *sin.* means left, does it not, and *dex.* means right?

Dr Dering: Dex. is right; *sin.* is left.

Lord Gardiner: On page 161 there are about half-a-dozen testicle cases together. Can you see them?

Dr Dering: Yes.

Lord Gardiner: The first man had both his testicles removed?

Dr Dering: Yes.

Lord Gardiner: By you, Dr Dering?

Dr Dering: Yes.

Lord Gardiner: And instead of putting it down as *sin.* and *dex.* was it sometimes put down as *amputatio testis uts.* which, I suggest, is short for *utriusque*, meaning 'on both sides'?

Dr Dering: Yes.

Lord Gardiner: And the difference between that and castration is that *castratio* is used where it is done to a potent man who has not been irradiated?

Dr Dering: Castration, healthy testicles removed. When healthy testicles removed, we call castration.

Lord Gardiner: And is the difference between the two that in the case where we find *amputatio* they have been X-rayed, whereas where we find *castratio* they have not been X-rayed?

Dr Dering: No, except one case which I explained.

He agreed that, on another page, an entry in his handwriting related to the castration of a potent man. He did the operation and Dr Grabczynski assisted. It was done under a German court sentence.

Lord Gardiner: Was it done against his will?

Dr Dering: I did not ask him.

Lord Gardiner: What do you think?

Dr Dering: It was not my duty to ask him for his will, whether he agrees or not.

Lord Gardiner: You see the 'Remarks' column. Was that operation performed in the presence of the German Dr Rohde?

Dr Dering said that the photograph was not clear. The register was passed to him: Yes. On orders and in presence of German Captain Doctor Rohde.

Lord Gardiner: Did you know that no German court had any legal right to make such an order merely because a man was a homosexual?

Dr Dering: I do not know what is German right. I was a prisoner. I could not argue and discuss with Germans any questions and problems.

Lord Gardiner: Did you know, if any such order was made, it could only be carried out in a hospital by doctors specified by the State Ministry of Justice?

Dr Dering: If I were in freedom I would follow this instructions and this regulations. I was not in freedom. I was in a camp, a horrible camp.

The Judge: The question is, 'Did you know that under Nazi law, as it existed then, castration could only be carried out in a hospital specified by the Ministry of Justice?'

Dr Dering: No. I did not.

Lord Gardiner: Did you ask to see the court order?

Dr Dering: No.

Lord Gardiner: You did not think, did you, that castrating this man could do him any possible good?

Dr Dering: Certainly not.

Lord Gardiner: You had no reason to think that the testicles were liable to develop cancer?

Dr Dering: No.

Lord Gardiner: You don't suggest that you asked your Polish doctors in the underground movement about the operation and they told you to do it?

Dr Dering: What Polish underground movement? I do not follow very much.

Lord Gardiner: I thought you said, in relation to Dr Schumann's experiments that you discussed them with some Polish doctors—whom you named—in the camp, and that they were in agreement with your doing them?

Dr Dering: Yes.

Lord Gardiner: You have not suggested so far that, in relation to these castration operations, you asked your Polish doctor friends?

Dr Dering: No.

Lord Gardiner: Why do you say you did this? You were not subject to German law, were you? Are you saying 'I did this simply because I should have been shot if I hadn't'? Is that right?

Dr Dering: I'm sorry, I don't follow.

Lord Gardiner: As a doctor you had taken the Hippocratic oath when you became a doctor?

Dr Dering: Yes.

Lord Gardiner: And you were here being asked to castrate a potent man against his will?

Dr Dering: Yes.

Lord Gardiner: That requires, does it not, some justification by a doctor?

Dr Dering: Yes.

Lord Gardiner: I am just asking you, is there any justification, in your view, except that you'd have been shot if you'd disobeyed the order?

Dr Dering: I would like to answer exactly to your question.

Since I entered Auschwitz all law, normal, human and God's law were finished. They were Germans' law. And this questions, Lord Gardiner, you put to me, they concern normal conditions. It is difficult to imagine the situation in life in the camp. So therefore it is difficult for me to give you short 'Yes' or 'No' to your questions.

Lord Gardiner: I want you, of course, to say anything you want to say. Am I right in thinking that, in regard to Dr Schumann's experimental cases, what you say is this: first, you discussed them with other Polish doctors; secondly, anyway it was very good for them to have irradiated organs removed, saving them from cancer and death; thirdly, that if you had not done it they would have been sent to the gas chamber; fourthly, if you had not done it, you would have been shot; and fifthly, if you had not done it, somebody else would? I just want to see, in relation to these castrations, which of those excuses applied. You say you did not discuss it with the doctors, and you do not suggest that removing a potent man's testicles against his will could do him any good. Is what you are really saying this: 'I did it because I'd have been shot if I had not'?

Dr Dering: I could not refuse. That is one point. The second point: it would be done, if not by me, by unskilled S.S. corporal.

Lord Gardiner: Let me take those two separately. On the first point—'I could not refuse because it was an order'—Captain Rohde was hanged for what he did; and was not his defence, 'If I had not done what I did my superior officer would have shot me'? Did you not know that?

Dr Dering: No.

Lord Gardiner: And, on your second point—if you hadn't done it someone else would have—it is a fact, is it not, that an addiction to drugs is a terrible thing?

Dr Dering: Yes.

Lord Gardiner: And the men who are drug pedlars and who are caught usually say 'If they had not got the drug from me they would have got it from somebody else'. But you feel that that is a good excuse, do you, for doing what you did—that if you had not done it somebody else probably would?

Dr Dering: Some unskilled people would do, and the people would suffer much more than done in proper way.

Lord Gardiner: Unless, of course, they were doctors. And I suggest that there were some in Auschwitz whom I shall be calling, who refused to carry out German orders.

Dr Dering: I can't remember one of them.

He agreed that case 'No. 2' on the list, on 12 April 1943, was a sterilization of a gypsy; it appeared to have been done by Entress, the S.S. doctor, while Dr Dering assisted.

Lord Gardiner: This was a man who had not been irradiated—a potent male?

Dr Dering: No. He would have some hereditary disease which I cannot specify now.

Lord Gardiner: Was this done with or without his consent?

Dr Dering: It was done on court orders.

Lord Gardiner: With or without his consent?

Dr Dering: He was not asked for his consent.

Lord Gardiner: Was there any medical reason for it?

Dr Dering: The diagnosis and sentence was based on the mental disability.

Lord Gardiner: Where do you find anything about his mental condition in the register? There is nothing in the register about a court order?

Dr Dering: Nothing in the register. No.

Lord Gardiner: In case 'No. 1' you put in the 'remarks' column that that was done in the presence of and on the order of Dr Rohde, but there is nothing of that sort in relation to 'No. 2'?

Dr Dering: No, but he arranged it.

Lord Gardiner: Why were you assisting in that operation?

Dr Dering: As prisoner in the surgical ward my duties were to prepare for any operation in the theatre the previous day and assist at the operation performed by S.S. doctor.

Lord Gardiner: If Dr Entress had said to you, 'I am going to sterilize this man. There is no court order at all, but that is what I am going to do, and you are to assist me', what would you have done?

Dr Dering: I would have assisted him, whether there was a court order or not.

Lord Gardiner: Was that because you were trying to work your passage with the Germans?

Dr Dering: Lord Gardiner, I was a prisoner and had to carry out what I was told, and as a doctor I had to do my best to save as many as possible people. I helped the patient in the first instance in seeing that the operation was performed in the proper manner. I helped not only as a human duty but I did as much as I could for these victims.

The Judge: Dr Dering, you have not answered Lord Gardiner's question. Perhaps it is because he put it in an idiomatic form. Do you understand what 'working your passage' means?

Lord Gardiner recapitulated. Dr Dering agreed that he started as a labourer, being beaten with the others; then became a medical orderly; then a prisoner-surgeon in control of all the hospital; and then surgeon-in-charge of the whole hospital.

Lord Gardiner: The Germans must have trusted you a good deal before they gave you that position, must they not?

Dr Dering: I did not discuss the matter with the Germans. Simply I was appointed and I had to accept this post against my will and wish.

Lord Gardiner: You ended up—you and Dr Grabczynski—for what you did to help in the experiments, as the only two prisoner doctors who were ever released from Auschwitz?

Dr Dering: No.

Lord Gardiner: You went to the cinema after you were released?

Dr Dering said that he had been in the civilian hospital as a prisoner and for the first seven weeks had no right to go out. Only later was he allowed to go to Church and occasionally to the cinema.

Lord Gardiner was studying the register again: Look at May the 6th. On that day fifteen men had their left testicles removed—seven by you and eight by Dr Grabczynski?

Dr Dering: Yes.

Lord Gardiner: These were not operations being performed for medical reasons, were they?

Dr Dering: All were X-rayed cases.

Lord Gardiner: These were not operations being performed for medical reasons, were they?

Dr Dering: It depends. It could be done in normal circumstances.

The Judge: Well, Dr Dering, *who* wanted these operations performed—Dr Schumann or the patient?

Dr Dering: Dr Schumann.

Lord Gardiner: And you knew Dr Schumann wanted them for his experiments?

Dr Dering: Yes.

Lord Gardiner: Then if you knew Dr Schumann wanted them for his experiments they were experimental operations, were they not?

Dr Dering: The experiments had been done before, by X-ray. That was the first step; and this was, if you like, the second step of his experiments.

Lord Gardiner: And therefore it was an experimental operation?

Dr Dering: In this way, Yes.

Lord Gardiner: Were they all young Jews?

Dr Dering: Yes.

Lord Gardiner: And were they brought to the hospital the night before?

Dr Dering: The night or two days before, maybe.

Lord Gardiner: And the day before, did they have a piece of wood put up their rectum in order to induce an ejaculation, to see that they were still potent?

Dr Dering: I don't know.

He did not remember one of them saying to him the night before, 'What am I here for? I am quite well. Why should I be operated on?', nor saying to one of them, 'If I don't take out yours they will take out mine', and that he was 'lucky to be alive', or words to that effect, and walking out.

Lord Gardiner: You don't suggest, do you, that you said to him: 'You have been irradiated—which is not my fault—and cancer may develop, and therefore it is for your own good that your testicle is to be removed'?

Dr Dering: I don't remember such a conversation.

Lord Gardiner: No. You did not say that, Dr Dering, I suggest, because you did not think that?

Dr Dering: Lord Gardiner, it is a difficult matter after twenty years to remember about each separate occasion, and what I did or told at the moment. These unfortunate cases were castrated by X-ray and I was convinced that if I did not follow the Germans' orders to remove destroyed testicles it is not only important what would happen to me but I would not save the prisoner. He would have had it done in any case. As Schumann threatened, he would have been sent to the gas chamber and the testicle would then be removed.

Lord Gardiner: You were operating on these young men as a doctor?

Dr Dering: As prisoner doctor, as before.

Lord Gardiner: And should a doctor always think of the welfare of his patients?

Dr Dering: It was impossible.

Lord Gardiner: I concede that on the Continent spinal anaesthesis was quite customary. But I suggest that in the circumstances with these young men knowing that they were going tc have a testicle removed against their will, it would have been kinder if you had used a general anaesthetic, so that they did not know what was happening while it was going on?

Dr Dering: Lord Gardiner, I had not always in abundance any kind of anaesthetics and I had no anaesthetist. The people who helped me in anaesthetics were simply schoolboys or students or journalists trained by me, and I had many sad experiences of complications due to ether anaesthetic. For those reasons I came to the conclusion that this way of anaesthetic was most suitable in the camp—and not only these 'experimental' cases, as you say, but also any other cases of operation for hernia, bladder and so on were always under spinal in the interests of the patient.

Lord Gardiner: These men were healthy young men, were they not?

Dr Dering: Yes, they were healthy young men.

Lord Gardiner: And therefore the sort of young men who would ordinarily be working in the camp, and not killed?

Dr Dering: Those were Dr Schumann's arguments—that he could take them to the gas chambers, but that in the interests of the Great German Reich he wanted to save them for work.

Lord Gardiner: You knew even at that time that Dr Schumann was engaged in experiments with a view to seeing how far after the war people could be sterilized in large numbers?

Dr Dering: It was mine and my colleagues' guess why these silly experiments were carried on.

Lord Gardiner: Pretty obvious?

Dr Dering: But I have truly said we had no influence. We could not change the situation.

Lord Gardiner reminded Dr Dering of his previous evidence that he had had only one personal encounter with Dr Schumann, Dr Dering agreed that he had seen him later on several occasions, and that he had known that the Germans were trying to discover the right strength of X-ray—which no one knew at that time—for sterilizing testicles.

Lord Gardiner: And the object of removing one testicle was to test it to see whether or not the X-ray had done its job?

Dr Dering: Yes. But may I tell you something? It was an old method, and we knew that by X-ray you could castrate completely or sterilize for some period. The doses were quite known. So these experiments were puzzling to us. But we had no chance to discuss and ask why they were doing these things.

Lord Gardiner: You don't dispute that you knew?

Dr Dering: It was my guess.

Lord Gardiner: If you say you realized that the reason why Dr Schumann wanted the X-rayed testicle removed was to see if the X-ray had done its work, I suggest that shows you realized that that meant that the testicles were not necessarily impotent?

Dr Dering: I had nothing to do with anything after the operation. Most probably he sent these specimens for microscopic examination, but I don't know.

The X-rays, he said, had been done by volunteers who pretended to be doctors, and that had caused much suffering. Many of the victims had burns from overdose. Most of the cases were so deeply X-rayed as to be impotent. Most of them, he agreed, had irradiation marks on both sides. He didn't know what the technique was.

Lord Gardiner: But you could see, by the time you had them, that both testicles had been irradiated?

Dr Dering: It was not always visible. Some of them had slight burns and some no marks at all.

Lord Gardiner: And where both sides were marked, you did not remove on any medical ground, but because Dr Schumann just wanted the left testicle removed first?

Dr Dering: There was a list saying which testicle, single or both, should be removed.

Lord Gardiner: Did you ever say to Dr Schumann: 'As these

testicles have been irradiated cancer may develop and therefore it would be in the man's interest to remove both'?

Dr Dering: No, I did not.

Lord Gardiner: What I have to suggest to you, Dr Dering, is that what you have said is medically quite wrong—that X-rays cause no danger at all such as to require the removal of the part X-rayed?

Dr Dering: It depends. If a patient comes to me today with X-rayed testicles I can advise him either to wait, and to see me frequently, or suggest removal.

Lord Gardiner: Do you know what 'to rationalize' means?

Dr Dering: No.

Lord Gardiner tried again. The Judge said 'May I help' and turned to Dr Dering: 'What Lord Gardiner and the jury want to know', he said, 'is this: When you were actually doing the operations, was that idea in your head? Or was it something you thought about later as a justification for what you had to do?'

Dr Dering: I thought already when I and my colleagues decided to carry out these operations in the interests of the patients—for various reasons.

Lord Gardiner referred to the register and 'No. 10' on the list—the first castration—and asked: Did you do that?

Dr Dering: Yes.

Lord Gardiner: What was the patient? A German Jew?

Dr Dering: I don't know if he was a German or other Jew; but he was X-rayed.

Lord Gardiner: Anyway, he was a Jew?

Dr Dering: He was a Jew.

Lord Gardiner: Why do you say that was not an experimental operation? It was, wasn't it?

Dr Dering: It was not an experimental operation but just the removal of something that was destroyed—like a crushed finger which cannot be saved and must be amputated. Am I not right to amputate?

Lord Gardiner: First of all, the answer is No, unless you have the patient's consent, isn't it? That is clear, isn't it?

Dr Dering: Not in concentration camps. Perhaps in normal conditions.

He studied the register again, and then conceded that though the entry for 'No. 10' was *castratio*, which meant the complete removal of testicles by surgery, it was not done under a court order. This, and two other cases, had been wrongly written up by him. The castration had been done by X-ray beforehand.

Lord Gardiner: Look at page 125. Were eleven more left testicles removed by you and Dr Grabczynski?

Dr Dering: Yes.

Lord Gardiner: Jewish testicles?

Dr Dering: They were mostly Jewish people.

It was not true that some time after that date he had attributed to Dr Grabczynski operations which he himself had done in order to help Dr Grabczynski 'work his passage'. Dr Grabczynski was a very experienced surgeon. It would have been a waste of time for one of them to assist the other.

Lord Gardiner: Do you remember one of the patients trying to get off the table and you slapping him down?

Dr Dering: No. I cannot remember and I don't think it was possible. It was normal procedure in every operation for the patient to be so placed that he could not have done that.

The next series of questions moved time back to Warsaw in 1928 and the racial persecution of the twentieth century. Dr Dering agreed that when he had first met Dr Alina Brewda she was a medical student, and that he had first come into contact with her through a fellow student, Krystyna Ossowska, who was his fiancée and whom he had later married. He agreed that at some time in 1922 or 1923—at the beginning of his student career—non-Jewish medical students had insisted on Jewish medical students sitting in a different part of the class room.

Lord Gardiner: It is right to say that you had no trouble or complications with Dr Brewda at that time?

Dr Dering agreed. He was, he said, already in the camp when the Germans had sent all Polish Jews to the Warsaw Ghetto. He knew that Auschwitz was the centre of a ring of forty camps, many of which were work camps, with some three million people doing forced labour.

Lord Gardiner: Auschwitz was both the headquarters of the forty camps, and also the murder surgery?

Dr Dering agreed. He knew that people from all over Europe had come to Auschwitz, and that some—'but not many'—were members of European resistance movements who had been caught by the Germans. He had not personally seen the way people arriving in the cattle trucks had been divided into two groups.

Lord Gardiner: I don't suggest you saw it, but as head of the underground you knew everything that went on; and you know it now?

Dr Dering: Yes.

He also knew, through the underground, that those over forty and the children, were never registered because they were sent straight to the gas chambers, and that they went into the gas chambers naked.

At first, the camp hospital had had German doctors in charge 'much less qualified' than he, but there had been a change of policy later and prisoner-doctors were allowed to work in the hospital.

Lord Gardiner: Of course, the Jewish doctors were not allowed to work as doctors, but only as orderlies?

Dr Dering: No. They worked as doctors.

Lord Gardiner: I suggest that the prisoner-doctors were non-Jewish and nearly all the Jewish doctors had to work as orderlies?

Dr Dering: We had 316 hospital staff, about sixty doctors of various nationalities. The rest were dressers.

Lord Gardiner: It was the exception that a Jewish doctor would be allowed to work as a doctor?

Dr Dering: We started as dressers and Jewish doctors came. German orders were that all doctors had to work in hospital either as doctor or as dresser.

The Judge: You still have not answered the question, Dr Dering. Lord Gardiner is asking you whether or not only a minority of Jewish prisoners who were doctors were allowed to work as doctors?

Dr Dering: As many as we needed in the hospital worked as doctors.

The Judge: Let us put it in a very simple way. You said there were about sixty doctors working in the hospital. How many were Jews, to your knowledge.

Dr Dering: I think maybe ten or twelve.

Lord Gardiner: Are all the doctors whose names are in your register officer-type non-Jewish Poles?

Dr Dering: Yes.

He knew that a large number of women in Block 10—at first about 100 and finally about 400 of fourteen different nationalities—had been in Block 10 for medical experiments; but he knew nothing about Dr Wirths' 'cancer research' except what he had heard from Dr Brewda.

Lord Gardiner: (mildly): But I thought that through the underground you knew everything that went on?

Dr Dering: Yes. I knew that there were operations on the cervix.

Lord Gardiner: Do you remember Dr Hautval—a French woman, a very religious Frenchwoman, not a Jew?

Dr Dering: No, I don't.

Lord Gardiner: She says, you see, that in May, long before Dr Brewda arrived, she asked you about the operations which Dr Wirths was doing, and you said you thought they could be dangerous for the women.

Dr Dering: I don't remember Dr Hautval and I don't remember any such conversation.

Lord Gardiner: And you knew Dr Clauberg as the doctor in charge of this mass sterilization programme and were very friendly with him?

Dr Dering: I am surprised to learn that I was friendly with Dr Clauberg.

Lord Gardiner: But you were an 'associate'[1] of his, were you not?

Dr Dering: As much as a prisoner can be associate with a Gestapo.

Lord Gardiner: You knew Dr Clauberg had got about 150 women on whom he was conducting sterilization experiments?

Dr Dering: I knew about some experiments he carried out there.

Lord Gardiner: Did you know they were of two kinds—first by injections of caustic fluid into the Fallopian tubes to see if they sterilized them, and, secondly, the experiments Dr Schumann was carrying out under him in relation to X-raying sexual organs?

Dr Dering: I guessed or heard rumours. I did not know what the experiments were.

Lord Gardiner: Have you since seen an indictment against Dr

[1] A reference to the statement of claim. Appendix, page 278.

Clauberg who was arrested as a war criminal but committed suicide before his trial?

Dr Dering: Yes.

Lord Gardiner: Have you read the indictment against Dr Schumann? He escaped to Ghana, did he not?

Dr Dering: I think so.

'Where he still is', added Lord Gardiner.

Lord Gardiner asked about Dr Samuel, a Jewish doctor. Dr Dering said that he did not know that Dr Samuel had removed irradiated ovaries under a general anaesthetic; but he did know that Dr Samuel had been sent to the gas chambers by the Germans. There were various rumours why. 'Presumably he was arrogant and he knew too much and he started one quarrel as with doctors . . .'

Lord Gardiner: I suggest—and I will hand you a copy—that you wrote a letter, and the view you express in it was not that he knew too much, but that he was 'old and useless and covered with eczema'.

Dr Dering: That is right.

Lord Gardiner read to Dr Dering the contents of two documents which had been translated from German into English and had been included among Dr Dering's pre-trial papers. Lord Gardiner, picking up the first document, read: 'Headquarters of the Fuehrer. July, 1942. Secret Reich's Matters,—single copy. On 7.7.42 a conference was held . . . object of the discussions being the sterilization of Jewesses, Himmler confirmed to . . . Professor Doctor Klauberg [Clauberg] that the concentration camp Auschwitz is at his disposal for his experiments on human beings and animals. On the basis of some fundamental experiments a method is to be found for causing sterilization without the person concerned noticing it. As soon as the result of these experiments is known [Himmler] wants a report transmitted to him in order that the sterilization of Jewesses can virtually be started. Moreover it should be tested preferably under consultation of Professor Dr Hohlfelder, who is an expert on X-rays in Germany, in what way a sterilization of male persons can be achieved by application of X-rays. [Himmler] stressed to all those present that the most secret matters are involved which can only be discussed internally, and whereby, in each case, all those participating in the experiments or discussions must be pledged to secrecy'.

Turning to the second document, Lord Gardiner read: To [Himmler] . . . as far as the question is concerned which you put to me a year ago, i.e. what time is required to carry out sterilization on 1,000 women in that way I am able to predict today the following: If the experiments which I have been carrying on continue to come off as well as hitherto—and there is no reason to suppose that they will not—the time is not very far off when I will be able to tell you, "by a properly trained doctor, in a properly fitted place (with assistant personnel of perhaps ten—the number of assistants depending upon the desired speed of the proceedings) most probably several hundred, if not thousand in one day" . . . Heil Hitler . . . Dr Clauberg'.

After inquiring why those documents had been included in Dr Dering's list among others relevant to the issues in the action Lord Gardiner asked: You know now that this was called the 'final solution of the Jewish problem'; that it was for the half- and quarter-Jews—when all the Jews had been murdered—who would still be left and would have to be dealt with, and that Hitler felt that to kill them all would cause difficulties with all their Aryan relations, and so the plan was to sterilize them. You know, now, do you not, that that was the object of the whole thing?

Dr Dering: Yes.

Lord Gardiner: At the time you realized that the experiments which were being done by X-rays and so forth, were being done to ascertain how far a particular race could be made to cease to exist by mass sterilization, did you not?

Dr Dering: I follow; I understand. May I explain? These documents were found after the war; nobody knew about them before.

Lord Gardiner: I am not suggesting for a moment that you knew about these documents at the time. Of course you did not.

The Judge: Members of the jury, these two documents were read to you for the purpose of finding out why Dr Dering included them in his list of documents which he thought were relevant to the issues in the trial. The documents by themselves do not begin to be evidence against Dr Dering.

Lord Gardiner returned to the register and asked: If this register had not been smuggled out by the underground, this case would largely be a question whether you are telling the truth, or Dr Brewda is, and it would be limited to some ten girls and a man. Has that not occurred to you?

Dr Dering: No.

Lord Gardiner: Did you think that all these people would be dead, and no one would be found?

Dr Dering: On the contrary.. I am pretty sure that I saved their lives.

Lord Gardiner: Did you not realize that, if somebody had not smuggled out the register, none of these people could ever have been found—if any of them were alive?

Dr Dering: They would. They are very well organized all over the world.

Lord Gardiner: Were you not doing these testicles operations to demonstrate how quickly you could do them?

Dr Dering: No. There was no question of speed.

Lord Gardiner: Were you not very proud about the speed with which you could remove these Jewish testicles?

Dr Dering: Not at all.

It would not be true, he said, if a doctor stated he had seen Dr Dering with Dr Entress removing the testicles from a young Jew, and about twelve others waiting in the passage. It was 'not allowed' to gather in the corridor. If a doctor were to say that he had come from the infectious diseases block to Block 21 and had seen Dr Dering operating on a male Jew, it would not be true, because he was 'not allowed to come from infectious diseases block to spread diseases'.

Lord Gardiner: Did you feel that as these testicles cases were Jewish men it did not much matter?

Dr Dering: We were very sorry for the Jews. We were suffering too.

Lord Gardiner: You were, I suggest, rather surprised at the speed at which you were doing the operation?

Dr Dering: The speed depended on the technique of the surgeon.

Lord Gardiner: Do you remember saying to a doctor, 'I have taken another twenty eggs off young Jews today'?

Dr Dering: No. I do not. I could not remember it nearly twenty years ago.

Lord Gardiner: 'Plenty of eggs for scrambling?'

Dr Dering: No. I read this allegation and know where from it comes.

Lord Gardiner: After Dr Brewda arrived in September 1943, she sent you a message asking you to come and see her at Block 10, and you did not arrive?

Dr Dering: I could not go by myself.

Dr Brewda might be telling the truth, he said, if she said she had told him that he seemed to have put on weight, and if she said that he had his hair short, but not shaved, and that his uniform looked as though it was tailor-made. He always made time to get up half-an-hour earlier to shave, wash and clean. People who neglected themselves broke down. As a surgeon he had to keep himself clean. He was wearing leather shoes; but at that time everyone had leather shoes. He had met Dr Brewda when she came to the hospital to have some equipment sterilized. He had told her that he had been doing 'much surgery', between 16,000 and 17,000 operations. The girl patients in Block 10 did not knit him a white pullover in return for extra rations.

Lord Gardiner returned to the register. Dr Dering repeated that he would accept as accurate only those entries in his own handwriting. Seventeen years ago, in Brixton, he had remembered altogether about eighty-five cases of the kind under consideration; and—strangely enough—that was about the number now appearing in his handwriting. He had two objections to a page showing that he had assisted Dr Grabczynski in six testicle operations: first, they were not in his handwriting; and, secondly, he and Dr Grabczynski had seldom assisted each other even in major operations, so that it was unlikely that they would do so in minor operations. 'We had a number of young surgeons who had need to exercise their fingers.' [This was accompanied by a gesture and flexing of the fingers.] He said that he did not know that a tall man called Blankenburg had reported that 'Dr Dering could remove testicles so quickly that there was not much point in messing about with X-rays'.

'SHE IS ALIVE AND HAS BEEN FOUND'

Lord Gardiner turned to the operations on the ten young Greek Jewish girls. He suggested that all ten had been done by Dr Dering.

Dr Dering: Even a register which I query shows that I performed only five. Why should it be suggested that I did ten?

If he had operated, he said, *he* would have given the spinal anaesthetic. It was Dr Brewda's duty to see that patients were premedicated in the ward. He knew the day's programme and would have ordered that.

Lord Gardiner: I suggest that the spinal injection was done in the ante-room?

Dr Dering: No. It was done when the operation was going on.

The patient was put on the table immediately after arrival. The other girls, he said, were either in Block 10 or outside the theatre in the corridor of Block 21.

He was cross-examined about the surgical details of ovariectomy and whether the proper thing to do was to cover the pedicle by using the flap of the peritoneum.

Dr Dering: As a matter of fact, there is not a peritoneal flap to use. It can be done with one broad stitch.

He sought to explain the surgery. The nature of the operation, with a short incision, was such that even an assistant could not see what he was doing. 'I am surprised that Dr Brewda could have X-ray eyes to see what I was doing when it was impossible to see.'

He was reminded that he had told Mr Duncan that nobody could have seen the detail of the surgery 'except the theatre staff'. He replied that his nearest assistant who was actually holding the hooks would eventually see the moment when he was ligating. In practice no one else could.

He denied that the last two girls had unhealed irradiation burns.

Lord Gardiner: You remember Dr. Brewda saying: 'Leave them alone. They have suffered enough already' and you said 'Shut up. I have my orders. They will kill me. I have to do it'?

Dr Dering: No. No. No. I could be strict, but I was never rude, especially to women. Remember I had no anaesthetist.

Lord Gardiner: But, Dr Dering, there are hundreds and hundreds and hundreds of cases showing you giving a *general* anaesthetic. I suggest it is not true that you were short of anaesthetists, because the register shows that a large number of abdominal operations were done under a general anaesthetic.

Dr Dering began to explain the nature of operations requiring a general anaesthetic.

The Judge: Never mind what the type of operation was. I understood you to say earlier today that one of the reasons why you gave these cases of amputation of testicles a spinal anaesthetic was that you had not got the services of an anesthetist. Lord Gardiner is pointing out that in the register, in your handwriting, time and time again, there are cases where a general anaesthetic was given. No doubt the inference which the jury are asked to draw from that is that you did have, on those occasions, the services of an anaesthetist?

Dr Dering: I had later on the services of some doctor. For a longer operation I applied general anaesthetic. But this is a matter of choice. A surgeon can use whichever anaesthetic is most suitable in a particular case.

Lord Gardiner: Then the reason you gave for not giving a general anaesthetic in this case—that you had not got an anaesthetist—is untrue?

Dr Dering: Not exactly. I did even operations on doctors and most doctors preferred spinal because they knew what could happen if an unqualified assistant should apply general anaesthetic.

Lord Gardiner: Those were operations done with the patients' consent?

Dr Dering: Yes.

Lord Gardiner: I suggest that if these girls were struggling and screaming, it might have been kinder to give them a general anaesthetic?

Dr Dering: General anaesthetic takes time. It takes at least twenty minutes. We had not the time. We worked from six in the morning to six at night in very great rush, so I could not wait any time for operations I did not want.

Lord Gardiner: But you had time to give the others on this page a general anaesthetic?

There was no audible reply.

Later Dr Dering said that Dr Brewda had not remembered these things soon after the concentration camp, but now after twenty years she had concluded that 'such and such conversations' took place.

Lord Gardiner: You say no such conversation took place at all because she was never there and the whole thing is an invention of Dr Brewda's?

Dr Dering: Yes.

It was not true that when the last two girls arrived it was plain that their left ovaries had already been removed. He did not remember a single case operated 'for the second time'. All had been 'for the first time'.

Lord Gardiner: Do you remember, when the last but one was on the table, that, after you started the operation, she was still moving?

Dr Dering: I do not remember. But for a surgeon with experience when a patient is anaesthetized by spinal there is no movement.

Lord Gardiner: I suggest that in the last two cases, the spinal, for some reason, seemed to be wearing off; that none of the others felt anything while the operation was going on, but that the last two girls did. Can you suggest any reason for that?

Dr Dering: I do not remember such situation, and if the patient moved or complained of pain something could have been done by way of general anaesthetic.

Lord Gardiner: I suggest you did do something—that when the last girl but one moved, you hit her and said, 'You damned Jewess, keep still until I have finished'.

Dr Dering: I strongly deny these allegations. It is conspiracy against me. If I may prove Dr Brewda's truthfulness . . .

The Judge: One moment. Will you answer the question and not make accusations.

Lord Gardiner (in the gentlest inquiring voice): This is another invention of Dr Brewda's is it?

Dr Dering: Yes.

Lord Gardiner: Why do you think that?

Dr Dering: Dr Brewda as medical officer of secret police in Warsaw produced horrible accusations against me. This is now in Mr Uris's book. Seventeen years ago she produced photograph of my prison photograph put on Gestapo cap and uniform, and sent it to London as proof that I was not only *Volksdeutsch* but also Gestapo officer.

Lord Gardiner: You are not suggesting that Dr Brewda has said to anyone that you hit this girl and called her a damned Jewess? Why do you suggest it was an invention of Dr Brewda?

There was a pause.

Lord Gardiner turned his head very slightly and looked over his left shoulder to the crowded court behind him and said: I think it is fair to say that this girl is alive and has been found; and it is *she* who says what you did to her, and that while Dr Brewda was sitting there on the stool you hit the girl.

Dr Dering seemed not to understand. 'You have Dr Brewda's word', he said.

Lord Gardiner: No. I am not relying on Dr Brewda's word but on the word of the girl who has been found and is alive and is here. Is it true or not?

Dr Dering: It is untrue.

The Judge intervened. He must explain to the jury what was happening. Lord Gardiner sat down. Then the Judge told the jury that they had to try this case on the evidence. Evidence consisted of what the witnesses said in the witness box and any documents or other articles which might be produced. What Lord Gardiner was now putting to Dr Dering as facts was not evidence. It would only become evidence if either Dr Dering agreed with it, or some other witness proved the facts which Lord Gardiner was putting. They must keep that very clearly in their minds.

Mr Duncan pointed out that the very last matter put to Dr Dering had not been pleaded as justification and therefore could not be the subject of cross-examination.

Lord Gardiner said that it was his duty to put to the witness the evidence which he would be calling. He turned to Dr Dering again: 'Do you know that the last girl of all developed a haemorrhage that night, and that Dr Brewda will say that she sent you a message and you did not come and the girl died during the night?'

Dr Dering: I did not know anything about it.

Lord Gardiner: If it is true, she must have died as a result of the operation?

Dr Dering: It is a great IF!

Now Dr Dering was being asked about the resistance movements in the camp. Was there an international movement called the Auschwitz Fighting Group, and were not its four leaders an Austrian called Langbein, and a Pole called Cyrankiewiecz, 'who later became Prime Minister of Poland', and another Pole called Haluk, and an Austrian called Burger 'who was found out by the

Germans and hanged'? He agreed that by the end of 1943 such a movement had emerged and that those were its leaders.

Lord Gardiner: And the clique of Polish-Army-officer type always refused to join it and formed a little group of their own?

Dr Dering: No. And I would like to tell you, Lord Gardiner, that it was not a clique of Polish officers, but a large organization since autumn of 1940, when Mr Langbein and Cyrankiewiecz were not yet in the camp.

Lord Gardiner turned back to motive. If what was done was otherwise morally wrong, would Dr Dering have thought himself justified in doing it because of what the other Polish doctors said? He replied that they had either to do it or face disaster for themselves and for the underground movement; and there was also the medical justification already explained.

Lord Gardiner: I am calling some distinguished English surgeons on this, so I must put it to you that they say there is not now and was not then any justification for removing either testicle or ovary merely because it had been irradiated.

Dr Dering: It could happen something or it could happen nothing. In camp conditions I could not take the risk.

Lord Gardiner: But if you had refused to do it, and unless somebody else did it, they would simply have been sent back to work?

Dr Dering: If they recovered.

Lord Gardiner: But if they recovered *with* an operation, they would recover all the quicker without one. You could not reasonably have thought that you would have been sent to the gas chambers yourself?

Dr Dering: It could be done. It was quite possible.

Lord Gardiner: But, I suggest, wildly unlikely—in view of your position with the Germans?

Dr Dering: My relations with Germans were just as any other prisoner who did what he had to do. I was working on both fronts. I had to do my medical job and my underground movement jobs. I could not run through the camp with Polish national white and red flag. I had to be careful with all my movements. I could not be brusque to Germans and give them rude reply. It would have been the end of me and of very important underground work which helped thousands and thousands of people.

Lord Gardiner suggested that the likelihood of being punished by death was wrong; first, because, with the exception of Dr Samuel, no prisoner-doctor had been sent to the gas chambers; and secondly, there was a very good example in Dr Dering's own evidence of refusal to obey an order, 'When you were directly ordered by your German superiors to give that phenol injection, you, to your credit, absolutely refused. You were told that you would be punished. And you were punished—by not being allowed to go outside the camp on your "half-day" for a fortnight'?

Dr Dering: That is right.

Lord Gardiner: That was when you were less dominant with the Germans than you were in November 1943?

Dr Dering: Yes. But there is a big difference between that refusal and operation. In that case I would have killed the man I refused. In the other case I would save the man—and I did it.

Lord Gardiner reverted to the visit to Block 10 after the operations and asked: Did Dr Brewda complain to you that she had only got paper bandages?

Dr Dering: It is absolutely untrue. At that time no one had paper bandages.

Lord Gardiner: But she knew you had proper bandages?

Dr Dering: If *she* had not, it was her fault.

Lord Gardiner: But she knew *you* had proper bandages, and was pointing out to you that she had only paper bandages. She asked if you could give her something for the girls?

Dr Dering: On my visit to Block 10 I was surrounded by these six nice young pleasant girls, who were very friendly, including Dr Brewda herself, and they just joked with me. I looked at the patients. Everything was all right. No temperature; no dirty or septic wounds. What should I do more? I was satisfied and left the block.

Lord Gardiner: How many did you see, do you remember?

Dr Dering: I saw all the operations.

Lord Gardiner: Do you mean all ten?

Dr Dering: I cannot remember now—ten or more or less.

Lord Gardiner: But I thought you said you saw your five?

Dr Dering: If I went there I probably saw all operated on same day.

Lord Gardiner: I suggest you saw all those who remained alive. Do you still say you only operated on five and not ten?

Dr Dering: Yes.

Then Lord Gardiner was asking about January 1944; and Dr Dering agreed that he had then been released from Auschwitz 'for one year' to help Dr Clauberg.

Lord Gardiner: And did you make yourself so useful to Dr Clauberg that he succeeded in keeping you after the end of the year?

Dr Dering: Six days before my term came, Clauberg escaped and I remained myself without him. Between January and April 1945, when there was fighting between Russians and Germans, I did not know which day I would be captured by the Gestapo and removed to Germany.

Lord Gardiner: But you never did have to go back to Auschwitz?

Dr Dering: It was liquidated some time in January.

Now the questions were about Dr Dering in post-war Poland. Lord Gardiner asked: Was there a day in Warsaw when you heard that Dr Brewda and other doctors had survived and were in Warsaw, and on that day you fled to Italy?

Dr Dering denied it. He had been warned by a friend that Dr Brewda was chief deputy medical officer to the secret police, that she was furious with him, and had promised to liquidate him mercilessly. He had seen her name on the door of the 'secret police office'. So he had changed his name and continued to work underground until November 1945. He had been in hospital for two months under a false name, being treated for troubles developed in the camp; and when he recovered he walked on crutches. He had been 'simply shocked' when Dr Brewda, through her powerful friends, had denounced him as a war criminal. He had not known what to do as between his underground duties and the new régime in Poland.

His voice grew tired and he faltered: 'I worked hard for my people, but just through the ambition of one bad woman who wanted to cover up her own experience in Block 10 . . .' He stopped.

Lord Gardiner waited until Dr Dering was composed again. Then he said: 'I do appreciate that some of the things I have to put to you may be painful for you. But you *do* realize that it is *you* who have brought this action for damages against a novelist whose whole Auschwitz episode in his novel occupies one page?'

Dr Dering: Lord Gardiner, the one sentence is exactly the same as Dr Brewda put in her accusations against me seventeen years ago—with the same 'h' in the middle of the name, the same '17,000 experimental operations' and with mortality 100 per cent. which is again fantastic.

The Judge: That is not the accusation with which the jury are concerned. There is no suggestion that all your patients died.

Dr Dering: But that is the beginning of Dr Brewda's accusation.

Lord Gardiner: Could you tell me, before I finally pass from the register, how many of the operations of an experimental nature which you did for Dr Schumann do you admit having taken part in?

Dr Dering: So far as I can remember, checking by the entries in my handwriting, eighty-five with colleagues. How many by myself I must check again. [He looked at the register lists.] Not more than thirty-three. We had to assist German doctors.

STATEMENTS TO THE HOME OFFICE

Lord Gardiner: Did you make a number of statements in Brixton Prison?

Mr Duncan intervened to say that after the Treasury Solicitor had been subpoenaed to produce the documents, the parties had agreed copies. Copies of documents were handed to Dr Dering. Lord Gardiner began to put to him for comment statements from the documents: 'I had certainly also heard that Dr Brewda said she would finish me. She in fact performed experimental operations on prisoners under the directions of the Germans. I myself performed no experimental operation. Dr Brewda is now acting as the doctor for the secret police in Poland'. Lord Gardiner paused, and asked: Quite untrue, I suppose?

Dr Dering: I still say that what I performed was to remove the glands destroyed by experiments in *bona fides* to save people's lives and suffering. It was not experimental on my side.

Lord Gardiner: Of course, at the time you made this statement you did not know that any relevant person except Dr Brewda had survived?

Dr Dering: I can imagine that many survived. About January the 19th, 1945, some people from the concentration camp at

Auschwitz were transferred to the hospital where I was. I saw a lot passing through and I was able to help some of them—even some Jewish people.

A document headed 'My Replies to the Accusations made by Dr Brewda' was under analysis. Lord Gardiner read: 'I had been very careful to record even the most simple cases so as to have evidence in the future', and 'all the operations performed were medically indicated'. Then Lord Gardiner asked: Is it still being denied that any of Dr Schumann's experimental operations took place in your block?

Dr Dering: The medical indication was to remove their organs.

Lord Gardiner continued relentlessly: '. . . in every case the sick were anaesthetised by chlorylethyl'. That is a general anaesthetic, is it not?

Dr Dering: It could not be applied for these operations.

The Judge: Maybe it could not; but the patient would have been completely unconscious.

Lord Gardiner went on reading: 'It is not true that in the presence of Dr Brewda I boasted of making sixty removals of testicles in two hours' and 'even a stranger to medicine would conclude that ten or twelve minutes would be a terrifically short time for such a job'. Lord Gardiner then commented: And you said the same in relation to the women. You are saying now, are you not, that the testicles were removed in ten or twelve minutes and that that is a perfectly proper time?

Dr Dering: I think it could be removed . . .

The Judge: I thought you said that that was what you were doing?

Dr Dering: Yes.

Lord Gardiner: Then you were wrong in saying that 'ten or twelve minutes would be a terrifically short time for such a job'?

Dr Dering: Dr Brewda said sixty in two hours.

Lord Gardiner: Then you declared 'only five operations performed on women'?

Dr Dering: At that time I remembered only five.

Lord Gardiner continued reading: 'They'—that is the Germans—'tried to persuade me to go on *Volkslist*', and you repeatedly refused. Then you say: 'They took me on one occasion in 1944 out of concentration camp and ordered me to work in an ordinary

German hospital. I did not change my mind, and I was sent back to the concentration camp'. That was a quite untrue account you were putting forward to the Home Office, was it not?

Dr Dering: Yes.

Lord Gardiner: The truth is that you had been released for a year to help Professor Clauberg and in fact never went back to the camp?

Dr Dering: I was kept on concentration camp list.

Lord Gardiner: Then that last sentence is untrue?

Dr Dering: This last sentence is strange, because I was not sent back.

Lord Gardiner: And you say you were 'freed by the Russians on April the 1st, 1945'. That would lead the Home Office to think that except for a period of a day or two you never left Auschwitz?

Dr Dering: It is something I cannot understand.

Lord Gardiner: Is the reason for it that you did not want the Home Office to know that you had been released from Auschwitz to help Dr Clauberg?

Dr Dering: I retained the status of prisoner to the end.

Lord Gardiner repeated the question. Dr Dering replied: 'I was taken as prisoner from the camp and handed to Professor Clauberg in the miners' hospital'.

Lord Gardiner began to repeat the question a third time. Dr Dering interrupted him, saying: 'I did tell the truth'.

Lord Gardiner: But this is not the truth in the last paragraph.

Dr Dering: I never came back.

Lord Gardiner asked him why he had not said frankly that he was released to help Professor Clauberg but had instead put in this false story. He replied: 'I cannot answer that question'.

Lord Gardiner: Is there any reason except that you did not want the Home Office to know . . .

Dr Dering interrupted: I confessed everything to the Home Office—everything that happened there.

Another passage, dated 26 July 1947, went under counsel's microscopic examination. In it Dr Dering had denied that he was performing sterilization or castration operations 'at Block 21 or elsewhere'. Dr Dering said he had tried to explain to the Home Office that they were 'Germans sentenced by German court, and as prisoner I had to do what I was told'. Lord Gardiner pointed out that that was not what he had said. What he had said was, 'It is not true'.

Lord Gardiner: Look at the photograph of the register—at page 112—number 10, on May the 20th. That was a castration performed by you?

Dr Dering: No, because this man was X-rayed. He was already castrated.

Lord Gardiner: You end up by saying 'I did not perform any such operations'. That is not true, is it?

Dr Dering: From this point of view you are right to say that I 'performed'; but I did no experiments carried out by myself. They were not chosen by me or carried out by me. I had no possibility to refuse or to convince Germans not to carry out this operation.

Lord Gardiner: But you don't say that to the Home Office.

Dr Dering said that Lord Gardiner was taking extracts from one statement which sounded 'as not true'.

Lord Gardiner referred to another passage. 'The removal of one testicle is neither sterilization nor castration but just removal of a dead body from the human organism without any further influence . . .', and said: I have already put to you that from the medical point of view, such an organ is not dead but merely non-functioning?

Dr Dering: It is not functioning. It means it is not normal—non-functioning.

Lord Gardiner: After the change of life in women, the sex organs no longer function. But they are not dead and we don't remove them, do we?

Dr Dering: They are non-functioning.

Lord Gardiner: And you have agreed that no one could tell for certain whether a man who had been X-rayed was potent or not, and that the object of removing a testicle was to find out?

Dr Dering: The object was just German purpose to carry out further experiments.

Lord Gardiner: To test it, to find out whether the X-rays made it impotent or not?

Dr Dering: What they wanted to find I don't know. I could logically come to a conclusion, but they did not tell me.

Lord Gardiner: I thought you agreed that you realized at the time that the object of taking out these testicles and putting them in bottles was to see if the X-rays had succeeded in rendering them impotent or not?

Dr Dering: Maybe that was the purpose.

Lord Gardiner went on reading. After a reference to operations on eighty-five men and five women there was this: 'I categorically declare that no one was ever performing in Block 21 any other operations while the Block was under my supervision. The best documents would, of course, be the surgical diary for which I cared so very much, thinking of its usefulness in the future. Alas! it disappeared!'

Why, asked Lord Gardiner, had Dr Dering said all that?

He replied that he had not had the register with him in Brixton Prison in 1947. The figure of ninety had stuck in his memory. That was in agreement with the part of the register now available in his handwriting. He was convinced that the rest of the 130 cases now being considered were not by him.

The Judge: As I understand it, you have said that from time to time S.S. doctors performed operations in Block 21. Now, in the light of that passage, will you explain how it came about that you told the Home Office that no one ever performed 'any other operations in Block 21'?

Dr Dering: My Lord, in many places I did inform the Home Office about this kind of operation. I did not hide it at all. I can see now that this page you have read could give an impression that I had not performed the operations.

Then Lord Gardiner read a passage about Dr Dering's punishment for refusal in 1941 to give the lethal injection of phenol. 'I was forbidden to leave the block for two weeks or go for walks.' To your credit, you refused altogether to execute that order?

Dr Dering: It was just luck. It could have been much worse.

Lord Gardiner: It was a very trivial punishment for an Auschwitz prisoner, wasn't it?

There was no reply.

Lord Gardiner continued reading: 'Personally I do not remember removing more than one testicle'. He asked: We know now that you did, on a number of occasions. Are you saying you had forgotten them?

Dr Dering: I was convinced until not long ago when I checked in the register.

Lord Gardiner: You made the statement that no testicle which had not undergone X-ray treatment was ever removed by you. That was untrue, was it not?

Dr Dering: As we know it now; but at Brixton I could only rely on my memory.

Lord Gardiner: Are you telling my Lord and the jury that when you wrote that, you had completely forgotten about all the court order cases?

Dr Dering: I think so.

The Judge: You are saying that you had forgotten that, on two occasions, according to the exhibit, you had removed healthy testicles under a German court order?

Dr Dering said that that was so.

Lord Gardiner: 'We doctors knew that if we did not perform these operations the men would be sent to the gas chamber and their testicles would be removed after death.' That, I suggest, *nobody* in Auschwitz could have thought. Obviously the gas chambers would have been described to you?

Dr Dering: I did not see the gas chambers I could by description imagine them.

Lord Gardiner: You can well imagine, with some thousands of bodies being released from a gas chamber together, to be conveyed to a crematorium, that to suggest that someone could find some particular body in order to remove testicles is absurd?

Dr Dering: We had threats from Dr Schumann that it might happen if we did not carry out orders.

Lord Gardiner: But you did not really think, knowing the sort of picture presented by a gas chamber when it was opened, that someone was really going to try to find one particular body in order to remove the testicles from it?

Dr Dering: It was just theoretical how they would do it—a special mark somehow, so that they would have no difficulty.

Lord Gardiner: Out of some thousands of bodies, to find one particular one?

There was no reply.

Lord Gardiner referring to a page in 'Additional Statements' to the Home Office in 1948: You told the Home Office this time that you had been given fourteen days 'solitary confinement' as a punishment for refusing to give a lethal injection of phenol. That was not true, was it?

Dr Dering explained that this document was a translation from Polish. By 'solitary confinement' he had meant that he stayed in the block and could not go out.

The Judge asked whether anyone from the Home Office was present for the assistance of the court. It had occurred to him that the original statement was in Polish, and even very good translations contained mistakes.

Lord Gardiner said that these were Dr Dering's own documents, disclosed by him. They had been lodged with the Home Office in English and not in German or Polish.

Lord Gardiner then handed to Dr Dering two documents and told the court that they were copies of a letter from Dr Dering's solicitors to the Home Office, at the date of the extradition inquiry, and of a statement prepared by 'leading counsel' on Dr Dering's instructions in 1948, putting his case to the Home Office 'in the best possible way'. Dr Dering was asked to read it to himself carefully. He did so.

Lord Gardiner: That is 'Dr Dering's case setting out the reasons on which it is urged that the deportation order should be cancelled', is it not?

The Judge: Try to think about this, Dr Dering. Read it carefully before you answer any of Lord Gardiner's questions.

Dr Dering said that he did not remember whether the statement had been written with his authority or whether he had seen leading counsel at the time. Some people from the underground movement had tried to help him and had approached leading counsel. He had only heard about their action in prison. The deportation order had been postponed because of it.

Lord Gardiner asked him to look again at the document. Was there anything there that did not express his point of view? Dr Dering said that the expression that he had been 'friendly with' Dr Clauberg sounded strange. His relations with Dr Clauberg had simply been those of a prisoner. Dr Clauberg had not beaten or hit him but had treated him in a normal way. He had been working quite hard, doing a lot of jobs for Clauberg.

The Judge: Is there nothing else there to which you wish to object? Take your time.

There was a lapse of some minutes while Dr Dering studied the document.

The Judge: Is there anything else you don't accept as being your case?

Dr Dering: I think once more I am surprised at this 'friendly terms'.

The Judge: Then this document, having been accepted, may be marked as an exhibit as also may the Home Office letter.

Lord Gardiner (to Dr Dering): Then it was right to describe you as 'an admitted anti-Semite'?

Dr Dering: I was called by some people—rather a small group—anti-Semitic, but I can say I have still today very sincerely Jewish friends.

Lord Gardiner: His Lordship asked you to say whether there was anything else which did not represent your views. It was *your* document; and it says: 'The victims in Block 10 were Jewesses, as were the doctors, whereas Dr Dering, by contrast, was an admitted anti-Semite'.

The reply was inaudible.

Then Lord Gardiner read a passage from 'counsel's statement' of 1948: 'The evidence against Dr Dering is mainly founded on Mr G's revelation that both his testicles were removed by Dr Dering'.

'A lot of statements on both sides,' Lord Gardiner said, 'were sent to the Home Office; and then one man, Mr G—a Pole living in Paris—was sent to identify you, because he said you were the man who had removed his testicles, and there was a hearing at Bow Street?'

Dr Dering agreed.

Lord Gardiner: And, having come to identify you, he said, when he saw you, 'I not only cannot identify this man, but this was not the man who operated on me'. If that was to be the test, that is why you were released, is it not?

Dr Dering: Yes.

Lord Gardiner: Now see Case No. 10 on page 112 of the register. That is another 'Mr G'. You told us that that was an operation performed by you under the heading *casus explorativus*—a castration. You did that one, didn't you?

Dr Dering: Yes.

Lord Gardiner: And the very next one was done by Dr Grabczynski?

Dr Dering: Yes.

Lord Gardiner: And that was on the Mr G who came to identify you?

Dr Dering: Yes.

Lord Gardiner: So Mr G was right in saying that 'This was not the man who did it'?

Dr Dering: Yes. But he could have recognized me easily because I was often in the ward: and he said at once that I did not do it.

Lord Gardiner: But if the previous case—also Mr G—had come over, the test would have ended in a different way?

Mr Duncan objected to the question.

Lord Gardiner put it another way: Or if, instead of stopping at that point and letting Dr Grabczynski do the next one, you had done it, he could have identified you?

Dr Dering: Yes.

In further answers Dr Dering agreed that what Mr Duncan had described in his opening speech as 'the Home Office apology' was a letter in which it was stated that the Home Secretary had 'now decided that there is not sufficient evidence to support a *prima facie* case for the surrender of Dr Dering to the Polish Government as a war criminal'; and that had been after the Bow Street hearing when Mr G had not identified him.

Had he, Lord Gardiner asked, seen the passage about himself in Tenenbaum's *Underground* published in 1952?

He said that he had read the relevant passage when it had been produced by the defendants on discovery.

Lord Gardiner: It is substantially the same as in *Exodus*, is it not?

Dr Dering: Yes. It is a very well organized action.

Lord Gardiner read from pages 272–273 of Tenenbaum's *Underground* and said: 'That was published in 1952 and had a large sale in English-speaking countries. Do you say that no one brought it to your attention?'

Dr Dering: No. I was in Africa for ten years. I think I saw the book.

Lord Gardiner: Your name is spelt with an 'H'. And you say you did not read *This was Auschwitz* by Dr Friedmann in London in 1946?

Dr Dering: No.

Lord Gardiner: And you were not interested to read about the medical trials at Nuremberg?

Dr Dering: I was myself in gaol at the time.

Lord Gardiner: But they were published in 1949, when you were free and in England?

Dr Dering: I was occupied in getting my daily food and had no time to read.

Copies of the novel *Exodus* were then handed to members of the jury in a paper-back edition which Mr Duncan said were identical in content with the defendant publishers' hard-back edition.

Lord Gardiner pointed out that the paper-back was not published by them and the Judge told the jury to remember that, although the author of the paper-back was the first defendant.

Dr Dering agreed that *Exodus* was a long novel.

Lord Gardiner: The Auschwitz episode in the book is a very small episode in a work which purports to be a work of fiction, is it not?

Dr Dering: It is not fiction. It is very anti-Polish and anti-English, of course.

He agreed that the operations *casus explorativus* were all on Jewish men and women and that the Greek girls had done nothing wrong. When he found that the men and women were all Jewish, he did not think that that was accidental. They had been chosen by the Germans. 'I would like to tell you', said Dr Dering, 'that in Ravensbrück experiments the guinea-pigs were Polish women. What nationality the Germans chose, we had no influence. It just happened that in Auschwitz they chose people of Jewish nationality.'

Lord Gardiner: Did you think they had chosen Jews for these experiments because they were Jews, or simply that there were more Jews than any others in the camp?

Dr Dering: That was just bad luck for them. We were sorry for them.

He would not have hesitated, he said, for the same reasons, to castrate Polish officers.

He was removed from Auschwitz in January, 1944, without being asked. He was not working for his release before November 1943. It was natural to want to escape from hell, but he wanted to stay to the end because the underground had 'important things' in preparation, which he had had to leave behind.

Lord Gardiner: No one is blaming you for wanting to get out of Auschwitz, but I am suggesting that, perfectly naturally, you were wanting to work your passage and obtain your release?

Dr Dering: I did not work my passage. The Germans had empty place they wanted to fill by slave labour, and they used me. Dr Clauberg had free help.

It was just coincidental, said Dr Dering in answer to Lord Gardiner's closing questions, that by the time he left Auschwitz he had done the operations on the ovaries and testicles.

Lord Gardiner sat down. Dr Dering had been under cross-examination for seven hours.

CHAPTER VII

Re-examination and Judge's Questions

MR DUNCAN re-examined Dr Dering about the Home Office statements. He said that he had given them in Polish at a time when his knowledge of English was less than it now was. His 'categorical' statement that 'no other operations' were performed while Block 21 was under his supervision had been accompanied by the further statement about the eighty-five men and five women about which he had already written; and apart from those ninety operations, and a few court sentences cases, all the operations were dictated by normal life and were medically justified.

The allegation against him made to the Home Office that he had carried out operations in two minutes was 'physically impossible'. At Auschwitz there had been no way of finding out whether the effect of radiation of the genitals had been slight or grave, and if he had to choose now, in the conditions obtaining at Auschwitz, whether to leave in or take out such an organ, he would take it out.

He could see at all times when operating in the theatre whether anyone else was there. Dr Klodzinski had never been there during one of his operations; of that he was 'absolutely certain'.

Dr Dering restated his reasons for doing the operations given in evidence and cross-examination. The register, he said, gave the name of the anaesthetist, and in no single case was a qualified anaesthetist there. Those shown as giving the anaesthetics were unqualified though trained by the prisoner-doctors. He could not remember cases of general anaesthetics being used for operations below the navel, though there might have been some; but his view was that for ovariectomy and the removal of testicles, spinal anaesthesia was preferable from all points of view.

Mr Duncan: Are you still of that opinion?

Dr Dering: Yes.

Mr Duncan sat down at 2.31 p.m. on the fourth day of the hearing.

Before Dr Dering left the witness box, the Judge said that he would like to ask some questions. He read the words from *Exodus* and asked: As I understand it, you are saying that Dr Schumann, Dr Wirths and Dr Clauberg, referred to in that passage, were S.S. doctors, and were, in fact, doing what the book says they were doing?

Dr Dering: Yes.

The Judge: Your complaint is, as I understand it, that you were in an entirely different position from them, because they were S.S. doctors, whereas you were a prisoner?

Dr Dering: Yes.

The Judge: What you are saying is that it was quite untrue that you performed 17,000 experiments in surgery without anaesthetic?

Dr Dering: Yes.

The Judge: And you say that because of that untrue statement you have been defamed?

Dr Dering: Yes.

The Judge: The defendants, on the other hand, say that you have not been defamed because, in substance, what they said about you is true: that you performed 130 operations in conditions of brutality, using a spinal anaesthetic without doing it in a proper way?

Dr Dering: Yes.

The Judge: I want the jury to get a picture of the position as best they can. Will you take the register, and open it at the first entry? What is the serial number of the first entry?

Dr Dering (reading): 14,139.

The Judge: Now turn forward in the register to the last entry in your handwriting. What is the serial number?

Dr Dering: 18,064.

The Judge: There are 3,925 operations in that book which you agree you did or assisted at or were present at?

Dr Dering: Yes.

The Judge: Of which according to the particulars forty-six [in your handwriting] are said to be experiments without proper anaesthetic or procedure?

Dr Dering: Yes.

The Judge: Now turn to the last entry with which this court is concerned. What is the serial number of the last entry on November the 10th, 1943? That is 19,521, is it not?

Dr Dering: Yes.

The Judge: I want the jury to see what you were doing in an ordinary, typical, day's work. Will you put the register on the box in front of you? (*Dr Dering did so.*) Now close it. (*He did so.*) Now open it at random between the cover and the point I have flagged. Put it on the ledge so that we can all see what is happening. Stand up. Read out the number of the page at which you have opened it.

Dr Dering: Page 112.

The Judge: That happens to be one of the pages we have actually been looking at. Now start at the top of the page and read out, putting into English, the diagnosis in respect of each patient.

Dr Dering read a list of operations: Glands in the neck. The next is the same; Septic thigh. Bruises of upper part of left thigh—

The Judge: The sort of bruises from a Gestapo beating?

Dr Dering: Yes.

He continued the list: Boils . . . Suppurating bursa . . . Cellulitis of the right leg . . . Condition after operation for hernia . . . Tubercular neck glands . . . Suppurating ear . . . Septic nose boil . . . Abscess of breast . . . Abscess of forearm . . . Abscess of abdominal wall . . . Neck carbuncle . . . Septic foot . . . Septic index finger . . . Face abscess . . . Abscess of right hand . . . Abscess of arm . . . of thigh . . . Septic knee . . . Septic buttock.

The Judge: So it goes on until at the bottom of the page, the jury can see that there are three cases in which you were said to be co-operating in experimental operations?

Dr Dering: Agreed.

The Judge: Were any other of those experimental in either the ordinary or the suggested meaning of the word—or your meaning of the word?

Dr Dering: Not at all anything to do with experiments. Just normal operations.

The Judge: The very last entry in your handwriting in the register is numbered 18,064? And you started the register?

Dr Dering: Yes.

The Judge: What proportion of them were of the type of diagnosis you have given us?

Dr Dering: Most of them were minor operations.

Dr Dering had made his case and had had it subjected to fine, almost surgical, analysis. But as the events showed he was to have another opportunity of being heard again by the jury—in rebuttal of new evidence introduced by the defendants.

CHAPTER VIII

English Anaesthetist

DR Christopher Hewer, M.B., M.R.C.P., F.F.A.R.S., questioned by Mr Neill, and giving evidence as an expert on anaesthesia, said that he had had forty-three years' experience in anaesthesia, and was senior anaesthetist at St Bartholomew's Hospital, and consultant to the Tropical Diseases branch of University College Hospital, and two other hospitals. He was the author of ten editions of *Recent Advances in Anaesthesia*, first published in 1932. He was also editor of *Anaesthesia*, a quarterly journal.

He said that spinal anaesthesia had been in common use for abdominal operations in America and on the Continent until the end of the last war, though not so much in this country. He had used it in more than five hundred cases. Premedication was usual by hypodermic injection of morphine or morphine derivative about an hour beforehand; that was, in his experience, preferable to a preliminary injection in the path of the main injection. A spinal anaesthetic, if given properly with a sharp needle, caused very little discomfort. In the hypothetical situation of having no qualified anaesthetist available for a lower abdominal operation he would, as a matter of choice, prefer to give a spinal rather than a general inhalant anaesthetic.

Asked about the practice of strapping patients to secure them to the operating table, Dr Hewer said that for certain types of spinal anaesthesia the table was tilted into a slight 'head-down' position when the anaesthetic was administered, and the patient had to be secured to the table. Straps round the legs was one such method.

Cross-examined by Lord Gardiner, Dr Hewer said that he had heard Dr Dering reading to the Judge a list of minor operations done on two successive days, and had noted that they had all been done under a general anaesthetic. It would be almost impossible, of course, to use spinal anaesthesia for an abscess in the neck.

Lord Gardiner: Is not a general anaesthetic particularly indicated where the patient is fearful, so that it is humane to enable her to lose consciousness?

Dr Hewer: Other things being equal.

Lord Gardiner: If the patient could see in the reflection of the operating lamp the nature of the operation being carried out—for instance, the removal of a testicle in the case of males—that would be likely to be a horrifying experience, would it not?

Dr Hewer: Yes, but I cannot imagine that happening. If it did happen, yes.

Lord Gardiner: Then failure to administer a general anaesthetic would show a lack of humanity?

Dr Hewer said that bandaging of the eyes was a very simple method of avoiding that.

Lord Gardiner: If a patient has had proper premedication, is it necessary to strap him down to the table?

Dr Hewer: Not from the point of view of the patient moving, but only if the table is tilted for the anaesthetic.

Lord Gardiner: But in the ordinary way are they strapped down for such operations?

Dr Hewer: No, sir, not in this country.

If patients had had a quarter of a grain of morphia thirty minutes before an operation, Dr Hewer said, he would not expect to find them either screaming or struggling, nor would he expect such patients to be able to stand in a queue before operation, for they would be extremely giddy.

Lord Gardiner: Were all the answers which you gave Mr Duncan given on the footing that the operations were done with the patient's consent?

Dr Hewer: Yes.

Lord Gardiner: Then if the patients knew what was being done, and could see what was being done, but it was being done against their will, that would be relevant to the question whether or not there should be a general anaesthetic?

Dr Hewer: If they had a quarter of a grain of morphine beforehand I would not expect them to be apprehensive at all. If they had had no morphine, they might well be.

Lord Gardiner sat down. In re-examination Dr Hewer said that, if he had been at Auschwitz twenty years ago and a patient was going to have an operation of the kind under discussion and in the circumstances described, he would have considered spinal anaesthesia the best method. A patient who had had premedication with morphine might be able to walk and talk for from ten to fifteen minutes afterwards. He did not know whether it was now the practice on the Continent to strap a patient to the table for a spinal anaesthetic; it might have been twenty years ago.

CHAPTER IX

Polish Prisoners

THE NEXT witness was a Pole, living in Chiswick. He took the oath on the Douai version and gave evidence in English. He told of his experiences in Auschwitz, to which he had been sent in 1940. He had injured his hand while in the camp and there was talk of amputation. A prisoner with only one hand would have had little chance of survival there, but Dr Dering had operated and saved his hand. The witness was not cross-examined.

The next witness, the court was told, was also Polish and would require the services of an interpreter.

The Judge: Before we have the interpreter sworn, can you tell me, Mr Neill, to what issue of fact this evidence is directed?

Mr Neill said that it was to the general background of the camp and the circumstances in which these operations had been performed.

The Judge: I would not say that that was irrelevant, but I should have thought, from the way Lord Gardiner has conducted this case, that it is common ground that Auschwitz was an indescribable hell. Is it necessary to go on proving that?

Mr Neill said that some of the questions addressed to Dr Dering —for instance, the question whether he had asked for and seen the orders of the German court—made it important for the jury to have fully in mind the sort of duress and the circumstances in which he had had to carry out other operations.

The Judge: I have indicated that I take the view that this kind of background evidence is relevant. But is it necessary for the jury and the witnesses to go through the harrowing experience of having all this in a lot of detail? However, let the interpreter come forward.

A Polish woman interpreter was sworn. The witness, also living in London, said that, when he had typhus, Dr Dering had visited the ward several times to make sure that patients had enough to eat. On one occasion he had seen male nurses hiding a living patient underneath corpses in the washroom, and he had been told to 'get out and keep quiet'. Some of the prisoners had said that was 'the work of Dr Dering'. Dr Dering used to give him requests on pieces of paper for supplies and the witness used to steal them from the S.S. hospital where he worked. The witness was not cross-examined.

A third Polish witness, living in England, said that he had had to have two operations in the Auschwitz hospital, one in 1940 and the other in 1942. The second followed corporal punishment.

Lord Gardiner, cross-examining: I gather that both the operations you had were under general anaesthetic, and done with your consent?

The witness: I wanted to be cured.

Lord Gardiner: You knew that Dr Dering was trying to do his best for you?

The witness: As he tried for everybody.

Lord Gardiner: And you knew that the operation was the right thing?

The witness: I am not a doctor.

A fourth Polish witness was called. The Judge demurred. Did Mr Duncan want to go on asking whether Dr Dering was kind to people? No doubt he was kind to certain people.

Mr Duncan said that it was not quite that. One of the things which the jury would have to consider was whether the sting of the libel had been established. He had told the jury that they might conclude that the ordinary meaning of the words complained of was that Dr Dering was a monster. It was, therefore, valuable for the jury to have not only the general background to Auschwitz but also evidence of acts of a humane character by Dr Dering.

The Judge said that he fully understood why these witnesses had been called; but Lord Gardiner had not suggested in any way that, so far as Polish men and women were concerned, Dr Dering had done anything other than his job. What was suggested was that, when it came to Jewish prisoners, he was indifferent to their welfare.

CHAPTER X

Surgeon from Poland

THE next witness was a surprise witness. Mr Duncan said 'Call Dr Grabczynski' and, as a quiet, neat man, short of stature, and dressed in grey made his way into the witness box, there was a stir throughout the court. Mr Duncan told the Judge that Dr Grabczynski knew no English, and the Judge asked whether this was the man whose name had cropped up frequently during Dr Dering's hours in the witness box.

Dr Grabczynski gave evidence in Polish through the woman interpreter, and gave his address in Cracow. He had arrived from Poland the previous day in order to give evidence at this trial. He was a doctor of medicine, having qualified in 1932, had since practised as a surgeon, and was now director of the surgical department in a hospital for railwaymen in Cracow, having held that appointment for the last seven years.

He had been arrested and imprisoned by the Gestapo in German-occupied Poland in October 1942 and, in December, transported to Auschwitz. He had been ill at the time; two days after his arrival he was transferred to the camp hospital and later to Block 21, as a sick person. There he had met Dr Dering whom he had neither known nor seen before.

Dr Grabczynski had at first worked as a male nurse, but after he had been in Block 21 for a few days, he had been called before the camp S.S. doctor, Entress, who asked about his special qualifications. After that he worked as a prisoner-doctor with Dr Dering until Dr Dering left the camp. Dr Grabczynski had started on the first floor where 'dirty' surgery was done, while Dr Dering was on the ground floor in the so-called 'clean' theatre.

Mr Duncan: From what you observed, how do you say Dr Dering treated his patients—badly or well?

Dr Grabczynski: Dr Dering treated his patients well. He looked after them properly.

Mr Duncan: So far as you were able to see, did he make any distinction between races or religions or anything of that kind?

Dr Grabczynski: We treated all patients as sick people and we did not take any notice of religion or race.

Dr Grabczynski said that Dr Dering was the senior doctor in the Block by reason of his camp number, and other doctors and nurses were under his orders. He treated his staff 'rightly', but was demanding in his work.

Dr Grabczynski said that he had been moved to the 'clean' theatre in January 1943, and operated there nearly every day until the end of his stay as a prisoner at Auschwitz. He remembered that in August 1943, Dr Dering had been made the elder ['*Lagerälteste*'] of the hospital. He also remembered an operation register which was kept in the theatre.

The original register was handed to Dr Grabczynski who identified it, and said that he had last seen it three days after the camp was liberated in 1945.

Dr Grabczynski said that he had never himself made any entries in the registers. He recognized as Dr Dering's the handwriting in the register for all the entries down to 28 August 1943, but did not know the writing after that date; it was not his own. Between August 1943 and January 1944, Dr Dering had gradually ceased to operate because of the change in his duties.

Mr Duncan: You remember Doctor, or Professor, Schumann?

Dr Grabczynski: Doctor. I remember.

Mr Duncan: Do you remember that Dr Schumann required certain kinds of operation to be performed?

Dr Grabczynski: Yes.

Mr Duncan: Was there a discussion among the doctors, or some of them, at Auschwitz about carrying out those operations?

Dr Grabczynski: Yes.

Mr Duncan: Was Dr Dering one of the doctors who was present at those discussions?

Dr Grabczynski: Yes.

He remembered two other doctors who were present at the discussions—a Polish physician called Diem, and a Dr Steinberg—

but after twenty-one years he no longer remembered any other names. They had discussed what Dr Schumann was doing.

Mr Duncan: Did you personally have any instructions from, or discussions with, Dr Schumann?

Dr Grabczynski: Personally, no. But Dr Dering told us that he had received an order from Dr Schumann.

Mr Duncan: Will you tell us what, after these discussions, the doctors decided was the proper thing for them to do?

Dr Grabczynski: As Dr Schumann had given the explicit order that these operations were to be performed, it would have fallen to the S.S. corporal or a nurse to perform them. Therefore the doctors were of opinion that, for the sake of those who were to be operated on, there would be much less risk if they were operated on by doctors. The hospital nurses and S.S. personnel were wholly untrained for performing surgical operations.

'One of the colleagues', Dr Grabczynski continued, 'was worrying and wondering if the organs which had been treated with X-ray would not develop other complications.'

Mr Duncan: Were these views about the interests of the patients your own views too?

Dr Grabczynski: Yes. It was my opinion too.

Mr Duncan: And now in 1964, have you changed your opinion, or are you still of the same opinion?

Dr Grabczynski: I am still of the same opinion.

Mr Duncan: You knew the character of the operations that Dr Schumann was requiring?

Dr Grabczynski: Yes I did.

Mr Duncan: Who was the colleague who expressed those doubts whether complications might result if an organ subjected to X-ray was not removed? Do you remember?

Dr Grabczynski: Today I cannot remember. My own opinion was that there could be complications, but my main worry was about the patients being operated on by untrained personnel.

Mr Duncan: Did the surgeons discuss what might happen to themselves if they refused to carry out the operations?

Dr Grabczynski: During that conversation we did not discuss the lesser points.

Mr Duncan: Do you mean that the possible fate of the surgeons was one of the 'lesser' points?

Dr Grabczynski: Yes. It was important, but first of all we were discussing what to do about the patients.

Mr Duncan: What do you think—based on your experience at Auschwitz—would have been the result for you if you had refused to carry out an operation of this kind ordered by Dr Schumann?

Dr Grabczynski: I would certainly have had to do with the political branch of the concentration camp at Auschwitz.

Mr Duncan: What does that mean?

Dr Grabczynski: The Gestapo of the camp.

Mr Duncan: At that time did you allow yourself to think what might happen to you or your brother surgeons if they refused?

Dr Grabczynski: First of all I was thinking of the sick.

Mr Duncan commented that that was really not an answer; but he did not want to pursue the question unnecessarily.

The Judge: If you 'had to do' with the political branch of the camp, what would you have expected that to mean for you?

Dr Grabczynski said that the political branch could break camp rules and punish 'from Block 11 to the death sentence'. ['Block 11' was the punishment and execution block adjoining Block 10.] He remembered performing operations for the removal of irradiated ovaries and testicles. He thought he had removed testicles 'some tens of times'.

He was referred to page 319 of the register, recording the ten ovariectomies in November 1943—the first five by Dr Dering, with Dr Grabczynski assisting, and the second five by Dr Grabczynski, with Dr Dering assisting. Dr Grabczynski said that he did not remember personally doing any of those ten. He was able to recall things now only because he had been shown the date and the register and because operations on women were rather rare.

Lord Gardiner intervened to say that he had already suggested to Dr Dering that he had himself performed all ten operations and had attributed some of them to Dr Grabczynski in the register. The Judge commented that because of the importance of these operations in the defence particulars it might be possible to get more certain evidence on the point by asking about the nationality of the patients. Could Mr Duncan approach it from that angle?

Mr Duncan: Dr Grabczynski, these seem to be all women or girls. Do you know what was their nationality?

Dr Grabczynski: I think they were Greek Jewesses.

He was then asked to tell in his own words everything he could remember about these particular operations. He said that he was in the operating theatre before the girls were brought in and when the spinal injection was given. He could not remember whether the patient was carried in on a special trolley or brought in; but she was brought in and put on the operating table, held by the nurse, bent forward with the spine arched, and given the anaesthetic with a special needle. The needle was then drawn out and the site of injection covered with sterile gauze. The patient was laid on the table and her legs and hands were tied down. After the site of the operation had been cleaned the operation was performed. The ovary, after removal, was put into what appeared to be a preservative in a container sent by Dr Schumann. The incision was stitched up, covered with gauze, and sealed with a special sealing liquid. Then the patient was untied, put on a stretcher, and taken out of the theatre. Present in the theatre, in addition to Dr Dering and himself, there were usually the theatre male nurse, a Pole [who was named] and a male instrument orderly.

Mr Duncan: Apart from the patient, was there ever a woman in the operating theatre while the operation was taking place?

Dr Grabczynski: During the operation itself—I don't remember.

He knew Dr Brewda.

Mr Duncan: Was she ever present while these operations were taking place when you were there?

Dr Grabczynski: She was not during the operation itself. She could have been there when they were taking the patient away.

Mr Duncan: Giving us the benefit of your surgical and medical experience, were the operations badly or successfully performed, or what?

Dr Grabczynski: These operations were performed according to the rules.

The Judge: The rules of what?

Dr Grabczynski: According to the rules of surgery.

The Judge: Doctor, this was Auschwitz. Was there anything different, and if so, what, from such operations in normal conditions?

Dr Grabczynski: I have already said No, and that the operations were performed according to the rules of surgical practice.

Mr Duncan: What was the general condition of the women or girls when they were brought to the theatre?

Dr Grabczynski: They were lying on a stretcher.

The Judge: What was their emotional condition?

Dr Grabczynski: That I don't know.

The Judge: Did anything happen in that operating theatre which distressed you as a doctor?

Dr Grabczynski: I don't remember anyone screaming—no, I don't remember.

Lord Gardiner's carefully phrased first questions in cross-examination were provocative and misunderstood.

He asked: Dr Grabczynski, were you a Christian before the war?

Dr Grabczynski: I was baptized.

Lord Gardiner: When you qualified, Hitler had not come to power in Germany, had he?

Dr Grabczynski: He was already there in 1932. He was Führer in 1933.

Lord Gardiner: Before the days of Hitler we should have agreed, should we not, that the most civilized and cultured group of countries in the world were the Christian countries of Western Europe?

Dr Grabczynski said that he 'did not know the statistics'. The interpreter, realizing that there was a misunderstanding, put the question correctly. Dr Grabczynski apologized, 'I thought you were speaking about sterilization, not civilization', he said. [There was a wretched little burst of laughter in court. It was an ironic misunderstanding.] The Judge said that there must be no laughter while this witness was in the box, for he could not understand what we were laughing at and it might embarrass him. Lord Gardiner repeated the question. The Judge intervened. 'Lord Gardiner', he said, 'it is not for me to give you advice, but is not that question a little embarrassing? How is it going to read in the *New York Times*? Put the question in broader language.'

Lord Gardiner: Do you agree that before Hitler came to power in Germany, the centre of civilization in the world was the Christian countries of the west?

Dr Grabczynski: Maybe.

Lord Gardiner: Do you agree that if at that time we had been told that within a short time one of those countries would murder two-and-a-half million people—mainly old people and children—by sending them naked into gas chambers we should all have refused to believe it?

Dr Grabczynski: Yes, I agree.

Lord Gardiner: Particularly if all that the murdered people had done was to be the children of their parents?

Dr Grabczynski: Yes.

Lord Gardiner: And if we had been told that experiments would be carried out to irradiate and then remove sexual organs of men and women when they were conscious of what was being done, in order to see whether the remainder could be sterilized *en masse*, we should equally have refused to believe it?

Dr. Grabczynski: Maybe.

Lord Gardiner: And we should have said, 'They could never find a doctor who had taken the Hippocratic oath to take part in such experiments'?

Dr Grabczynski said that he would like shorter questions.

The Judge suggested to Lord Gardiner that the phrase 'take part in' wanted some qualification in the context of this case. One of the problems arising was what was meant by 'taking part in', either as a voluntary or as an involuntary act.

Lord Gardiner: By 'taking part in,' I mean a surgeon actually removing the sexual organ?

Dr Grabczynski agreed. He also agreed that he knew that something like two-and-a-half million people had been murdered in the gas chambers; that men and women had had their sexual organs irradiated; and that there were doctors who actually removed the sexual organs. He knew, too, that it was being done for Dr Schumann's experiments, though he did not then know the nature of the experiments.

Lord Gardiner: Were the two doctors who actually removed most of the sexual organs of both men and women two Polish doctors, Dr Dering and yourself, Dr Grabczynski?

Dr Grabczynski: Yes.

He said that he had never met Dr Clauberg. He had met Dr Wirths many times after April 1944, for in that month he had been put at Dr Wirths' disposal. He had seen Dr Schumann because he had come to the theatre occasionally when operations 'commanded' by him were being performed. He knew Dr Klodzinski but did not remember his ever being in the operating theatre in Block 21.

Lord Gardiner: Did you obtain your release from Auschwitz?

Dr Grabczynski: Yes, on March the 18th, 1944.

Lord Gardiner: Do you know that Dr Dering was released?

Dr Grabczynski: Dr Dering was released before me.

Lord Gardiner: Do you think there were any special reasons why the Germans might feel that you and Dr Dering had earned your release?

Dr Grabczynski: With regard to myself there were stated reasons.

Lord Gardiner: What were they?

Dr Grabczynski said that Dr Wirths wanted him to supervise the building of an operating theatre and sterilizing room at a hospital near the concentration camp, and 'I was ordered to go there'. He had been under orders to report to the camp Gestapo once a week. He had escaped from the hospital on 5 August 1944, and hid himself near Cracow in various places. He had had no contact whatever at that time with any irregular Polish resistance movement.

'DURESS'

The Judge turned to Lord Gardiner: 'I am very anxious', he said, 'that the jury should grasp the fundamental issues in this case at the earliest possible moment. Is it your case that Dr Dering was a willing tool of the S.S. doctors in the sense that he was trying to ingratiate himself with them and was quite ready to do what they asked him for his own purposes? Is that the way you are putting it?'

Lord Gardiner said that it was a question of degree.

The Judge: But are you saying that the mere fact that he physically performed the operations which he has in the witness box admitted performing justifies the libel?

Lord Gardiner said that since the House of Lords decision in Lewis's case[1] the jury had to decide the meaning, and also the sting or gist of the libel. If in fact Dr Dering performed the operations, then what had been said was true.

The Judge: Physically performed them—even though he felt under duress—and justifiably so?

Lord Gardiner said that everything done by the Germans in the war was done by an individual. The defence at Nuremberg had been: 'I was told to by my superior German officers'.

[1] *Lewis* v. *Daily Telegraph Ltd.* [1964] A.C. 234.

The Judge: But these happen to be the Royal Courts of Justice and this is going to be dealt with by the common law of England.

Still under cross-examination, Dr Grabczynski said that he had been put in charge of Block 21 when Dr Dering became head of the hospital, but did not know who kept the register. It was 'possible' that the entries in the register correctly recorded what had happened.

Lord Gardiner: Is not the ordinary meaning of *casus explorativus* an operation done to assist diagnosis?

Dr Grabczynski: More or less, yes.

Lord Gardiner: In this book, did not *casus explorativus* mean operations done on Dr Schumann's orders?

Dr Grabczynski: Yes.

Lord Gardiner: Do you ever remember castrating, or helping Dr Dering to remove testicles from anyone as a punishment?

Dr Grabczynski: Was it by court order?

Lord Gardiner: Whether by court order or not?

Dr Grabczynski: Usually those condemned by German tribunals were operated on by German doctors.

Lord Gardiner: Do you remember, although there was no court order, an order from Dr Schumann for the removal of testicles as a punishment?

Dr Grabczynski: I don't remember.

He agreed that he assisted Dr Dering in removing both testicles from a potent man against whom there was an entry *vita sexualis anormalis*, meaning 'abnormal sex life', and who had not been irradiated.

Lord Gardiner: When Dr Dering was asked by Dr Schumann to remove those testicles, if Dr Dering had said 'I am not going to do this. I have disobeyed an order before and nothing much happened to me. I shall disobey again', would you have done the operation.

Dr Grabczynski: No. I would not.

Lord Gardiner: If Dr Dering had refused you would have refused?

Dr Grabczynski: Yes.

Lord Gardiner: And do you think it probable that other prisoner-doctors would have refused?

Dr Grabczynski: It is possible.

Lord Gardiner: Would Dr Schumann have done them himself?

Dr Grabczynski: No. He had threatened that he would order S.S. men to operate, and they had no medical experience.

Lord Gardiner: You realize that the testicles were wanted for scientific examination, and therefore they would be useless unless the operation was properly done?

Dr Grabczynski said that the testicles would have been 'sent away' in any case; but the chances of post-operative infection, if operations were done by S.S. men, were very real, and 'that was the main factor why during discussions with other doctors we decided to carry out the operations'.

Dr Grabczynski was asked whether a spinal anaesthetic was suitable for a patient who was mentally or emotionally upset. The Judge intervened.

The Judge: If a patient is crying, distressed, or distraught, do you think it a proper case for use of a spinal anaesthetic?

Dr Grabczynski: If the patient has been premedicated properly he should have calmed down.

The Judge: If the patient has not calmed down, would a spinal anaesthetic be the proper anaesthetic?

Dr Grabczynski: One had to take into consideration the fact that general anaesthetics were rather rare about that time.

The Judge: The witness has not answered the question. I must leave it to you, Lord Gardiner.

Dr Grabczynski said that he would not expect a girl of eighteen having an ovariectomy against her will to be calm. But before the ten ovariectomies all the girls had had premedication with whatever was available. He did not do it himself. There was no anaesthetist; but there would have been a written order.

Lord Gardiner: If patients were standing in a queue in a passage, that would show, would it not, that they had not had an injection of morphia?

Dr Grabczynski: One can have a morphia injection and stand.

There was usually an arch and a sheet to prevent the patient from seeing the operation.

Lord Gardiner: Was it dangerous to operate if a girl was already suffering from an irradiation burn?

Dr Grabczynski: If it were a serious burn of the skin it would reflect on the healing of the wound.

Lord Gardiner: Was the operation dangerous?

Dr Grabczynski: No. It could only reflect on the healing of the wound. It would heal in a worse way.

Lord Gardiner: Infection might develop, might it not?

Dr Grabczynski: No. Just more difficult healing.

Lord Gardiner: Do you remember, at any time, one of the girls moving, and Dr Dering hitting her and saying something rude?

Dr Grabczynski: I have never seen Dr Dering hit any sick person.

He did not remember Dr Schumann being there during part of the time while the operations were carried out on the girls, but Schumann used to give the number, the side, and the ovary to be removed. He did not remember any operation on a girl who had already had an abdominal operation for removal of an ovary. He would have remembered had it happened.

Lord Gardiner: On the day of the operation on the Greek girls, did you see Dr Brewda with any girls, or do you not remember?

Dr Grabczynski: With the patients, no. But she might have come into the operating theatre while one patient was being removed and another being brought in.

Mr Duncan questioned Dr Grabczynski in re-examination. He said that, in all the sexual operations which he performed or assisted at on girls or men, he could tell from their demeanour that they had had premedication. He did not remember a single case without it. If there had been any crying, distressed or distraught patients, he thought that he would have noticed. 'I don't remember such cases.'

If Dr Brewda had been in the theatre during the operations he thought he would have seen her. The rules in the hospital were not written; the only unwritten law was not to enter the theatre during operations. He would not have forgotten if Dr Dering had ever hit a patient.

Dr Grabczynski's evidence was concluded at 3.38 p.m. Mr Duncan was in a slight difficulty: no other witness for the plaintiff was in court. The Judge thought that neither side had provided themselves with the forensic equivalent of the cricketing night watchman; but nobody would break their hearts if, on a Friday afternoon, the hearing was adjourned early. The court rose at 3.45 p.m.

'UNTHINKABLE'

The case entered its second week with Dr Josep Mezyk, a medical practitioner from Chicago, as the last witness for Dr Dering. In 1939 he had been a medical student in Poland and had been sent to Auschwitz in July 1941, where he soon met Dr Dering. Later, when he was put on to medical work in Block 20, the infectious diseases block, he used to go to Block 21 to see operations on his own patients performed by Dr Dering. He had watched Dr Dering doing spinal anaesthetics, and in Dr Mezyk's view Dr Dering operated extremely skilfully, his speed being high.

Some of the other doctors had been Jewish. One had survived, and Dr Mezyk had met him in Belgium after the war. There had also been Jewish male nurses in the infectious diseases department and a Jewish messenger boy; and the majority of the patients were Jewish.

Mr Neill: Was any distinction made between Jewish and non-Jewish patients?

Dr Mezyk: The German S.S. made the distinction. We did not.

Selections were made in Block 20 for the gas chambers. Being in charge of the ward, he had had to present patients to the S.S. doctor for dispatch to the gas chambers. 'As soon as we knew selection was to be made we tried to discharge as many as possible.' Others were hidden, or sent to some place where the selection had already been made. When Dr Dering was in charge of the hospital he would warn Dr Mezyk that there would be 'selection tomorrow' and tell him to do everything possible to keep the numbers down. Patients saved in that way were of all races; but most of those to benefit were Jewish.

Several doctors, other than Dr Dering and Dr Grabczynski, had been released from Auschwitz; one from Cracow and another from Warsaw; and, he thought, several more. 'I was supposed to be discharged, but the political department of the camp disqualified me, saying I was absolutely necessary for the camp.'

Mr Neill: Did you see operations on testicles by Dr Dering?

Dr Mezyk: No. I did not.

Mr Neill: What would have been the result of refusing to obey an order?

Dr. Mezyk: To refuse would not have solved the problem.

The Judge: That was not what you were asked. From your knowledge of conditions in the hospital, can you help the court by telling us what would happen to a doctor who was given an order by an S.S. doctor, if he refused to operate?

Dr Mezyk: The straight orders could not be refused. The S.S. man could kill on the spot if he so desired. If not he would have to report, and the penalty was, for dirty ward, shooting on the spot punishment; ordinary penalty, flogging—twenty-five flogs—hanging perhaps fifty minutes with the hands up; that was the customary punishment for any violation of the camp rules. I know doctors who were hanged thirty minutes by the feet from the fact that the ward was not clean. So a straight refusal of a straight order was unthinkable.

Mr Neill sat down, echoing the word 'Unthinkable'.

Lord Gardiner cross-examined Dr Mezyk, who said that he watched operations in Block 21 from August 1941 onwards.

Lord Gardiner: When you were in Block 20?

Dr Mezyk: I was in Block 20. They were fairly near, separated by about eighty feet distance.

Lord Gardiner: Sometimes you walked across?

Dr Mezyk: Yes.

Very few Jewish prisoner-doctors, he said, worked as doctors; they worked as orderlies. It was the practice for any new man to start as an orderly. 'I so started; so did Dr Grabczynski.' There was not always a vacancy on the list of doctors.

Lord Gardiner: Do you agree or disagree with Dr Dering that, out of the sixty prison doctors, ten or eleven were Jewish?

Dr Mezyk: I agree.

Questioned about the percentage of Jews to non-Jews in the camp, Dr Mezyk said that in the Autumn of 1943, it was about sixty per cent.

Dr Mezyk wrote down the names of two doctors released from Auschwitz in 1941, one a surgeon, the other a physician in charge of contagious diseases. Some people had been released from Auschwitz because their families went to the German authorities and demanded it. Bribery and many other means were used.

Lord Gardiner: Did you know that tests of male semen were carried out in Block 28?

Dr Mezyk: Yes, we knew; and we knew that Dr Schumann was carrying out experiments.

In answer to Lord Gardiner's suggestion that, in 1943, there was an international underground in the camp which the 'Polish professional gentlemen never joined', Dr Mezyk said that the only other underground group was largely Communist—Germans, Austrians and some Spaniards. He did not regard Communists and Jews as 'mostly the same'. Many of the Germans had been arrested when Hitler gained power, and they took pride in being Communists and 'old-timers' in the camp.

Lord Gardiner: By the Spring of 1943, was the whole of the running of the hospital dependent on the prisoner-doctors?

Dr Mezyk said that in 1943 the key administration was in the prisoner-doctors' hands. There was a shortage of doctors. The hospital was run by the S.S. doctors, the prisoner-doctors being under their orders.

Lord Gardiner: Did you know that Dr Dering was ordered to give a phenol injection and refused?

Dr Mezyk: No.

Lord Gardiner: Do you know that, when he refused to obey an order to perform the injection, he was punished by not being allowed out of the camp for a fortnight?

Dr Mezyk: I do not know.

Lord Gardiner: Does it surprise you?

Dr Mezyk did not answer, and Lord Gardiner repeated the question.

Dr Mezyk: No.

The Judge: Why?

Dr Mezyk: There were so many details in the complicated situation in the camp that I would expect all unexpected features. Certain things were not discussed. The doctors refused phenol injections; and non-doctors did them.

Mr Duncan re-examined Dr Mezyk and said that subject to any evidence in rebuttal that was Dr Dering's case.

The time was 11.20 a.m. on the sixth day.

PART III: DEFENCE BEGINS

CHAPTER XI

Lord Gardiner for the Defendants

Lord Gardiner, addressing the jury, said that he agreed with what Mr Duncan had said about Auschwitz and also that this was a very serious case.

Dr Dering was really saying two things; first that the gist or substance of the words of which he complained was untrue and, secondly that it was a case for very large damages. The defendants said that the gist was true, and in any case the circumstances were such that the appropriate award of damages would be 'the smallest coin of the realm'.

The jury had first to decide how people understood the words.

Everybody at some time or another had read about Auschwitz—about what happened in concentration camps.

That should not be minimized. The jury would have observed that, when Dr Dering quite properly spent some time in describing what conditions at Auschwitz were really like, Lord Gardiner, far from challenging him, had asked questions to enlarge and emphasize it, in order to make quite plain that the defence did not dispute what Auschwitz was like.

They entirely agreed that if, on any issue, it was necessary to judge Dr Dering's conduct, it must be realized that everything which he did he did as a prisoner-doctor under German domination at Auschwitz.

It was very easy for us, sitting in comfortable England, to criticize what people did or did not do in a situation of that kind—but could any of us be sure how we would have acted in similar conditions?

What was Auschwitz? What would readers of varying experience think, while reading the book? What had been put to Dr Grabczynski was right: if, in the 1920s anybody had asked, 'Where in the world is the most civilized and cultured group of countries?', it would show no disrespect for the United States or our own Commonwealth to say, 'Really it is the Christian countries of Western Europe which are the flower of civilization and culture—the highest point to which man has yet developed'. And if anybody had asked, 'Do you think it possible that, within relatively few years, one of these countries will drive millions of old people and children literally naked into gas chambers?', everybody would have said 'Absolutely impossible'. In Germany, after all, the Kaiser had gone, and all that militarism, and they had an ordinary, Western democratic government. And we should have said (should we not?) 'Impossible, for two reasons. First, one cannot conceive of any reason why anybody should do this. They would bring on themselves the loathing of the world for a generation. If they did it in a peacetime situation, they would soon be at war, because everybody would go to stop them. If they did it in a wartime situation, what could they possibly have to gain to justify conduct of that kind and the opprobrium it would bring—and rightly—for a generation?' And secondly, we should have said, 'You'll never get the people to do it. After all, a conscript army is made up of people from homes and factories, who have women and children of their own. Can you imagine that you would ever get men with children of their own to drive children in tens of thousands into gas chambers?'

If it had been said or suggested that, on top of that, human beings would be used as guinea-pigs, and have their sexual organs removed literally in front of their eyes while they were conscious, as experiments to see whether men and women could be sterilized *en masse*, again we would have said, 'It is impossible—and apart from that, a thing like that could only be done by doctors, and where could you find any doctors to do it?'

'Well, we'd have been wrong—because there was a doctor, an anti-Semitic, Polish doctor, the present plaintiff, Dr Dering, who did it. And if I say "a" doctor it is because, on the evidence, it is pretty clear that, with his dominating position in the hospital and his dominating personality, it really depended on him, on Dr Dering.' As Dr Grabczynski had said, 'Of course, if Dr Dering had refused to do it, I should have refused to do it'.

Why would we have been wrong? For two reasons. First, there was a cause which was thought to justify it: anti-Semitism. We ourselves believed that men and women had qualities different from any other created being. Members of religions would say, 'This is because only men and women have souls'; while those who had no religious beliefs might say, 'It is because their intellect is developed to a point wholly different from that of any other creature and they have the ability to recognize the difference between right and wrong, and free will'.

But, of course, if once you allowed yourself to think that there was some body of men who, because of their race or colour, were not really human beings, then you were justified in imposing every sort of disability on them—very useful to rulers who, if they found anything going wrong, could lay it at their doors—the universal scapegoat. If once you thought that you were justified in treating any such groups as if they were animals, and said, 'Well, we slaughter animals'—then Auschwitz was simply the logical end of that particular road.

The second reason why we should have been wrong was that when it came to the point there were not enough people who refused to obey orders to drive children into a gas chamber—and old people—who had done nothing except to be the children of their parents. There *were* people who said: 'I'm not going to do this and live, because I would not like to live and have this on my conscience. I'm not going to do it and then say, "Well, I was acting under orders". I am not going to push them into gas chambers and then say, "Well, they're going to be pushed into gas chambers anyhow. I can't stop that. The other people would probably do it much more cruelly. I shall do it much more kindly, and, therefore, it is really in their interest that I should do it rather than these other people".' The trouble was that when it came to the point there were not enough of such people.

This camp hospital in Block 21 was not there for the benefit of the prisoners. It was there for the benefit of the Germans. They needed able-bodied people as slave labour and it was not sense, if a man had a septic thumb or foot, not to have a place where it could be put right, so that he could be got back to work—although, if it was going to take over six weeks, it might be simpler to send him to the gas chamber.

The Germans needed doctors more and more, and, gradually the prisoner-doctors really ran the whole thing. It could not have been continued without them. Dr Dering, having finally been appointed head of the whole hospital, was, the jury might think, the one man who was really indispensable to the Germans. He was, apparently, on his own evidence, the best surgeon there; he ran the whole place extremely well with almost German-like efficiency, and nobody questioned it at all.

The jury had heard what happened to him so far as punishments were concerned. When he did disobey an order, as early as January 1941, when he was a very, very junior doctor on the staff, when he was told to give that phenol injection, and refused, all that actually happened was that, after he had been threatened, he was told that he could not go outside the grounds for a fortnight in his spare time.

On Dr Dering's own evidence, this was simply not a case in which he was in anything remotely like the position of the members of the German armed forces. Everyone knew what would have happened to them if they had mutinied in war and disobeyed an order.

This man was invaluable to the Germans. Indeed, they were competing for him, because, as the jury knew, Dr Wirths, medical head of the whole of the camp, desperately wanted to keep him to run the hospital, while Professor Clauberg, who was apparently Mrs Himmler's doctor, wanted to get him for his clinic. There was a battle going on in Berlin about him, ultimately decided in Berlin. The jury could imagine what would have happened in Berlin if, at the very time when Dr Clauberg was trying to get Dr Dering for himself, he had been liquidated by the prison authorities.

A murderer was none the less a murderer if he committed one instead of ten or eleven murders. It was quite clear that the number, 17,000, had been fantastically exaggerated. The figure was copied from another book; possibly, though that was not known, the author of the other book got it from Dr Brewda, who misunderstood Dr Dering when he told her that he had done 17,000, operations. The paragraph was also quite wrong in stating that the operations were done 'without anaesthetic'. Again the meaning of the words was entirely a matter for the jury.

Dr Grabczynski was one of the doctors who had been 'worrying and wondering' whether the organs which had been treated with X-rays might not develop other complications. The jury, when they had heard the evidence, would be invited to say that no complications would have arisen. Although Dr Dering was practising in England, he had called no medical evidence to suggest that an irradiated testicle was likely to cause the slightest trouble.

'I suppose, if the thing has been rendered impotent, it's been rendered impotent. I shall call English doctors before you to say that there was not in 1943, and there is not now, the slightest reason to think that, because a testicle or ovary had been irradiated, it would cause the slightest trouble.'

There were other reasons why this reason given by Dr Dering could not be true. He had always referred to the organs as 'dead'; but he had had to agree that he removed the testicle in order for it to be discovered whether it was dead.

Then there was the case of the potent man. 'I am calling before you one man, both of whose testicles were irradiated, and one of which Dr Dering removed; and since then he has had two children, because Dr Dering did not remove both. It is perfectly clear that, as the whole object of the experiment was to find out whether the X-rays had rendered the testicles impotent or not, nobody could have told whether they were or not.'

Could the jury imagine any doctor of any sort of humanity at all—however anti-Semitic he was, and even though these were Jewish patients, if he *really* thought that there was a medical justification, if he *really* thought that the testicle which had been irradiated would have developed gangrene or cancer—who, seeing their distress, would not have said to them, 'Well, unfortunately these have been irradiated by the Germans. As you know, that's not my fault; but trouble *can* develop, you see, now it has been irradiated, and, really, it's in your own interest that you should have this out, and it's a very good thing for you that it's coming out'. Dr Dering agreed that he never suggested that to a patient at all.

In the court order cases, of course, a potent man was castrated. There was no suggestion that that was being done for his own benefit. The jury would remember too that Dr Dering had been asked whether he would have removed a testicle if Dr Entress had said there was no court order but that he wanted Dr Dering to do it; and he had said that he would.

'I shall invite you to say that so far as he seeks to justify all this on the ground that it was a very dangerous thing to leave this testicle in one's body, and that it was medically justified, and a jolly good thing to have it out, that simply is not true.'

Then it was said: 'Oh, well, they'd have been sent to the gas chamber, or the S.S. corporal would have done it'. Though the jury had not yet heard all the evidence it would show that these 'guinea-pigs' were naturally safeguarded. The last thing the Germans would have wanted would have been to have them sent to the gas chambers. There was no evidence from Dr Dering that Dr Schumann would have got the S.S. corporal to do it. No doubt Dr Schumann or Dr Rohde or Dr Entress would have done it. The register showed that S.S. doctors removed about twenty testicles, so they were quite capable of doing it. But of course the jury could not form a view about all this until they had first decided what the facts were. And there was a very strong conflict on the facts.

Had it not been for the register, the jury would have had to decide between Dr Dering and Dr Brewda. But the register contained names, and so it had been possible for a search to be made throughout the world.

The jury could take into account politics, religion, and anything else which they thought relevant. The defence witnesses were of many different types. There were doctors, who knew something about these girls.

One was Dr Kleinova, a dedicated Communist who never pretended to be anything else. She went as a doctor with the International Brigade to Spain, and could not go back to Poland, so she became a doctor in France, and after the German occupation joined the French resistance movement. She was ultimately found out and sent to Auschwitz. Subsequently she was decorated by General de Gaulle with the Croix-de-Guerre and Star. The jury would see her and could decide what sort of person she was.

Then there was Dr Brewda. She said that it was 'absolute lies' to suggest that she was something to do with the Polish secret police. The only thing she had ever been interested in was medicine. She had never been a member of any political party at all, and when she found after the war that Poland was a Communist country she came to England because she did not wish to live in a Communist country, and had lived here ever since. If the jury thought that she had exaggerated anything they could say so. It might not be surprising, in a sense, if she did feel strongly about what she saw at Auschwitz.

Then there was Dr Hautval, a deeply religious French Protestant. She, being a woman of courage and character, told the Gestapo exactly what she thought about the way they were treating Jews, so they said, 'Oh, well, if that is what you think', and they pinned a thing on her saying *Amie des juifs*—'Friend of the Jews'—and said, 'Well, if you are so fond of them, you can go to Auschwitz with them'; and she had to go.

The jury might consider her evidence of some importance, because she herself had taken part in one or two experimental operations, and then she absolutely refused to take part in any more. After all, it was a strong part of Dr Dering's case that if a prisoner-doctor refused to do that, he would be shot or sent to the gas chamber—even though he had himself also told the jury that, after a certain time, apart from a very old man who became useless, no prisoner-doctor had been sent to the gas chambers. She refused, and she was alive. The trouble was that there were not enough Dr Hautvals. There was a violent conflict of evidence, and it was for the jury to say whose evidence was reliable.

Evidence was then called for the defendants.

CHAPTER XII

Evidence from Auschwitz

'THIS I CANNOT FORGET'

THE first defence witness—'the first woman'—gave evidence in Hebrew which was interpreted. She said that she was born in Salonika in 1925. She was taken to Auschwitz in 1943.

Lord Gardiner: Were you tattooed?

The first woman: Yes.

Lord Gardiner: Do you remember your number?

The first woman: Yes.

The Judge: Have you still got it?

She drew up the left sleeve of the tweed coat she was wearing, exposing her forearm and a series of numbers.

Lord Gardiner: Repeat the number?

The woman bent her arm for the interpreter to see, and he read out '40574'. This was checked in the register.

She said that she was sent first to Birkenau and worked very hard. Her sister was with her, but did not stay with her. She was beaten. After three months they brought her to Auschwitz, where she was in Block 10 with other girls. Then she was sent back to Birkenau for a day, and 'they' brought her to a place where she saw a big machine. 'They put two plates—there was electricity—one on my abdomen, one on the back.'

A number of girls went together. (She recited nine names.) The effect of the machine was that the spot was dark and coloured, and she vomited. The effects lasted about four weeks. 'Afterwards they called us again. They took us, and we had to take a bath. Afterwards they sent us to a place opposite Block 10; that was Block 21. I entered in the block, and two men came and made me an injection in the column. Because of the pains I shouted, screamed, and they took me to another room, put me on a table. There was a kind of screen before my face. There was a big lamp. I saw the reflections in the lamp. I felt they were doing something, but did not realize what. Dr Brewda was there. I do not remember how any other doctors were dressed. I remember what Dr Brewda was doing. She patted my cheeks and told me "Don't be afraid. It will pass quickly".'

She understood the word 'injection'. She had received no other injection than the one in the back. She had not received one in the arm. After the operation was over they took her on a stretcher to Block 10. The operation wound remained open a long time. The same thing happened with the other girls. One girl, Bella, died the same night.

After she had been ill for some months she was sent back to Birkenau to work on ammunitions. Later she was sent to Ravensbrück. At that time she was eighteen. She had married since her liberation, and lived in Israel.

With no change in his even, dispassionate voice, Lord Gardiner asked: Have you any children?

The first woman: No. [The effect of the simple question and the finality of the answer could be felt—people in court wept openly—and the effect was scarcely lessened when this question was put to witness after witness, and the same answer given.]

Lord Gardiner: I believe that you have adopted a girl?

The first woman: Yes.

Lord Gardiner: What has been the effect of the operation on your health?

The first woman: I don't feel well always.

Mr Duncan cross-examined her. She said that, at Birkenau, she was beaten three or four times.

Mr Duncan: After three months were you moved to Auschwitz?

The first woman: There was no exact date for us. It was about July or the beginning of August.

Mr Duncan: Were you working in Block 10?

The first woman: No. [Clearly this was an unexpected answer.]

Mr Duncan: Tell the court what you were doing in Block 10 in Auschwitz if you were not working?

The first woman: I did nothing. I only slept and ate.

Mr Duncan: For the first month, before the electrical treatment, was anything else medical being done?

The first woman: No. I did nothing. When we were tired we went to bed and when we were not tired we got up. Personnel gave us to eat and watched us. Before the operation I do not remember seeing Dr Brewda.

She knew who was meant by 'Dr Schumann'.

Mr Duncan: Did you know, before you went to Birkenau, that Dr Schumann was carrying out experiments?

The first woman: No.

Mr Duncan: Did you know that you were to have electrical treatment, or was it a surprise?

The first woman: It was a surprise.

Though they talked about the electrical treatment, the girls did not know what the result would be. 'We were too young to know that', she added.

Mr Duncan: And when the time came for you to have your operation you say you were taken to have a bath?

The interpreter told the court that the woman was 'ashamed to tell what had been done'. There had been some 'cleaning'. The first woman herself then said that this cleaning and bath took place before she was sent to Block 21.

Mr Duncan: Did you know in November 1943, after you had had your bath, that you were going to have a surgical operation?

The first woman: No. (She shook her head).

Mr Duncan: You must have been a very worried, frightened woman?

The first woman: Yes.

She thought she had been taken to Block 21 some time in the afternoon in November but could not remember exactly. The girls had been taken 'two by two'. That meant, she explained, that after one girl have been given the spinal injection, the other was brought in, and as one was brought out of the theatre, the other was taken in. She did not remember who had told the girls to go from Block 10 to Block 21, nor whether anyone had taken them. It was over twenty years ago.

Mr Duncan: A lot has happened since then?

The first woman: They operated on me and then brought me back to Block 10.

Mr Duncan: A lot has happened to you in the twenty years since then?

The first woman: I don't feel well, and it was told to me that my feeling ill is the consequence of the operation I suffered in Auschwitz.

She did not have morphia before the operation.

Mr Duncan: And when you went to Block 21, what room did you go to first?

There were two rooms side by side. They had taken her into one room where there were two men 'like male nurses'. One man had held her while she was standing up and bent her head over to her knees, while the other gave the injection into her back.

Mr Duncan: I suggest that the injection was given actually in the operating theatre. What do you say?

The first woman: No.

Mr Duncan: You say it was outside in the waiting room, and that it caused you some pain?

The first woman: At the moment I received the injection I screamed; but afterwards I did not feel the lower part of my body.

Mr Duncan: Just one moment's shock and pain?

The first woman: Yes.

She thought that there had been some minutes between the injection and being taken into the theatre. She did not remember how she was taken into the theatre—whether it was on a stretcher or a trolley—but only that half her body was dead.

Mr Duncan: But it was the bottom half that was dead and not your brain?

The first woman: Yes.

Mr Duncan: I am suggesting to you, madam, that in fact at that time you were already very drowsy.

The first woman: No, I could not walk, but the upper half of me was quite all right. I was not drowsy.

Mr Duncan: Was it in the theatre when you were distressed and called out that Dr Brewda patted your cheeks?

The first woman: I felt that she stood behind me because I was quite aware of my upper part of my body and was not sleepy—and she put her hand on my cheek and consoled me.

Mr Duncan: Am I right in thinking that at that time in 1943 there was no common language between you and Dr Brewda such that you could understand one another?

The first woman: There was French. She told me: '*N'aie pas peur, mon enfant*'. I understand a little French and '*N'aie pas peur*' means 'Don't be afraid'.

Mr Duncan: How many people were in the operating theatre when you got in?

The first woman: I remember only Dr Brewda at my side, but I saw some people in the theatre. I don't remember exactly how many.

Mr Duncan: Do you remember, some days after the operation, the surgeon coming to see you in Block 10?

The first woman: Someone came, but I don't remember who it was.

Mr Duncan: Whoever it was, did he look at the scar?

The first woman: Not very much. We were all lying side by side and he passed our bunks and looked, but did not approach us.

Mr Duncan: Do you mean he did not look at the wound?

The first woman: No, he did not.

Mr Duncan: Did he speak to you, or the one beside you?

The first woman: No.

Mr Duncan: You don't really remember after all these years?

The first woman: This, I cannot forget.

Asked by Lord Gardiner in re-examination whether there was anything by which she would recognize 'Dr Schumann', she said, after reflection, that there was a sign, a scar, on his face on one side, 'as if after an operation'.

The Judge: At the time of this operation in 1943 what languages did you speak?

The first woman: I knew a little French, some Italian, Spanish—or Spanioli—which is my language—and Greek.

The Judge: Have you given evidence at any trial other than this about what happened in Auschwitz?

The first woman: No.

The second woman, living in Los Angeles, and bearing a tattoo mark 38762 gave evidence in Judeo-Spanish which was translated by her husband who was sworn in as interpreter.

She had been taken from Salonika in March 1943, to Birkenau, where she had been put to work destroying houses and carting the materials away.

She had been taken to Block 10 with a group of some ten girls. She had been irradiated and taken from Block 10 to Block 21, where she had been given a spinal injection in a room that was not the operating theatre. The injection was very painful and she could do nothing but scream.

In the theatre the table had been tilted with her head down, and Dr Brewda had been behind her head, comforting her and saying: 'My child, courage'.

During the week after the operation her wound was open and bleeding and 'some dirt coming out'; and it had been bad for about two months. She remembered a girl, Bella, who died the night after the operation, and another, 'Marta', who had been operated on twice; and another, Buena, who 'screamed very much and was taken out of the room and I never saw her again'.

Her bandages after the operation had been 'only papers', and the stench of the wounds was such that 'no one could stay in front of us because it was so unpleasant'. When the doctor came round to see them after the operation, her wound was uncovered, though she did not remember by whom. The doctor had not examined it, but had merely passed the foot of her bunk.

The Judge said that he would like to know, in respect of each of the witnesses who had been the victims of these operations, whether any of them had given evidence at any other trial, and also how many of the girls who had had the operations, so far as this witness knew, were ever able to get back to work in the camp.

The second woman said that she had not been able to work again, though some of the other girls did. She had never given evidence in any other court about this matter. She had married her husband in 1946.

Mr Hirst: Have you had any children?

The second woman: No children.

Mr Hirst: What effect has that operation had on your life since 1945 and up to today?

The second woman: Most of my time is in bed.

Cross-examined by Mr Duncan, the second woman said that nobody knew why they were not working at the time. She knew now that the women in Block 10 had been there for experimental purposes.

She could not see much of what was going on in the theatre from the ante-room, because she was 'half-dead' and 'a little unconscious' from the injection.

Mr Duncan: I suppose it is not much good really asking you about the people in the theatre since you were almost unconscious by that time?

The second woman: Dr Brewda was in the operating room.

Mr Duncan: I suggest that that is a mistake, that you are wrong about that?

The second woman: No, it is not a mistake.

Mr Duncan: How do you know that Bella died the same day?

The second woman: We asked about Bella and they told us she is dead.

She knew Bella had been operated on twice. Bella had told her that Dr Samuel had done the first operation. 'Marta' had also been operated on twice.

Mr Duncan: Who told you about the first operation?

The second woman: I was told.

Mr Duncan: Did Dr Brewda tell you about that?

The second woman: No. 'Marta' told me.

Mr Duncan: And the girl you did not see again—Buena—the one who was screaming very much and was taken out of the room. How long was that after the operation?

The second woman: I don't remember exactly.

Mr Duncan: Do you say that all the ten girls were screaming or crying after the operation—all of them?

The second woman: Yes.

The Judge: When you came round from the operation and were conscious again, had you any idea what kind of operation had been performed on you?

The second woman: No.

The Judge: When did you first learn that what had happened was that one of your ovaries had been removed?

The second woman: After my liberation when I went to Israel.

The Judge: And had you any idea that the operation was connected in any way with the X-ray treatment you had had earlier?

The second woman: No, I did not know that.

Mr Duncan: You know Dr Dering by sight now?

The second woman: I do not know him.

Mr Duncan: I suggest he was the surgeon who came round to Block 10 a few days after the operation?

The second woman: I don't remember him at all.

NEW ALLEGATIONS

The first man was called. He was now thirty-eight and lived in Israel. He was born in Salonika, and was at High School when the Germans came. They took him to Poland about the beginning of April 1943. He was with his parents in the same wagon until they got to Poland where they separated the men and the women. His mother did not want to be separated from him. He was taken to Birkenau and the next morning they 'made a number in his forearm'.

Undoing his cufflinks—his fingers seemed all thumbs, and he took some time about this—he exposed a tattooed number, which the interpreter read to the court as '114302'.

Mr Hirst: Within a very few days after your arrival at Birkenau did a German officer visit your Block?

The first man: Yes. A German officer came. He asked for two men of each age group between sixteen and thirty.

He was chosen as one of two eighteen-year-olds, but had no idea then why he was being selected.

Mr Hirst: Who did the selection?

The first man: The German officer gave the order, and the Block elder had to perform the order—the choice.

That happened after he had been at Birkenau for two days. He did no work there. The next morning he was taken with a group of others to Block 12 at Birkenau. There they were given special clothes, and every morning a doctor took their temperature and pulse. 'They took us to the camp of the women and did irradiations.' The room into which they were taken, one by one, had a table; it was not very dark. An officer of the *Luftwaffe* was in charge and later the first man learned that the officer's name was Dr Schumann; he was tall, and there was a sign—a scar—on his cheek.

When his turn came, he was told to take off his clothes, and was naked. 'They told me that I should put my genital organ, together with the scrotum, on a machine.' The machine was over his genital organs. There was the noise of a motor. He stood there, with the motor running, for from five to eight minutes. The machine was directed, so far as he could judge, to the centre. Afterwards he was told to leave the room. All the others stood in front of the machine.

When it was over, they were taken to Block 12. He was examined every day afterwards to see if there were any signs on his organs.

His organs were not stained. 'I saw that on the organs of my comrades were dark stains. Generally, after the irradiation, I had not pains specially, but I had a general ill feeling.'

One morning he was taken away with five others by ambulance to a place which, he later learnt, was Block 28, Auschwitz. He was taken with another of the men to the first room on the left, a doctor's room.

Mr Hirst: Who was present?

The first man: Dr Dering. *This* Dr Dering. (The man pointed to the plaintiff.) At that time I did not know his name, but I now recognize him. Dr Schumann was also there. Dr Dering had on a white gown.

Mr Hirst: Was anything done?

The first man: Yes.

Mr Hirst: Describe what was done.

The first man: They told both of us to take off all our clothes. Afterwards they gave us a piece of glass. Dr Dering came with a sort of club and put it into my rectum.

Mr Duncan immediately objected that this piece of evidence had not been pleaded nor put to Dr Dering; and eventually this, and other evidence, was incorporated in Supplementary Particulars of Justification.[1]

Mr Hirst: What happened after you were given the glass?

The first man: When he introduced the stick into my rectum, some drops came out of my member.

Mr Hirst: Who is 'he'?

The first man: Dr Dering.

He, and the five others, were taken to Block 21, to a room with beds. Nobody came to see them that day. He saw Dr Dering the following morning, and they spoke in French, which the first man then spoke fluently. He had begun the conversation.

Mr Hirst: What did you say?

The first man: I did not know what they would do to me. When I came to know that I was to be operated on then I said, 'Why are you operating on me? I am fit, not sick'. He answered me in French, 'If I take not the testicle off you they will take it off me'.

[1] See Appendix, pages 281–2.

After that conversation they put him on a stretcher and took him to the operating theatre. He was able to walk, and did not want to go on the stretcher because he was afraid; he resisted. Men 'took' him. They were wearing white gowns. He did not remember whether there was one room or two rooms, but there were two tables for operating. He was sitting on the stretcher, and male nurses held him and wanted to give a spinal injection. He resisted; and the needle broke. The first time, when the needle broke, they started to curse in Polish.

Mr Hirst: Who were 'they'?

The first man: I could not see who, but I only heard words in Polish. I was bent over.

A further, successful, attempt was made to give him a spinal injection. He had 'terrible pains', which continued until the lower half of his body was paralysed. He had no other injection of any kind in Block 21 on that day. After the lower half of his body went dead they put him on the operating table. He was fully conscious.

Mr Hirst: What happened?

The first man: They took off the shirt I had, and put iodine on the skin, the left side of the lower abdomen. I was lying back. I saw the doctor putting the iodine on with a swab. After some minutes I saw Dr Dering when he had my testicle in his hand and showed it to Dr Schumann, who was present. I felt no pains during the operation.

Mr Hirst: How, if at all, did you react to the pain at the time of the injection?

The first man: What could I do? I felt pains. I continued to speak in French, saying 'Don't do this'.

After the operation he remained in bed a couple of days. Dr Dering came 'maybe every morning', lifted the bedclothes and looked.

Mr Hirst: Was he friendly or unfriendly?

The first man: Not the one, not the other.

He had stayed in Block 21 about two weeks longer than the others because he had an infection. Afterwards he worked as a carpenter. He stayed in Auschwitz until the end. Now he was married for the second time. He gave the dates of his marriages. He had no child by either marriage.

Mr Hirst: What was the effect on your general health of the operation and irradiation?

The first man: I don't feel as a human being at all.

He had never given evidence in any court or before any tribunal about these matters.

Mr Duncan cross-examined. The first man said that thirty men had gone to Block 12. They had asked each other: 'Why did they take us here?' but 'could not imagine the answer'. When he had the treatment with the machine he did not know why his genitals were being irradiated. Dr Schumann looked to see that he did not move. Dr Schumann said nothing during the irradiation. He himself had no idea whether the irradiation was done well or properly or badly. 'I didn't know at all what they do to me.' The others waited outside; and each went in in turn.

They asked afterwards what would happen 'but nobody wanted to tell us'. They asked the prisoner-doctors in Block 12, but they would not tell them anything. Until he was taken from Block 12 he did not know that he was going to have 'some kind of operation'.

The first time he saw Dr Dering was in the doctor's room in Block 28.

Mr Duncan: I am going to suggest that you are mistaken in saying that Dr Dering was there?

The first man: He was so.

Mr Duncan: I suggest that you are entirely wrong in saying that Dr Dering did this thing with a piece of wood.

The first man: He himself showed the stick to Dr Schumann and said, 'That is the instrument'.

The proceedings in Block 28 had lasted about twenty minutes.

The conversation he had had with Dr Dering in Block 21 took place in the presence of a male nurse.

Mr Duncan: I suggest that you are mistaken, and that you never had a conversation with Dr Dering.

The first man: I tell only the truth and the whole truth, and I remember quite well that I spoke to him in French.

Mr Duncan: I suggest that you are quite mistaken in your recollection about the needle breaking?

The first man: I am quite sure, because they cursed in Polish, and put me again in the same position.

Mr Duncan: Who were 'they'?

The first man: They were some people. I don't know if Dr Dering cursed. I only know that I heard curses in Polish. I only saw people in white overalls and the only one I recognize was Dr Dering. I saw Dr Dering every day after the operation when he came to see me, and while I was in Auschwitz I saw him frequently.

Mr Duncan: You told us that at the time of the injection you felt a terrible pain. That was the actual pain of the injection, of the needle going in, was it?

The first man: There was a pain when they did the injection in a brutal manner, and I was upset and shouted and screamed and resisted.

Mr Duncan: In what way was the actual injection done in a brutal manner?

The first man: Today if they want to give an injection they give it with consent, but they took me by force. I resisted and they gave me the injection.

Mr Duncan: If you are right, the needle broke because you were struggling?

The first man: Yes.

He could not remember exactly how long after the second injection ('if there was a second injection', said Mr Duncan) he ceased to have pain; possibly some minutes. There was a screen before his face for the operation, but he tore it down. Somebody put it up again but he took it off again.

The operation lasted from ten to twelve minutes. He felt no pain during it. When Dr Dering came to see him and before he took off the clips, Dr Dering told him that everything was all right; but he had an infection.

Mr Duncan: You were pretty badly treated by the Germans?

The first man: Surely.

Mr Duncan sat down, and Mr Hirst re-examined.

Mr Hirst: Do you know what happened to the bit of broken needle?

The first man: I do not know.

He did not remember which hurt more, the first or second injection. He had seen Dr Dering with Dr Schumann on two occasions, first in Block 28 when fluid was taken from him, and again in the theatre when Dr Dering showed Dr Schumann what had been removed from his body.

Mr Hirst: What was Dr Dering's attitude to Dr Schumann on those two occasions?

The first man: Very friendly and smiling.

RESISTANCE LEADER

Herr Hermann Langbein, of Vienna, who spoke in German, which was interpreted, and who had come from Frankfurt where he was giving evidence in the Auschwitz trials, said that he was a writer by profession and general secretary of the International Auschwitz Committee from its formation in 1954 until 1960. He had become a member of the Communist Party in 1933 in the week in which Hitler came to power, and remained in the party until after the suppression of the Hungarian revolt. 'Then I was excluded from the Party because I made opposition to this.'

In May 1941, he had been sent to Dachau, and in August 1942, to Auschwitz. At that time male nurses were needed at Auschwitz because of a typhus epidemic. His tattooed number was 60355; and at first he did night shift work in the hospital office but later was made clerk to Dr Wirths, the chief of the S.S. medical staff at the camp.

He worked in the S.S. department outside the base camp, and outside the electrified barbed wire. He went back to Block 21 almost daily. 'I went most of time when I was in camp and in evening after roll call. I had many friends in the building with whom I kept in contact in order to be informed as much as possible.' He had seen Dr Dering very often. Dr Dering was dressed in prisoners' dress. The clothes and shoes of the personnel in the hospital building were 'better than those of ordinary prisoner'. Dr Dering spoke 'mostly Polish; but we talked in German'.

When he got to Auschwitz there were several resistance groups. About the spring of 1943 a general group called the Auschwitz Fighting Group had been formed. There were four leaders—two Poles, Josef Cyrankiewicz and Tadeusz Haluk, and two Austrians, Ernst Bürger and himself. Josef Cyrankiewicz was the present Prime Minister of Poland.

They had achieved 'quite a bit. As the programme of our opponents was murder, we saw our chief task as the preservation of life.

We attempted to put sand into the machine of death. We achieved, for instance, the discontinuance of fatal injections, which were given to many prisoners who were ill'. They organized escapes, and sought and found contact with the Polish underground movement. Lists of the names of S.S. personnel were sent to London via Cracow and were then broadcast by the B.B.C. 'S.S. men listened, and then their courage to commit murder was slightly restricted after that publication.'

There were two chains of sentries in Auschwitz—'the small and the large'. The large chain was there when prisoners went out to work; the small chain surrounded the camp itself. 'It was known to us that, when a flight alarm was given, the large chain had orders to stay on the spot for three days. We found hiding places inside the large chain.' Escaped prisoners were given food and medical supplies for three days while they were in the hideout, and maps, and addresses at which they could call. There were many prisoners who had no idea that there were resistance groups in the camp. The work had to be done secretly.

There were many Polish members, and many doctors at the hospital joined. It was difficult for him to say whether there was any group which did not join.

In the autumn of 1943 the position had greatly improved owing to a change in the commandant's office, and the removal of 'the most notorious of all camp doctors, Dr Entress', who went to Mauthausen.

He had kept his position as Dr Wirths' secretary most of the time, but was punished in the autumn of 1943. Ernst Burger was hanged, together with others, in Auschwitz by the Germans on 30 December 1944.

Cross-examined by Mr Duncan, Herr Langbein said that the international organization was in existence in the spring of 1943. Between 1940 and 1943 other organizations had been doing their best in much the same way.

Mr Duncan: I expect that you knew that Dr Dering was one who had been associated with these activities when he first arrived at the camp?

Herr Langbein: When I made the acquaintance of Dr Dering he enjoyed a good reputation in the prisoners' hospital building.

Mr Duncan: Thank you very much. Prisoners, whether doctors or not, did not choose the clothes they wore?

Herr Langbein: Well, everyone who had possibility saw to it that he got good clothes.

Mr Duncan: If he could. But Dr Dering had to wear the clothes he was given, is not that right?

Herr Langbein: Whoever held position in camp had, by means of that position, a chance to exchange for better clothes. I, too, used to wear clean clothing.

MEDICAL STUDENT KLODZINSKI

The next witness was Dr Stanislaw Klodzinski, whose name had appeared in the original particulars of justification. He spoke in Polish, which was interpreted, and said that he was a practising Roman Catholic. He had been sent to Auschwitz in August 1941, when he was twenty-one and had completed his third year as a medical student. He felt ill and was sent to the camp hospital. After he recovered he had stayed in the hospital, helping in the room, and later as a porter, in Block 20, and finally as a doctor. Block 20 was mainly for infectious diseases.

He had first met Dr Dering at the end of 1941. 'At beginning I realized that Dr Dering had some contact with illegal organizations. I had such contacts. They concerned health, medicine and equipment for hospital. I sent out illegal news from Auschwitz and received answers.' In 1942 there had been a change in the organization of the resistance movement. The camp had become an international camp. He lived and worked in Block 20.

Mr Hirst: While you were in Block 20 did you ever go to Block 21?

Dr Klodzinski: Very often.

He had gone several times a day, for sterilizing material for dressings for his patients, and he had colleagues there. No one suggested that he should not go into Block 21.

He had made a drawing of Block 21, showing how it was divided, and was asked about each of the rooms, and the layout.

In the middle of 1943, he had seen a group of young men in Block 21, standing along a corridor, near the bath. He spoke to them. From what he saw and in conversation, he was sure that they had not had morphia. After he had spoken to them he went into the ante-room of the operating theatre. Preparations were being made for operations in the ante-room, and a patient in the theatre, lying on the table, was undergoing castration.

Mr Hirst: Did you see who the surgeon was?

Dr Klodzinski: Yes. Dr Dering.

Mr Hirst: Do you remember who else was there?

Dr Klodzinski: Probably Dr Entress and some orderlies.

Mr Duncan cross-examined: Although you were able to go to Block 21, you were not allowed to go to the operating theatre, were you?

Dr Klodzinski: Yes. I was allowed.

Sometimes he was allowed in when operations were going on. 'On the whole not allowed, but as student of medicine I was allowed. Dr Dering was allowing me to enter operating theatre.' The general rule that infectious ward employees were not allowed in the theatre was merely 'theoretical'. There were various infectious diseases in Block 21, where 'asepsis was not very strictly kept'.

Mr Duncan: Those events occurred twenty years ago?

Dr Klodzinski: Twenty-two.

He agreed that, in October 1962, he had by arrangement met Mrs Dering at a restaurant in Cracow. She had wanted to know what he had said about her husband at the time of the extradition proceedings. He did not remember whether she had asked particularly if he had seen her husband operating on testicles or ovaries.

Mr Duncan: You said 'Not ever'?

Dr Klodzinski: That I did not say. I definitely said that Dr Dering had carried out and I had seen it.

Mr Duncan: In 1962 did you tell Mrs Dering that her husband had been very good about getting food and medicines from outside the camp?

Dr Klodzinski: Yes.

Re-examined, he said that he had seen appendicitis operations in Block 21. Dr Dering had never objected to his watching. On the occasion of the castration he had watched for a few minutes.

Mr Hirst: What did you see?

Dr Klodzinski: The incision, removal of testicle, and the placing of testicle in kidney-shaped dish.

THE THIRD WOMAN

The third woman said that she could not give her age because all her papers had been lost; she was either thirty-nine or forty. She had been taken from Salonika and sent to Birkenau in March 1943; her tattooed number was 38782. She was irradiated in the summer. On the same day she was sent to Block 10 where the doctor was Dr Brewda, who was kind.

On the day of the operation 'before I was injected, I screamed, and during it I called "Father and mother" '. She had been frightened. The only injection she had that day was given by a male nurse and was painful. 'When I was on the operating table there was a big lamp like a mirror, and I could see blood, but not exactly what they did to me.' Dr Brewda was at her head. She asked Dr Brewda what was happening. Dr Brewda said '*Patience, patience, mon enfant*'. Dr Schumann was in uniform and did not have a white overall. After the operation she was in great pain, and her wound opened after a day or two and remained open for at least one month. In the night 'Bella shouted for water' and was taken out of the room. She knew that Bella and 'Marta' had been operated on twice. She herself had many 'signs' of burns after the irradiation. Even today one or two were still red. She had married but had no children of her own; she had adopted a child. She had never given evidence before about her experiences.

After the operation, when she was in bed, a doctor passed by with Dr Brewda. She did not remember his face. 'He did not examine my wound. He only passed and looked. He did not speak to me, nor I to him.'

She was cross-examined by Mr Duncan.

Mr Duncan: You were a girl of eighteen or nineteen when you were taken away to Birkenau, and were put to work, hard work. You were badly treated, I suppose?

The third woman: There was a very hard life.

She was punished and beaten; it was a horrible experience.

Mr Duncan: Long before you got even to the irradiation, let alone the operation, you were a frightened, miserable girl, I suppose?

The third woman: I worked. I had no choice.

Mr Duncan: Were you a frightened, miserable girl?

The third woman: I was healthy, and I worked hard.

Mr Duncan: In March 1943, were you moved from Birkenau to Block 10 in Auschwitz?

The third woman: I went in mid-summer. In the camp we did not know the exact date.

Mr Duncan: Did you girls talk to one another about what you were doing in Block 10 with no work?

The third woman: Yes, because we found there many other women, none of them working.

Mr Duncan: Was it common talk that the women were there for some kind of experiments?

The third woman: Yes.

Mr Duncan: That made you more frightened and miserable still?

The third woman: I was afraid.

The third woman was still in the witness box when the court adjourned at the end of the seventh day. Next morning she said that she would like to add something to her evidence. It was that 'they' had intended that she should be one of those to be operated on by Dr Samuel in Block 10; but because there were still little stains on her skin she had been sent back to Birkenau. Then orders came that five of her group should go back to Block 10, and they had been called 'by their numbers' and sent back to Auschwitz for operation by Dr Samuel. Then they had changed their minds about her, and only 'Marta' and Bella had been taken.

Then Mr Duncan asked: 'Now about the time when you went to Block 21, in November 1943 . . .'

The third woman, stolid and middle-aged, who had been giving her answers in a clear and composed voice, suddenly burst into uncontrolled sobbing. She covered her face with her hands and put her head down on the table.

The Judge: (to the interpreter): Explain to the witness that she can go out for a few minutes.

She was helped out of her seat by the interpreter and turned to go down the steps leading to the body of the court, supporting herself by putting her hand against the panelled wall of the court. There she stopped, and turned her face to the wall, with her arms upstretched, in an attitude of silent grief. At once the interpreter took her by the arm and led her out of court.

The Judge told Lord Gardiner that when she had recovered she could perhaps return to the witness box. Meanwhile the next witness might be called.

Mr Duncan said that he did not propose to subject the woman who had just left to further cross-examination and understood that no point would be taken for the defence if he did not challenge her further.

The Judge: Then will someone go out and tell the lady that she won't be required any more?

CHAPTER XIII

Expert on Anaesthesia Interposed

THE tension of the preceding two days was eased a little when Dr John David Ebsworth, an expert witness on anaesthesia, went into the box. He gave his qualifications as the Diploma of Anaesthetics, a Fellow of the Faculty of Anaesthetics of the Royal College of Surgeons, consultant at University College Hospital since 1947, and teacher of students at University College Medical School.

He told Mr Hirst that there were two main methods of anaesthesia—general and local—and they could be used as alternatives or in combination. One form of local anaesthetic was by injection into the spinal cord. It was his practice, and normal practice, recommended in six standard textbooks, to try to minimize the discomfort of that procedure for the patient by putting in a little local anaesthetic beforehand with a very fine needle at the point of the main injection to render the tissues roundabout insensitive when the larger needle was introduced into the spinal cord. That preliminary injection was quite distinct from premedication by morphia.

In normal conditions in the early 1940s a spinal anaesthetic might have been used for patients who could tolerate being operated on while conscious and who had agreed to accept it; but one would as a matter of routine sedate the patient beforehand.

Mr Hirst: At University College Hospital, suppose the patient is nervous?

Dr Ebsworth: I would not inflict that form of anaesthetic on a nervous patient. I would use a general.

Mr Hirst: Let us now consider Auschwitz in 1943. Assuming that both general and local anaesthetics were available at any one time and that these patients were nervous, would that be an indication for a general or a spinal?

Dr Ebsworth: For a general.

If he knew that patients had not consented to the operation and were part and parcel of an experiment, the humane and proper thing to do would be to give them a general anaesthetic.

He had read Dr Hewer's evidence in this trial and noted that Dr Hewer had said he would approve of spinal anaesthesia in these cases.

Mr Hirst: Have you in court the book by Dr Hewer to which he referred in his evidence: *Recent Advances in Anaesthesia*?

Dr Ebsworth: Yes; the 1943 edition. Dr Hewer has some illuminating observations on the advisability of spinal anaesthesia when a patient is nervous.

Mr Duncan objected that this had not been put to Dr Hewer. Lord Gardiner replied that he had not known that Dr Hewer was going to be called and could not be expected to have read all the textbooks on anaesthetics in England.

The Judge said that, in his experience, if one called the attention of a witness to something he wrote twenty years ago, the witness usually said: 'Yes, but I have changed my mind since'. But if Mr Duncan thought it right, Dr Hewer could be recalled.

Dr Ebsworth then read from the book passages on '*Contra-indications to spinal anaesthesia*'.

Put in simple language, he said, they meant, 'If the patient is in any distress you should render the patient unconscious'.

Mr Hirst: If there is no preliminary injection at the site of the spinal injection, is it likely or unlikely to cause pain?

Dr Ebsworth: Likely to cause pain. It could be acute pain.

However expert the anaesthetist, it was not always easy to get a spinal injection in at the right place. It was not safe to carry out a spinal injection if a patient was struggling and resisting, for the actual placing of the needle had to be done with great accuracy. There would be great difficulty in directing the needle on a moving target, and the further risk of the needle breaking if the patient made a violent move.

Mr Hirst: You heard the male victim who described how the first needle broke when he was struggling. Did that strike you as consistent with what you might expect?

Dr Ebsworth: Yes.

The needle used for the preliminary injection was the finest possible needle and very short.

Dr Ebsworth produced a syringe with a needle, and said that it was of the type in use in 1940. It was marked as an exhibit. He knew that Dr Hewer had said that there was no point in giving a preliminary injection, because it caused two lots of pain instead of one; but there was no comparison between the pain caused by the fine needle which penetrated the skin readily, and the spinal needle which, being of a bigger bore, could cause great pain.

The effect of a spinal anaesthetic on the patient's general condition above the waist also varied. He had not been surprised to hear the second woman saying that she was sleepy. That could be entirely attributable to the effect of the spinal anaesthetic. If a patient was struggling, it would be more difficult to control the anaesthetic, for one might tend to push it in more quickly to get it over, and that might make the anaesthetic creep up a little, causing dizziness and even unconsciousness.

Premedication was always given for ordinary surgery, at least half an hour before operation. If a person were given an injection thirty minutes before, he would probably feel giddy, unsteady, and almost certainly nauseated, and those effects would be increased if the patient were already debilitated by brutal treatment or undernourishment. He would not have expected such a patient to be able to stand in a queue in a corridor waiting for operation. An experienced doctor could tell by looking at a patient whether or not he had been premedicated. Morphia contracted the pupils of the eyes.

The register was handed to Dr Ebsworth and he was referred to specific pages where the anaesthetic used for a number of operations was recorded as 'ether'. He said that ether was 'a safe and sound general anaesthetic'.

Mr Hirst: If ether was available, would that be preferable to a spinal for this kind of operation in these circumstances?

Dr Ebsworth: In my opinion, yes.

He noted, halfway down one page, a laparotomy performed under ether. A laparotomy could be very similar to the operation for the removal of an ovary.

Mr Hirst: From the point of view of an expert on anaesthetics, is there any sense in using a general anaesthetic for a laparotomy, which was presumably done with the patient's consent, and a spinal anaesthetic for the removal of an ovary done without the patient's consent?

Dr Ebsworth: I should use a general anaesthetic in those circumstances.

Dr Ebsworth noted, on pages 90 and 91, a number of operations for amputation of testicles, and that all but four of the operations on that page preceding the amputations had been done under ether.

Mr Hirst: And also—since we have been told that it was impossible to give a general because there was no assistant to give it—one Lawski appears to have administered all the ether anaesthesia and then to have changed his rôle and become assistant surgeon in six amputation operations. Now turn to the page of the ten girls' operations. It is right, is it not, that there are four operations under ether, on the same page at the bottom, on the following day?

Dr Ebsworth: Yes.

Cross-examined by Mr Duncan, Dr Ebsworth agreed that Dr Hewer was a considerable expert in the field of anaesthetics, and also that experts did not always agree.

Mr Duncan: It is quite clear, is it not, that a great deal of your evidence today is evidence with which Dr Hewer does not agree.

Dr Ebsworth: That may be so of Dr Hewer's evidence in this court, but not in his book. I agree with some of the evidence he gave.

He could not agree with Dr Hewer that a preliminary injection in the path of the main injection might increase the difficulty of giving the spinal injection; but he conceded that if that was Dr Hewer's view and his own was a contrary view, a great many other doctors might take one or the other view.

Mr Duncan: Whichever of you happens to be right—and perhaps both may be—the pain of the puncture is something which disappears with remarkable rapidity?

Dr Ebsworth: What puncture?

Mr Duncan: The spinal injection?

Dr Ebsworth: Not necessarily. When you carry out this particular operation you have to do it very deliberately and feel your way. It is not like pushing a needle two inches into a thigh. You have to be very precise and feel your way between the bones. If you strike the bones you may have to start all over again.

Mr Duncan: Assuming a spinal injection is being given—well or badly—and the needle is being withdrawn, I suggest that the pain is quickly over.

Dr Ebsworth: Yes; but I cannot agree that it would be of short duration. It may take an expert five to ten minutes to perform this manoeuvre. If you have to go on exploring it may be very painful. No expert can guarantee that he can just put a needle in and find the point.

Mr Duncan: But if the injection is done extremely well the pain disappears quickly?

Dr Ebsworth: Yes.

Mr Duncan: Assuming that there was no competent anaesthetist available, do you agree that it would be very unwise to use an inhalant anaesthetic?

Dr Ebsworth: Yes.

Mr Duncan: Do you accept the general proposition that, for an operation on the lower abdomen, a spinal injection is, in many cases, preferable?

Dr Ebsworth: From the surgeon's point of view perhaps, but not necessarily from the patient's point of view. Spinal anaesthesia produces, without any doubt at all, good operating conditions for the surgeon. But, in certain circumstances, those advantages may be completely outweighed by the general circumstances—in other words, the attitude and mental make-up of the patient, and the circumstances of the operation.

Mr Duncan: Nobody would suggest that there was anything strange about using spinal anaesthesia on the Continent? It was perfectly ordinary, was it not?

Dr Ebsworth: Yes.

The Judge: What was the normal form of anaesthesia on the Continent up to 1939 for an operation for appendicitis?

Dr Ebsworth: I was not on the Continent myself, but I can believe that it could be a spinal anaesthetic. It could be another anaesthetic. It was not necessarily confined to one anaesthetic only.

The Judge: Was that never the practice in this country?

Dr Ebsworth: Oh yes. But spinal anaesthetics have declined in popularity in this country during the last fifteen years or so.

The Judge: Was not that as the result of an action[1] in one of these courts?

Dr Ebsworth: Yes.

[1] *Roe* v. *Minister of Health* [1954] 2 Q.B. 66.

CHAPTER XIV

Further Victims

'HOW COULD I BE CHEERFUL?'

THE fourth woman, aged thirty-nine, came from Israel. She had been born in Salonika and taken to Auschwitz with her mother when she was seventeen. Her tattooed number was 41614. In Block 10 the beds were three-tier bunks and the windows were closed so that she could not see through them. One day Dr Schumann came and all the young girls stood in a queue and he picked some of them out for irradiation.

During the operation 'I was awake and I saw in the reflection of the lamp that they did something to me. I felt like vomiting. Then I felt the warm hand of Dr Brewda. She told me "*Encore un peu, mon enfant*". I cannot forget it. If it had not been for Dr Brewda I should not have lived'.

A few days after the operation a man doctor had entered the room where she was. 'The moment Dr Brewda told him my state was not in order I saw how he answered. He said words I could not understand. It was enough for me when I saw. . . . '(She made a pushing-away gesture.) 'Then he turned round and went past all the beds. When he was leaving the room Dr Brewda told him about my bad state again. Then he returned to my bed and tore away the plaster and bandages. That is right and the truth.'

After being in bed for months in Block 10 she was sent back to Birkenau and put to work filling sand into railway wagons, but later managed to get sent to a munitions factory. She had married after the war, had no children of her own, but had adopted a daughter.

She was cross-examined by Mr Neill: While you were in Block 10 what were you doing during the day?

The fourth woman: Nothing. That was experimental work. In the beginning I did not know it. Afterwards I knew.

Mr Neill: Who told you that?

The fourth woman: Nobody had to tell us because we were received like beasts.

Mr Neill: Did you see a female doctor?

The fourth woman: I want to know which woman doctor. I saw many. I know only Dr Brewda. She was at the most important moment of my life by my side.

Mr Neill: Is it hard for you to remember what happened that day?

The fourth woman: I remember and I shall till I die. During the operation towards the end, I felt like vomiting, and started to say 'Oh! Oh! mother', but then I felt the warm hand of the woman doctor Brewda, when she said '*Elle est finie, mon petit. Elle est finie*'.

Mr Neill: That was all you heard?

The fourth woman: Yes.

The fifth woman, born in Salonika in 1926 and taken to Birkenau in 1943, bore a tattooed number 43339, and gave evidence of what had happened up to the point of the spinal injection in the ante-room. Her head had been quite clear during the operation, and she remembered Dr Brewda being present 'sitting at my head, like a mother'. Her wound had become infected, as had those of other girls. She remembered Bella being taken from her bed the same night and 'I never saw her again'. After the war she had married in Italy and she and her husband went to Israel in 1946. Following treatment in Israel, her menstrual periods, which had stopped after the operation, had started again, and she had twice become pregnant in 1948 and 1949; but 'the pregnancies were not successful because of the operation'.

Mr Neill, cross-examining: Do you remember anything about the operation, madam?

The fifth woman: I remember the operation. I have the scar.

The sixth woman, born in Greece in 1925, bore the tattooed number 38968, said that she had married after the war, had no children of her own, but had adopted a boy. The effect of the operation on her health was that she never felt well, had headaches and had no energy.

Lord Gardiner: Do you have any difficulties in your married life?

The sixth woman: In the beginning I had many difficulties.

She was cross-examined by Mr Neill, who asked her how she knew the name of Dr Schumann. She replied: 'All of us knew his name. If I see him today I will recognize him immediately. He has a scar.' During the operation she had seen 'all red' in the theatre lamp. In re-examination by Lord Gardiner, she said that she knew Dr Schumann because when she came to Block 10 he had looked at her number, and she had asked who he was, and had been told.

Lord Gardiner then said that before this witness was released, he wished to draw the Judge's attention to the fact that Dr Dering's case, which was that the spinal injection did not take place in the ante-room at all but was done in the operating theatre on the table, and that no one screamed, was not being put to the witnesses. It had not been suggested to any of them that their evidence was completely untrue.

The Judge said that he had noticed that that aspect of their evidence was not being challenged.

Mr Neill said that he had not put every single point to the last witnesses.

The Judge: I think the jury are entitled to know whether your case is that this witness and a number of the other witnesses have really let their imaginations loose and imagined all this, or whether you are saying that they are in fact, as a result of what happened to them, confused and, though perfectly honest, cannot be relied on. What is the case for Dr Dering?

Mr Neill said that Dr Dering's evidence was that the injections were given in the operating theatre, by himself, and that, as these ladies were at the time girls of seventeen or eighteen, it was quite impossible for them, in the extremely distressing circumstances, to recollect in detail the evidence which they now sought to put before the jury.

The Judge: I rather gathered that that was how you would put it. You are not going to suggest to them that they are all telling a pack of lies?

Mr Neill: I do not think I can.

The Judge: Then I don't think you need have them all back and suggest to them that they are telling a pack of lies, if your case is that it is all such a long time ago that their recollection is not very good.

Lord Gardiner protested: The plaintiff's case, that when Dr

Dering called at Block 10 they were all laughing and joking and everyone was having a very nice time, has not been put to any of them. It is usual to put your case to a witness.

The Judge: It does not sound, from what they recollect—whether accurately or not—that they would say they were laughing or joking. (To Mr Neill): Do you want to put it specifically to this witness?

Mr Neill then asked the sixth woman, who had sat patiently in the witness box during this discussion which she did not understand, whether she had been given the spinal injection before or after being taken into the operating theatre. She replied that it was 'Before'.

The Judge: That is quite clear. Now put to her that after the operation all the girls were quite cheerful.

Mr Neill asked her whether she remembered the man doctor coming to Block 10 after the operations. She said that she did, but that he had not talked to her, nor had he been talking to the other girls.

Mr Neill: How were you? Were you cheerful? I suggest you were quite cheerful on that occasion.

The sixth woman: How could I be cheerful? I had strong pain.

The next witness was not called until after the Judge had allowed[1] the defence to deliver the supplementary particulars of justification, on the morning of the ninth day of the trial.

TWICE OPERATED

The seventh woman was the girl 'Marta', who had been mentioned frequently as having had two operations. She was born in 1923 and early in the war had gone through a marriage ceremony with a man in Salonika; but in April 1943, she was taken to Birkenau. [Her tattooed number—40204—was shown to the interpreter in the way now becoming familiar but never losing its effect.] She had been put to very hard work at Birkenau, but was then chosen for irradiation. After it she had great burns on her body which became infected and took about a month to heal. When they had been 'cured' she had gone back to Birkenau for a couple of days, and then she and four other girls (whose first names she gave) had been

[1] See Appendix, pages 281–2.

called out and taken back to Block 10; and she and one other, the girl Bella, had been put aside for operation, as she understood, by Dr Samuel 'on Schumann's orders'. Dr Samuel did the operation.

Mr Hirst: On that occasion what kind of anaesthetic did you have?

The seventh woman: Chloroform.

She had known nothing about the operation, as she was asleep 'during two hours'; but both she and Bella had been operated on on the same day. Her scar was horizontal. There had been complications, and also trouble with the burn on her back, and she had been kept in bed for three months. Then in November she was taken to Block 21 in a group of ten girls; Bella was one of them. They had gone on foot, all within the hour. She had been the last of the ten, 'after Bella'. She had been given an injection in the back by a male nurse, in a room next to the operating theatre, while she was in a sitting position, and 'they' bent her head down between the legs of another male nurse.

Mr Hirst: Was the moment of injection painless or painful?

The seventh woman: Certainly it hurt. I screamed at the moment of the injection. I did not want to be operated on twice.

Bella, the seventh woman said, had also screamed 'as I did'.

[She became disturbed, and was told to take her time.] When she was composed again, Mr Hirst asked: What effect did the injection have on the lower part of your body?

The seventh woman: It was not dead. I had only pains.

Mr Hirst: Did it ever go dead?

The seventh woman: No.

Mr Hirst: Was your brain clear or clouded?

The seventh woman: I was clear, and I spoke.

Mr Hirst: When you got on to the operating table, what happened?

The seventh woman: They operated on me.

Mr Hirst: What did you see with your eyes while they operated?

The seventh woman: I saw the lamp over me and it was full of only red. I screamed for very strong pains. Dr Brewda told me always: 'Don't be afraid. It will finish soon'.

Mr Hirst: Did you yourself have any conversation with either of the men in white?

The seventh woman: Yes.

Mr Hirst: Will you tell us what was said?

The seventh woman: I asked them to finish with me because I could not stand the pain longer, and he told me: 'Let me finish my work, *verfluchte Jüdin*'—that means 'damned Jewess'—and he gave me a blow on my breast. The doctoress stroked my hair. I was crying and sweating.

Mr Hirst: Did you see with your own eyes what was removed from your body?

The seventh woman: I heard they cut inside and I saw that they took out something.

After the operation she had been taken back to Block 10 and the following morning 'everything was open'. Before the operation she had had no injection other than the spinal injection.

Mr Hirst: Are you quite sure about that?

The seventh woman: I am ready to give my signature to it.

The scar from her second operation was vertical, so that the two scars were like a cross. Both were visible today. In the middle of the night after the operations, Bella had been taken away and she had never seen her again. She herself had been 'very bad' during that night and had not heard anything; but later she had seen for herself the condition of the other girls. They had been looked after by a female nurse and Dr Brewda—who had assured her that she would be 'cured'—just like a mother.

A man who came to the ward about a week after the operation had gone round with Dr Brewda but just looked at the girls from the foot of their bunks; he did not examine the wounds.

Mr Hirst: Which was worse—the pain after your first operation or that after your second operation?

The seventh woman: The second.

Mr Hirst: Which wound was the nastier?

The seventh woman: The second.

Mr Hirst: Can you tell us whether the man who came round the ward a week after the operation was the same man or a different man from the one who called you a 'damned Jewess'?

The seventh woman: I recognized him from his front.

She had settled in Israel after the war and had remarried. She had no children of her own, but she had adopted children.

Mr Hirst: What effect has the irradiation and the two operations had on your general health since the war?

The seventh woman: I had no periods. They made of me a beast.

Cross-examined by Mr Duncan, she agreed that when she was doing hard manual labour at the beginning in Birkenau she had often been beaten, and the food was very bad.

Mr Duncan: And soon after, you began to feel pretty ill and miserable?

The seventh woman: I felt lonely.

She was asked a series of questions about the first and the second operations.

Mr Duncan: It is a long time ago?

The seventh woman: Twenty years.

Mr Duncan: Do you think, perhaps, after all this time, that you are not very certain about what happened at which operation?

The seventh woman: What that means I don't know. If I look at myself I am destroyed—my whole life.

The Judge: What is being suggested to you is that with the passing of time and all the things that have happened to you, you have got confused about what happened at the first and the second operations?

The seventh woman: I know what happened at the first and the second operation. I know.

She had not known the purpose of the operations, but after the first, 'Dr Samuel said to me "If you will live, then you will be as all the others I operated on". He told me that he opened and closed the abdomen. That was all that he told me'. He looked after her every day for three months. The first operation was about September; the second about three months later.

Before the second operation, on the same day, she had been examined by Dr Schumann, who was alone. He told her that the operation of Dr Samuel 'was not in order', and that she had to have another operation by another doctor. When she went to Block 21 she knew that it was for an operation. She went crying and screaming. 'All of them cried, but I cried more because I did not want to enter the second time.'

Mr Duncan: Did you all walk across in one group?

The seventh woman: We went one after the other, within one hour, as guinea-pigs.

She burst into tears, and put a handkerchief to her eyes. The court waited. After a while she appeared more composed. Mr Duncan waited.

The Judge spoke to the interpreter. 'Ask her', said the Judge, 'if she is ready to go on.'

The interpreter spoke to her and she said several words.

The interpreter: Yes.

Mr Duncan: You had better interpret what she said.

The interpreter: Yes. I want to take vengeance.

Mr Duncan: I thought that it might be important!

The seventh woman said that she still had pain at the site of the operation and in her back.

Mr Duncan: Are you saying that, twenty years later, you still have pain from where you had the injection?

The seventh woman: I have pains in my back, also the abdomen. I have still other pains.

Mr Duncan: Do you remember how long after the spinal injection you were taken into the operating theatre?

The seventh woman: After about one hour.

Mr Duncan: You have told my Lord and the jury that at one stage one of them said, 'Let me finish my work, you damned Jewess'. Was it the man who was doing the operation?

The seventh woman: Yes.

Mr Duncan: What language did he say it in?

The seventh woman: In German.

Mr Duncan: You understand German, I suppose?

The seventh woman: We learnt such ugly words there.

The Judge: I can understand your learning the German words for 'damned Jewess'; but did you know enough German to understand what he meant when he said: 'Let me finish my work'?

The seventh woman: I learnt some German when I was beaten in the camp.

The Judge: We will have a little test. Perhaps the witness will now say in German 'Let me finish my work'.

The seventh woman: 'Lass mich fertig mein arbeit, verfluchte Jüdin'.

Mr Duncan: Do you recognize the man who came round the ward as Dr Dering, who is sitting in court today?

The seventh woman: After twenty years I cannot remember. I saw that Dr Brewda spoke to him.

The Judge asked her whether she, like the other girls from Salonika, spoke 'this Spaniole language'. She said that that was so, but that she also knew a little French, and she talked to Dr Brewda in French.

Before re-examining the seventh woman, Lord Gardiner said that he did not want to impose on the jury more evidence than was necessary. Once again, in the case of this seventh woman, it had never been suggested to her that her injections did not take place in the operating theatre, or that she had had premedication by morphia, or that her injection had been given when she was on the operating table, or that Dr Brewda had not been present at all. If it could be assumed from that that all those allegations had been abandoned, some time might be saved with other witnesses.

Mr Duncan said that he was not withdrawing what he had said.

The Judge: These subtleties are not very easy for the jury to follow. Are you suggesting that this witness comes into the category of 'liar' or of 'confused'?

Mr Duncan: I am not suggesting either one or the other, but I am suggesting that my client and his witnesses have been telling the truth. That is part of my duty.

The Judge: But is it not part of your duty, if you are suggesting that this witness is telling lies, to make that clear?

Mr Duncan: If I were suggesting that, I would do so.

The Judge: Do I gather that you have not suggested to this witness in terms that she has invented the story, but that you are going to say that your client is a reliable witness and this one is not?

Mr Duncan: Precisely. I hope that if I intended to convey to a witness that she had come here and committed perjury I would say so.

Lord Gardiner: I thought it was being suggested that they all suffered from hallucinations and that they saw Dr Brewda when she was not there at all.

The Judge: No doubt you will both address the jury.

Re-examining the seventh woman, Lord Gardiner asked her: You said that Dr Samuel told you, 'You will live and you will be like all the other ones'?

The seventh woman: Yes. He said: 'The others will have children'.

Lord Gardiner: And that you would be like them?

The seventh woman: Yes.

The Judge: You told us through the interpreter that you wanted vengeance. Do you want vengeance?

The seventh woman: Yes.

The Judge: On whom?

The seventh woman: Those who spoilt my life. All the Germans.

The Judge: What did you think was the nationality of the doctor who operated on you the second time?

The seventh woman: I don't remember his nationality.

The Judge: Did you think he was a German?

The seventh woman: No.

THE INTOLERABLE QUESTION

The next witness, the second man, living near Haifa, was quiet in manner and older than the others. He had been born in Poland in 1912 and had had a wife and family before the war but, just after September 1939, he was taken to a Jewish prisoner-of-war camp and had never seen them again. He had been sent to Auschwitz in 1942.

After radiation of his genital organ, he developed black stains and went to the camp prisoner-doctor for help, but had been told that he had orders not to help.

He had had two operations. Dr Dering was present at the first, which was performed by the S.S. Dr Entress. The second had been performed by Dr Dering himself.

The interpreter told the court that the second man wanted to say what had happened in the room after his second operation, but the Judge commented that there was nothing in the supplementary particulars about Dr Dering after the operation, and Lord Gardiner turned to a different subject.

Lord Gardiner: Have you remarried since the war?

The second man: Yes.

Lord Gardiner: Have you any children of your own?

The second man did not reply, but put his hand over his face, and wept. The Judge adjourned the trial for five minutes.

Afterwards, the second man said that he had given evidence about these matters for the Polish Government in the Court of

Haifa in 1950. He had made a statement for the purposes of this action some months ago.

Cross-examined by Mr Duncan, the second man said that on the occasion of the first operation he had been able through the door to see what was going on while he was waiting to be operated on.

Mr Duncan: I suggest to you that for the first operation the spinal injection was given to you by Dr Entress.

The second man: No *doctor* did the injection. The whole world knows about that.

It was quite untrue that the injection had been given in the theatre when he was on the table, or that there had been a screen between his chin and his lower abdomen during either operation. There had been no screen. It was quite untrue that Dr Dering had administered the spinal anaesthetic on either the first or second occasion. He had assisted at the first operation but 'never did Dr Dering do the injection'.

Lord Gardiner called his next witness. The second man, still in the witness box, said something to the interpreter, who told the Judge that he was asking whether he might be allowed to say something to the court. The Judge said that he could not.

FIRST OF THE TEN

The interpreter from Judeo-Spanish was sworn to interpret for the eighth woman, born in 1923 in Salonika, who said that she was still living there.

She had been married, eight days before the war spread to Greece, to a man to whom she had been engaged, to avoid being separated by the Germans; the marriage had never been consummated. She had been taken to Block 10 direct from the wagon and tattooed with a number, 41579.

She had been the first of the girls to be operated on in November 1943, and had been so placed during the operation that she could not see anything but the movement of hands. Towards the finish of the operation she had seen in the theatre a lady doctor—Dr Brewda—who had told her not to worry or be afraid. After the operation her wound had not been open, though she had felt very ill, and had remained in bed in Block 10 for three or four months.

She thought she remembered a male doctor from outside Block 10 visiting the ward 'just once' after the operations but he did not examine her wound and did not speak to her. She had married since the war in Salonika but had no children, and was in poor health.

Cross-examined by Mr Duncan, the eighth woman said that, though it was many years ago, she did remember some things quite well and was quite clear that she had had a spinal injection in the ante-room and that it had not been given by the surgeon in the theatre. She was quite sure that she had been taken into the theatre—more or less dragged in—by two men, and not carried on a stretcher.

Mr Duncan: Up to the day of the operation had you ever heard of Dr Dering?

The eighth woman: No, sir, nothing at all.

Mr Duncan: Do you, one way or the other, recognize him now as one of the four men who were in the theatre that day?

The eighth woman: I don't remember because they were all wearing masks.

Mr Duncan: Did you see Dr Brewda come into the theatre?

The eighth woman: No, I did not, because they were already operating on me. All I know is that she was not there at the beginning.

Dr Brewda had given her courage. The 'ladies' in the block treated wounds which were open; but her wound was not open.

Mr Duncan: Did the doctor, whoever he was—and I suggest it was Dr Dering—go up to the patients?

The eighth woman: Yes.

Mr Duncan: Was Dr Brewda with him all the time?

The eighth woman: I think so.

Mr Duncan: And were other nurses going round with him?

The eighth woman: I think so.

Mr Duncan: And as they went round the ward, were they talking to one another?

The eighth woman: Yes.

Mr Duncan: And in some cases laughing?

The eighth woman: I did not take any notice. I was very ill.

She knew a little Greek and a little French. She and Dr Brewda had talked to each other in French. Dr Brewda gave consolation.

Mr Duncan: Did you ever deliberately disobey any order given to you by the Germans?

The eighth woman: I could not do anything against their orders because they would have killed me.

Lord Gardiner, re-examining: Did they ever order you to do anything criminal?

The eighth woman did not understand what was meant by 'criminal'. She agreed that the orders given to her were in relation to her work.

'I WAS A JEW'

The third man, born in Poland in 1925, said that he lived near Tel Aviv, and bore the tattooed number 75278. He had had first his right and then his left testicle removed—the left by Dr Dering. He had gone alone to the operation on orders to do so. He had been given an injection, but could not say by whom; but he had had no earlier injection that day. When he was on the table, 'I saw when Dr Dering approached to operate, and I asked him: "Why do you operate on me? Is it not enough that they operated me once?" and he answered: "Dog, in any case you will die." '

The Judge: In what language did he speak those words?

The third man: In Polish.

Lord Gardiner asked the man to say the words in Polish.

The third man: 'Przestań szczekać jak pies, tak i tak umrzesz'. The Polish interpreter in the body of the Court translated the words as: 'Stop barking like a dog. You will die anyway.'

His testicle had been removed and put into a container which bore his number. He had gone back to work later.

He had given evidence at the Eichmann trial in Israel, and about a year ago he had read about the present case in the newspapers. As he knew Dr Dering, he had at once written to ask if he might give evidence at this trial.

The Judge then explained to the jury the effect of his ruling about the supplementary particulars.[1]

The third man, who had sat quietly through the Judge's observations to the jury, was then cross-examined.

Mr Neill: You feel very bitter about this, don't you?

[1] See page 32.

The third man: I don't feel good at all, and I feel pain in my heart and shame in my face.

After the first operation Dr Dering had come to see him in hospital, two or three times during the six or seven days he had been there.

The Judge: My understanding is that this witness is saying that after the first operation Dr Dering assiduously came to look at him every other day.

The third man agreed that many horrible things had been spoken to him at Auschwitz by Germans. Generally they swore and told the prisoners to work faster, or 'did not speak but only beat'.

Mr Neill: Are you sure that these words were not used on some other occasion by a German?

The third man: No. Only *he* said it.

Mr Neill: Are you saying that you can remember the exact words twenty years later?

The third man: Yes.

The Judge asked the man to repeat in Polish what he had stated that he had said to Dr Dering and what Dr Dering had replied, and directed that the words should be taken down by the Polish interpreter in writing, shown to Dr Dering, and then made an exhibit. That was done.

Lord Gardiner, re-examining: You have been asked whether you were not used to being spoken to rudely by the Germans?

The third man: The Germans always spoke rudely.

Lord Gardiner: Were you Polish?

The third man: I was a Jew.

Lord Gardiner: How long had your family been Polish citizens?

The third man: For generations.

Lord Gardiner: Did you expect to be spoken to like that by a Polish doctor?

The third man gave an answer in Hebrew, which the interpreter translated: 'He had always spoken in that rude manner. He was an anti-Semite'.

The Judge asked the jury to put the last bit of translation out of their minds. The question had been quite proper, but if his Lordship had understood the answer while it was being given he would have stopped it.

The fourth man, who said that he had given evidence at the Eichmann trial, had been only sixteen when the Germans took him from Salonika to Auschwitz. He bore the tattooed number 114563. He was in the youngest age group, and the Germans had selected boys from each age group for irradiation. He had been twice irradiated, once in the Gentiles' hospital block and once in the women's camp. Then two men had dragged him to the theatre for operation. He had not given evidence before about his experiences. He had come from Israel to England on 9 April and saw the English lawyers on 12 April, last Sunday week.

TWO CHILDREN

The fifth man, aged forty-eight, was one of two men aged twenty-six selected for irradiation. He had the tattooed mark 11220 with a triangle. He had had three separate irradiations over two weeks, and was then taken to Block 28 at Auschwitz.

Before the operation, he said, he was slapped in the face and then injected in the spine.

Mr Hirst: Did you have any conversation with anybody during the operation?

The fifth man: I spoke in Greek and said, 'Why did you bring me here. I am healthy man, and don't need an operation'. I spoke to those who were present. They said to me '*Ruhig!*' which means 'Silence!' The operation lasted about twenty to thirty minutes. I could not see what was happening.

The following morning he 'had pain' and Dr Dering ordered that he should have a tablet. After the war he went to Israel and married.

Mr Hirst: Are there any children of your marriage?

The fifth man: Yes. Two. [He gave their dates of birth.]

Mr Hirst: What has been the effect of the operation on your general state of health since the war?

The fifth man: Immediately after having been liberated from the concentration camp I started to receive medical treatment, which I receive still, and I shall continue to receive until I die.

Mr Hirst: On the day of your operation did you receive any injection other than the spinal injection?

The fifth man: No.

'RUHIG!'

Mr Hirst: Who said 'Silence'?

The fifth man: Dering himself.

Mr Hirst: Who slapped you?

The fifth man pointed at Dr Dering sitting in the well of the court, and said, in a voice deepened with emotion: 'He did'.

Mr Duncan cross-examined. The fifth man said that he first saw Dr Dering in the operating theatre, when the lower part of his face was covered with a mask.

Mr Duncan: If anybody slapped you it was, I suggest, in the adjoining room before you got to the operating theatre?

The fifth man: It was in the operating theatre. [The man again pointed to the well of the court where Dr Dering was sitting.]

Mr Duncan: I can see you pointing to Dr Dering, but you did not know him then?

The fifth man: I knew him the following morning.

Mr Duncan: Had you any knowledge that anyone in the room understood Greek?

The fifth man: I don't know. I didn't understand German.

Mr Duncan: The only answer you got was '*ruhig*'?

The fifth man: Yes. At that time I didn't know it was German. It was not a Greek word. After a couple of months I learnt some German.

Mr Duncan: May I suggest that what the German word, *ruhig*, means, is 'gently'?

The fifth man: It means 'Silence'.

The Judge asked whether the interpreter was a German scholar. He said that he was. Mr Duncan initiated a discussion on whether, in a pastoral context,[1] *ruhig* was more properly translated as 'gently', 'quietly' or 'silently'.

[1] '*Ruhig fliesst der Rhein*'.

PART IV: EVIDENCE OF THE DOCTORS

CHAPTER XV

The Communist: Dr Lorska

'I THINK I AM OBJECTIVE'

THE first of the women doctors mentioned by Lord Gardiner went into the witness box—Dr Dorota Lorska, aged about fifty, with a pleasant face, dark hair, and wearing a blue and black tweed suit.

Of Jewish origin and born at Kielce in Poland, she attended High School, but could not get into the University medical faculty, so she went to Prague where she qualified in medicine in 1937, and then married a Mr Klein, which made her name Kleinova. She volunteered as a doctor in the Spanish Civil War when she was twenty-four, and joined the Communist Party in Spain. She was still a member. When the Spanish war ended and the Second World War began, her husband had vanished in a concentration camp. She had stayed on in France, being unable to return to either Poland or Czechoslovakia. She joined the French Resistance movement at the very beginning and after the war General de Gaulle's government had awarded her the Croix de Guerre and Star.

She had been arrested by the French police who collaborated with the Gestapo and was deported with about 1,000 people, arriving at Auschwitz on 2 August 1943. 'A German S.S. doctor, Wirths, after events which were worse than Dante's Hell, turned to us and asked which of us were married women. Before I had time to reply he noticed on my sleeve a band with a red cross. He asked me whether I was a doctor. I said "Yes". Then he made me join a group of sixty women who declared themselves to be married. That was how I got into Block 10.' She was tattooed, her number being 52325 with a triangle underneath. She realized what was happening in that block, and decided that the best thing for her to do was to get herself included in the *kommando* of an S.S.

doctor, Weber, at the so-called 'institute of hygiene', examining blood and sputum in the laboratory.

Lord Gardiner: Did you ever take part in experimental operations?

Dr Lorska: Never.

She had known Dr Samuel, who was old and seemed 'mentally not quite right'. He was over sixty.

The only non-Jewish woman in Block 10 was Dr Hautval who had arrived before Dr Lorska. Dr Brewda arrived in September with pneumonia.

Lord Gardiner: Do you remember some Greek girls?

Dr Lorska: I remember, and all the more so because I could communicate with them easily. I spoke Spanish.

She understood Judeo-Spanish. She knew that some of these girls had been irradiated, and helped Dr Brewda with them. The first thing she knew about the operations was the girls coming back from the theatre. They were restless, crying and screaming. She and Dr Brewda had looked at all of them that evening and Dr Lorska had examined one, aged about sixteen, whose condition seemed exceptionally grave. She was pale, her pulse almost imperceptible; it looked as though she had an internal haemorrhage and that 'she could easily die'. Dr Lorska stayed with the girl during the evening but was not there when she died.

Lord Gardiner: Were the girls' wounds healing?

Dr Lorska: No. They did not heal in the usually accepted way. The skin was not growing together and there were suppurations.

Block 10 was next to Block 11, which was the execution block and for that reason the windows of Block 10 had not only bars but also wooden shutters, and the place was lit by electricity.

The Judge inquired what heating, if any, there was.

Dr Lorska said that in the beginning there had been ovens in which they used wood and coal. The warmth did not radiate, 'and if you were not near the oven you had to freeze'.

She had been sent away from Auschwitz in January 1945, at first on foot and then by train, to Ravensbrück. Some time after the war she returned to Poland, married a Dr Lorski, and was attached to the Tuberculosis Institute.

Mr Duncan cross-examined. He asked: There is no doubt in

your mind that those responsible for the running of Auschwitz behaved like fiends?

Dr Lorska: No. I have no doubt.

Mr Duncan: Can you think of anything much worse to say about a person than they were one of these fiends?

Dr Lorska: It is sufficient.

Mr Duncan: Nobody will blame you, but you feel very, very bitter about all these experiences, do you not?

Dr Lorska: I think that I am objective.

Mr Duncan: Would this be fair: you know nothing whatever about Dr Dering, either in his favour or against him, except what you have been told by other people?

Dr Lorska: I know from others.

Mr Duncan: You did tell—you were asked—about being a member of the Communist Party. Did that political feeling affect your feelings about other people at all?

Dr Lorska: I do not think so.

Mr Duncan: Did you know whether Dr Dering was a Communist?

Dr Lorska: I knew that he was not.

There had been about 400 women in Block 10; the majority of them were healthy. Dr Samuel had told her the nature of the operations he was doing—cutting out sections of the Fallopian tubes. He also told her that Dr Wirths was examining the early stages of cancer of the uterus, and pieces of uterus were being removed for that purpose, from women who, so far as she knew, did not have cancer—in other words, experimental operations.

Mr Duncan: How did Dr Samuel come into the picture?

Dr Lorska: Dr Wirths ordered Dr Samuel to do it; Dr Samuel was a prisoner-doctor, and Dr Wirths was an S.S. doctor.

The Judge: What nationality was Dr Samuel?

Dr Lorska: He was of Jewish origin, from Germany.

Mr Duncan: Did you know that Dr Samuel was executed by the Germans?

Dr Lorska: Yes. I heard that he went to the gas chambers while I was there.

Mr Duncan: Did you ever know why?

Dr Lorska: Because he knew that experimental operations were being carried out. That was what was being said in the camp.

Mr Duncan: Was it part of your duty to look after these unfortunate women?

Dr Lorska: No. It was not my duty; but, as a doctor, I could not do otherwise.

The Judge: Do I understand rightly that on the first floor of Block 10 there were about 400 women who were, so to speak, the raw material for the experiments?

Dr Lorska: Yes.

The Judge: And then, from time to time, they were called out for experiments and operated on?

Dr Lorska: Yes.

The Judge: So that these unfortunate women who were the raw material knew that at any moment they might be called down?

Dr Lorska: The older ones realized that.

The second week of the hearing had ended. The Judge asked the jury to take home with them the paper-back copies of *Exodus* and to read the eight pages before and after the paragraph complained of to see how it fitted into the book. 'Perhaps', he added, 'the jury will be good enough to have finished their homework by Monday.'

'LET US BEHAVE AS HUMAN BEINGS'

Mr Duncan asked Dr Lorska how long she was in Block 10 before she managed to get the laboratory job. She said that for about six weeks she had simply been waiting as 'raw material for experiments'.

Mr Duncan: And I suppose you managed to escape that because of your medical knowledge?

Dr Lorska replied that that was so 'up to a point'. What she had done was to find out what experiments were being carried out on the women, and if they were not dangerous experiments but merely unpleasant, she used to get one of her colleagues to carry them out on her. Before she went to the laboratory she learned that Dr Samuel was doing experiments on orders from Dr Wirths.

Mr Duncan: And I suppose, Dr Lorska, you knew that it was no good trying to stop him?

Dr Lorska: Dr Samuel did not refuse to carry out those operations. He knew too much. That was why he was sent to the gas chambers.

Mr Duncan: Did you yourself know that executions were going on?

Dr Lorska: I saw them. Although the windows of the laboratory had bars and planks, I could, through a chink, see people being led there and executed. They were shot.

She had also known that before her arrival there had been murders by phenol injections, and that prisoners were often beaten to death.

The Judge said that he wanted the jury to follow the working conditions of those in Blocks 10 and 21. How often, he asked Dr Lorska, did these executions take place in Block 11?

'During the first weeks of my stay in Block 10,' she said, 'two or three times a week'—not just one shot but mass executions, several scores of people at a time, women and children; so that when in Block 10 they heard firing everyone knew what it was all about; and though Block 21 was further away, and people working there might not hear the actual shots, they too, knew what was going on. The executions had become less frequent after the spring of 1944.

Mr Duncan: During the time these horrible things were going on, did you discuss what it was all about and why these people were being killed?

Dr Lorska: I did not know why the S.S. and the Nazis were killing each individual; but there was a general discussion as to why the Nazis were killing innocent people.

Mr Duncan: And you did not know what was in their horrible minds?

Dr Lorska: I thought they certainly had no human thoughts.

She agreed that people had been killed for the most trivial reasons or for no reason at all.

Mr Duncan: Did you hear me ask one of the women, 'Did you ever deliberately disobey any order given to you by the Germans?" and her answer: 'I could not do anything against their orders because they would have killed me'?

Dr Lorska: I understand that. But I know many who did not carry out the orders.

On the Judge's direction, a passage from the evidence of Dr Mezyk was read to Dr Lorska in which he gave the reasons why in his view 'a straight refusal to a straight order was unthinkable'.

The Judge: Was it your understanding that under the camp regulations S.S. men could shoot on the spot anyone who disobeyed an order?

Dr Lorska: That was not so simple in the camp.

The Judge: Was it your understanding that the ordinary penalty for disobeying an order was some severe torture by flogging or hanging up by the wrists or feet?

Dr Lorska: I know that one could by-pass the orders of the S.S. men in such a way as to avoid punishment.

Lord Gardiner re-examined her: You have told us about the executions and you said, 'I know many who did not carry out their orders'. Will you tell us who they were?

Dr Lorska: In the first place, Dr Hautval. Then there were those who did not refuse directly but did everything possible not to carry out the orders so that they would avoid doing permanent damage to their fellow prisoners.

She had, 'of course', taken the Hippocratic oath when she became a doctor. It was 'certainly not' in accordance with a doctor's ethical code to operate on patients against their will, even if it were in the patient's interest to operate.

Lord Gardiner: If you had been ordered to take part in experimental operations would you have done so?

Dr Lorska looked towards the Judge, and asked whether she might be allowed to say something.

The Judge: I think she is entitled to say something.

She then said: 'In the first days of my stay in Block 10, one evening I spoke with Dr Hautval. This conversation took place in the operating theatre. She explained to me as a doctor what was happening in Block 10. At the end of that conversation she told me that it was impossible that we should ever get out of the camp alive. "The Germans will not allow people who know what is happening here to get into touch with the outside world", Dr Hautval said, "so the only thing that is left to us is to behave, for the rest of the short time that remains to us, as human beings." I have never forgotten that conversation, and in all the difficult moments of my life I have remembered what she said to me'.

Lord Gardiner: And did you agree with her?

Dr Lorska: Completely.

The Judge said that the ordinary person was not a saint, and he wanted the jury to know how the ordinary man would behave. He asked Dr Lorska: If Professor Clauberg—who was an S.S. General, was he not?—had said to you, 'Tomorrow morning you will take that girl's left ovary out', I gather that you would have refused?

Dr Lorska: I think I would have committed suicide.

The Judge: But if you did not commit suicide, what would you have expected to happen to you for disobeying an order from someone with the status of Professor Clauberg?

Dr Lorska: My situation would have been worse, because I am Jewish.

The Judge: What would you have expected to happen to you?

Dr Lorska: Maybe I would have got into some heavy commando.

The Judge: Nothing more than that?

Dr Lorska: I don't think so.

CHAPTER XVI

The Accuser: Dr Brewda

SENT TO CALM THE GIRLS

THE next witness whose appearance in the witness box had been anticipated from the first day, was Dr Alina Brewda, a short, middle-aged woman in a dark blue suit. Born in Warsaw in 1905 of Polish-Jewish parents, she now lived in Brondesbury Park, London.

She had met Dr Dering when she was a medical student and he was houseman at the Warsaw University Clinic. They were quite friendly. He had married her fellow student, Krystyna Ossowska, some time after 1930. Dr Brewda had also met him from time to time when they were about the business of the Jewish and Polish Students' Associations, though there were not many social contacts between the two bodies. At that time she had been a member of the Democratic Party, 'the party in the middle'.

Mr Hirst: Are you now a member of any political party?

Dr Brewda: No.

Mr Hirst: Have you ever at any time been a member of the Communist Party?

Dr Brewda: Never.

After she qualified in 1930 she specialized in gynaecology and obstetrics and went to Paris. In September 1940 the Nazis had sent her to the Warsaw Ghetto where she lived until the uprising in April 1943. Then she had been taken as an ordinary prisoner to Majdanek with about 8,000 women. She had 'appointed herself' to work as a doctor; and, when she was sent to Block 10 at Auschwitz on 24 September it had been 'the same story'. She just started to examine patients. Her tattooed number was 62761. Dr Kleinova (Dr Lorska) had been a fellow prisoner in Block 10, but Dr Hautval was not there then.

Mr Hirst: Who gave you your day-to-day orders?

Dr Brewda: Nobody told me. I was not such a young doctor. I just started to see what I could do.

She had examined all the women in the block, upstairs and downstairs, and found that about 150 were being used for experiments in sterility by Wirths, and by Clauberg, who injected caustic fluid into the womb. Some of the women were bleeding.

Mr Hirst: What religion did the women profess?

Dr Brewda: They were all Jewesses of about fourteen nationalities.

She spoke Polish, Russian, German and French and so managed to communicate with most of them. She spoke to the Greek girls in very simple French; they were the youngest, some of them 'really only children'. It had always taken her a long time to get round to see the girls who were on the first floor because they were 'terribly afraid of any grown-up person', having by that time already been examined by the S.S. doctors—Wirths, Schumann and Clauberg.

Mr Hirst: When did you first hear that Dr Dering was in Auschwitz?

Dr Brewda: Not very long after my arrival—and to my astonishment.

When she heard that Dr Dering was the senior prisoner-doctor in the camp she was sure that he would help her to get drugs for her patients, and she tried to contact him by sending a message through the men who brought their food; but 'Dr Dering did not come'. She sent a second message. Then he came. She had met him in the corridor of Block 10. He was smartly dressed and clean-shaven, and wore leather shoes in good condition.

She started the conversation in Polish by asking about getting some milk for three young children. He said it was quite impossible. Then she asked him for white bread for patients recently arrived from Poland bringing an epidemic of scarlet fever. He offered her one diet only, for herself; but she was already on a diet, having had pneumonia.

Mr Hirst: Did Dr Dering tell you what he was doing in the camp?

Dr Brewda: Yes. He told me that he was a general surgeon and was operating.

Mr Hirst: Did he mention any number of operations he had done?

Dr Brewda: Yes. Thousands—16,000 or 17,000. I asked him

what kind of operations. He said 'abdominal', in Polish—which meant that they were major operations.

He told her the operations were gastrectomies, ovariectomies, appendicectomies, removal of testicles, and gynaecological. She asked him about his wife, and he said that she was still in Warsaw, probably in prison.

'I was surprised that it was possible, in a camp, to perform such a lot of operations, and I asked him whether the patients survived, He said that they did.'

After she had seen him operate on the ten Greek girls she concluded that probably the 17,000 operations were all unnecessary and, therefore, experimental, as were the ten she watched. She had never gone to the theatre in Block 21 before those operations. She was not allowed to leave Block 10 without an escort. She had never seen the register in Auschwitz. Dr Dering did not show it to her in the theatre. She had never seen the book at any time before this case and even now had seen only photographic copies of extracts. When Dr Dering came to Block 10 some of the girls were knitting, and she asked them to knit him a white pullover. When she saw him again in Block 10 she asked him for more diet for her patients, and gave him the pullover. 'He did not refuse it, and I got the diet. He took the pullover.'

Mr Hirst: It has been suggested by Dr Dering that the only thing you ever asked him for was some extra rations for yourself. Is that correct?

Dr Brewda: It is not correct.

The Greek girls had been on the first floor of Block 10. 'About twenty-five of those girls we used to call "Schumann's girls". The others belonged to Clauberg.' She had first examined them for scabies, but found that their skin was covered with suppurating blisters and realized straight away that they were the after-effects of irradiation—'a pretty big dose' and done by people without much knowledge of irradiation.

She had met Dr Samuel, who had disappeared from the block some three weeks after she arrived. He was 'an old man in a bad mental condition, bewildered, and unfit to act as a surgeon'. Dr Wirths told her that she was to take over from Dr Samuel to use a machine from Berlin, and that she must do for him 'what Dr Samuel had done'.

Mr Hirst: Did you ever, at any time, participate in any experimental operations?

Dr Brewda: Never.

Before the operations on the Greek girls, Dr Schumann had asked her how long it would take her to organize a proper theatre in Block 10. She did not know what to say, and simply said, 'I don't know. About three months'. In October, he had asked her whether she could remove ovaries, and how long it would take her to perform such an operation. 'I said about one and a half hours; and he said I was lying.'

Mr Hirst: Were you ever asked by Dr Schumann actually to perform any specific operation?

Dr Brewda: No. He did not ask me just straight to do this operation.

On the day of the Greek girls' operations in November she had met Schumann in the corridor. He told her that she must go with him 'to calm the girls'. He was in a 'furious state'. She went with him. Until then she had never been into Block 21. The first thing she heard in the corridor as she entered was screaming. 'I entered into the annexe. I saw two men holding a screaming girl sitting on a couch, and a second one crying. I saw two men and two girls. Dr Dering was washing his hands in the annexe.' The door of the theatre was open and she could see everything. A girl was lying strapped to the table. In the annexe Schumann told her that she was to 'calm the girls'.

The Judge: Could Dr Dering have heard what Schumann was saying to you?

Dr Brewda: I presume, Yes. It was quite a small room.

She had tried to tell Dr Dering that the girls had been irradiated. He said that he knew it. She asked him what he was doing. He said 'ovariectomies'. Dr Dering went into the theatre. She did the same, because the girl on the table was screaming and crying and trying to release herself. She took up a position at the head of the table, nearest to the door. Dr Dering then started to operate.

Mr Hirst: From their appearance—the two Greek girls in the ante-room and the one on the table—did you think that they had had any kind of morphia injection before they were taken to Block 21?

Dr Brewda: Of course not.

She had not given them any premedication and had not been asked to do so. Until Dr Schumann came over no one had told her that these operations were going to take place. She tried to calm the girl on the table by saying the simplest words in French.

As to the manner of the operation, she said that the incision was abnormally small. The stitching afterwards was done roughly and 'at terrific speed'. 'I told him there would be haemorrhage or peritonitis, and what should I do? He said I should not worry. The operation took about twelve minutes. I had never seen one of this kind done so quickly. I had a very good view, and I did understand what was being done.' The normal time would be about thirty minutes.

Dr Dering then went out of the theatre to the annexe and gave the second girl a spinal injection. 'I left the theatre, and when I got into the annexe I tried to comfort the girl somehow.' There had been a couple of minutes between the injection and the operation. The girl was struggling all the time.

Mr Hirst: Did Dr Dering wash his hands between the first and second operation?

Dr Brewda: Not so far as I remember.

Mr Hirst: Were the instruments sterilized between operations as far as you remember?

Dr Brewda: I don't think so.

After the second injection Dr Brewda went back into the theatre. The girl on the table was screaming and trying to escape. 'We had a common language. I kissed her and comforted her as much as I could. I tried to tell Dr Dering I had not seen anything like this. It was as though he was operating on corpses.'

Mr Hirst: What could you see Dr Dering doing during the first and second operations as to the covering or otherwise of the stump?

Dr Brewda: For that to be done, the parts would have had, at one moment or another, to be outside the abdomen.

Mr Hirst: Is that something you can see being done?

Dr Brewda: If it had been done—but it was not.

The Judge: I have no recollection of Lord Gardiner putting to Dr Dering that the ordinary routine of the operation was to raise the organ through the incision. It may be of some importance, because, as I understood Dr Dering and Dr Grabczynski, they were both saying that this witness could not have seen what was done because they were working down in the abdomen.

Mr Hirst: The actual lifting out of the organ was not put, but the failure to cover the stump was put.

Turning to Dr Brewda, Mr Hirst asked: Quite apart from any deduction from the size of the scar, could you see, with your own eyes, whether the pedicle was covered or not?

Dr Brewda: If it would have been covered I could see, because it had to be lifted out. But it was not.

At this point Lord Gardiner made a successful application for the hearing of a witness *in camera*, and the sixth man[1] was interposed, after the court was cleared.

When the hearing in open court was resumed, Dr Brewda said that the mode of performance of the second to the eighth operation had not been materially different from the first; and she had done exactly the same thing during and between each operation.

Mr Hirst: Do you remember which two girls came last of the ten?

Yes, she remembered them particularly—'Marta' and Bella—because they were almost the youngest and had already had one operation with a horizontal scar, the 'German school' of operation; and also they had unhealed irradiation wounds in the lumbar region so that lying on the hard table was terribly painful and they had been screaming. She also remembered telling Dr Dering that 'Marta' had already had one ovary removed, and 'If you remove the second she will be like a eunuch'.

Mr Hirst: What did Dr Dering say to that?

Dr Brewda: Nothing.

From the way in which Dr Dering had performed those ten operations, she had drawn the conclusion that it was 'just a shame to the medical profession' that such things could happen, and also—because it was a very highly organized procedure with everything going very smoothly and at terrific speed, ten girls done in two and a half to three hours in the afternoon—that Dr Dering had done previous operations of this kind. There had been no change of surgeon while she had been in the theatre. Dr Dering was in charge of these operations and he performed them all.

The Judge asked Lord Gardiner whether it was being suggested

[1] His evidence is referred to at pages 229 and 252.

that Dr Dering had done more than these ten ovariectomies. There was nothing about that in the particulars.

Lord Gardiner said that that had been alleged in the original particulars. Now that they had the register, and Dr Dering had seen it, it was not being said that he had done more than these ten. What Dr Brewda was now being asked was what she thought at the time; and it was relevant that she had been struck by the speed, and that that led her to think that Dr Dering must have done a good many similar operations.

After the operations, Dr Brewda said, the girls' condition had been 'terrible'. She had had nothing to treat them with during the night. She had had to steal some morphia from Professor Clauberg's rooms—he always had a supply of six morphia injections—but she had exhausted that supply quickly.

Mr Hirst: What happened to Bella during the night?

Dr Brewda: Bella died.

She and Dr Lorska had been with the girls, and they had both examined Bella. One did not need to be a very old doctor to diagnose internal haemorrhage. She had moved Bella out into the corridor and Bella died soon after. She also remembered Buena, who had died two or three days later—from 'shock after operation'. She admitted that when she was asked to charge her memory about these events for the purposes of this case she had recollected three girls dying and twelve operations; but now that she had heard the girls giving evidence and had seen the page of the register, she was saying that two out of ten had died after operation. The third Greek girl, who died about the same time, might have died of typhus. She had not discussed this case with the girls at all.

Two or three days after the operations, the girls' wounds started to open. No one in the block had anything but paper bandages. The wounds had also started to smell, and she could not move the other girls from the room. She had tried to send messages to Dr Dering through the porters, asking him for some sulphonamide drugs.

He came eventually—once—about the fifth day. She met him in the corridor and told him that she had had two deaths, and that no wounds were healing, and asked if he could help her in some way. He said nothing, but went with her into the ward.

Mr Hirst: What did he do?

Dr Brewda: He just passed by and looked at them.

'Possibly' he examined some of the girls, but a careful inspection was hardly necessary; by that time she had them all on the lower bunks, and they were close together; and anyway the wounds were necrotic. He had never sent any supplies. So far as she knew, he never came to see the girls again. Some of them were in bed for months—'nearly until the spring'.

Mr Hirst: Do you remember seeing anything through the window of Block 10 in January 1944?

Dr Brewda: Yes. I saw Dering leaving the camp. He was still wearing his prisoner's uniform and, I think, carrying two suitcases.

In July or August 1944, she had received punishment of solitary confinement in Block 11. The Nazis did not tell her why. She had stayed in Auschwitz until 18 January 1945.

The Judge asked to what issue these questions were directed.

Mr Hirst said that the jury should know briefly what had happened to Dr Brewda up to the present.

She said that she was liberated on 8 May 1945, and returned to Poland in July.

Mr Hirst: It has been suggested by Dr Dering that you had a post in the N.K.V.D. with either the Russian or the Polish secret police in Warsaw in 1945. Is that correct?

Dr Brewda: It is not correct.

Mr Hirst: Did you have any connection at all with any secret police at any time?

Dr Brewda: Never. I was not a Communist and no one suggested to me to take such a job.

Mr Hirst: It has been suggested that during that period you conducted a sort of personal vendetta to destroy Dr Dering. Did you?

Dr Brewda: Never.

In February 1947 she had left Poland for England where she had lived ever since. She had never given evidence about these matters in a proper court before, though when Professor Clauberg was caught she had gone to the magistrates' court in Kiel.

'I WAS THERE'

Cross-examined by Mr Duncan, Dr Brewda denied that she had ever been 'prepared to say anything against Dr Dering, however untrue'. In all the twenty or so years since those events she had always repeated what she was now saying.

The Judge: Let me put it in a more explicit way. Has there ever been a time since these appalling events when you have deliberately told lies about Dr Dering?

Dr Brewda: Never.

Mr Duncan: So that it may be in your mind between now and tomorrow, you made one or more statements at the time when Dr Dering was in prison at Brixton and extradition was being considered?

Dr Brewda: In 1947, Yes.

Mr Duncan: Are you now saying that all that you said . . .

Lord Gardiner intervened to say that if Mr Duncan was going to put a written statement to the witness, she was entitled to see it.

The Judge told the jury that this appeared to be a technical move to get Mr Duncan to play his ace now when he wanted to play it tomorrow.

Mr Duncan said he would not pursue it now. He asked her whether she was 'pretty bitter about all that happened' to her from 1940 to 1945 and she replied that she loved life and human beings.

Mr Duncan: You are bitter about the Nazis?

Dr Brewda: They don't exist any more. I belong to associations of Nazi camp survivors, and our aim is to forgive but not to forget.

On the twelfth day Dr Brewda was still under cross-examination. She said that she had gone to Block 10 as a doctor and not—like Dr Lorska—as 'raw material' for experiments. She had about 400 women as patients.

Mr Duncan: Were they all raw materials?

Dr Brewda: Not all for operations. All for experiments. The Block belonged to Clauberg.

Dr Lorska had tried to tell Dr Brewda what was going on while she was still ill with pneumonia; and when she recovered she discovered it with her own hands and eyes. The caustic fluid injections were 'ghastly things'. The Germans were trying to discover the earliest possible stages of cancer of the womb.

The Judge: Instead of treating the women, they just cut the part out, is that right?

Dr Brewda: Yes.

Mr Duncan: That was a ghastly thing to do, was it not?

Dr Brewda: Of course.

Mr Duncan: You were powerless to prevent them?

Dr Brewda: I could not help by saying to Dr Wirths, 'Don't do it'. When he asked me, I told him that it was the first time in my life I saw the instrument.

She did not think that anybody had any complaints about Dr Dering until the spring or autumn of 1943 and she had not been surprised to hear Herr Langbein express his view of Dr Dering's reputation. She confirmed it. The way in which he had been dressed when she first met him did not cause her to form an unfavourable impression—not unfavourable. She was surprised. She was not accustomed to seeing prisoners with their uniforms fitting and their trousers pressed. It was obvious that he was privileged. She did not think now that the white pullover episode reflected discredit on Dr Dering. 'It was the custom in the camp to try to bribe Nazis.'

Mr Duncan: It was a sort of bribe from you in the hope of getting a little extra milk?

Dr Brewda: It was that if I give him the pullover he would give it.

The Judge: Many people who lived through the war knew that margarine had its uses. Doubtless that applied to Auschwitz too.

She had had doubts at the time about Dr Dering's statement that he had done 16,000 or 17,000 operations and that patients had survived.

Mr Duncan: Did you have some doubt in your mind about even that later on?

Dr Brewda: Yes. I have some doubts.

After further questions by Mr Duncan, Dr Brewda was asked by the Judge: 'Are you saying that you thought he was "shooting a bit of a line" about the number?'

Dr Brewda: Yes.

The Judge: What Mr Duncan wants to know is whether, when Dr Dering told you about the character of the operations, and named them, you had any doubts about that at the time?

Dr Brewda: No. But after November, when I saw how he behaved and in what manner he performed the operations, I came to the conclusion—because *they* were experimental anyway—that he was taking part in experiments on human beings.

Mr Duncan: And jumped to the conclusion that he had performed 17,000 experimental operations?

Dr Brewda: I never said 17,000.

Mr Duncan: Do you hold this view today—on the assumption that 16,000 operations were performed by Dr Dering—that the majority of them were experimental?

Dr Brewda: I saw photographs of the register, and now I know that he was boasting. It was not major operations.

The Judge: Will you answer the question? It is important.

Mr Duncan repeated it: Do you think today that the majority of the 16,000 or 17,000 operations were in fact experimental?

Dr Brewda: I do not. I saw the photos of this book in the summer of 1963, and now I know that he was boasting to me—he was lying. He told me that he performed major operations.

The Judge: Let us get it quite clear. Do you think today that the majority of the operations he performed were experimental? Now the answer to that is either, Yes or No. Which is it?

Dr Brewda: No.

After further questions, Mr Duncan asked: 'What would you have done if Dr Clauberg had said to you: "Tomorrow you will take out that girl's ovary"?'

Dr Brewda: I would never do it. I would try to invent some lies, as I did with Wirths and Schumann, and hope for the best. I was already used to their methods. I was not very much afraid at this time. I was very lonely and I had lost my family. If he had asked me I would have refused and seen what he would do. In my experience from all those years under the Nazis, they were as big cowards as it is possible to imagine. I knew many many doctors, and I never heard but one who did such things. Everyone either refused or tried to escape or asked to be transported to another camp or made some excuses. It was possible, if someone was old and experienced enough.

Mr Duncan: Had you any doubt at all that if one of the S.S. personnel had ordered an ovary to be taken out of a woman and the surgeon had refused, it would have been taken out by someone else?

Dr Brewda: I doubt very much if it would have been done, if not by a surgeon prisoner. All I have heard until now is that Samuel performed these operations and nobody else in the camp until I saw Schumann. . . .

Mr Duncan: But if you had refused to carry it out, you say it would not have been carried out by anyone?

Dr Brewda: I am *nearly* sure. In the autumn of 1943 conditions were quite different from 1942 and 1941.

The Judge asked whether in 1943 they were not still using the gas chambers and still having executions in Block 11 two or three times a week. She said that that was so; but there had been a big change in the camp about that time.

Mr Duncan: I suppose you would agree that, from the patient's point of view, if this kind of operation was going to be done at all, it would be better to have it done by a skilled person than by an unskilled orderly?

Dr Brewda: Of course it would be better. But I never saw an orderly performing an ovariectomy or heard any suggestion of its being performed by an orderly.

The Judge told Dr Brewda that the jury might have to consider in this case this very difficult moral problem whether a doctor, in a place like Auschwitz, who really did believe that death or serious injury might follow the refusal to perform an operation, was justified in performing it. Did she regard it as a difficult moral problem for a doctor, or did she take the view that the answer was perfectly clear?

Dr Brewda: It is difficult, but in my mind and in the minds of many other doctors it was quite clear.

Mr Duncan: About the operations in November, you say that until Dr Schumann came over to Block 10 and told you that you were wanted to calm the girls you did not know they were being operated on?

Dr Brewda: That is true. We did not know anything about it.

Mr Duncan: They were prepared, in the sense that they were washed and shaved?

Dr Brewda said the girls had been shaved; and she guessed from their embarrassment in the witness box—for they were orthodox Jewesses—that it must have been done by a man; but she did not know who had done it.

Mr Duncan: You say Schumann was 'furious'?

Dr Brewda: He was not in a good mood.

Mr Duncan: Not in a mood in which one could reason with him very easily?

Dr Brewda: Probably if you knew him well you could.

When Schumann had told her to come over and calm the girls, he had not explained which girls. She had felt unhappy; but it was an order and she did not ask questions in such circumstances. It was better to obey and go and see with one's own eyes. She had seen all ten operations. She had heard, and agreed with Dr Dering when he said that he had given the spinal injection.

Mr Duncan: So when so many of these girls said that it was the orderly and not the surgeon, they were wrong?

Dr Brewda (with infinite tolerance): How could *they* know?

Mr Duncan: Dr Dering also said that they all took place in the theatre and not in the annexe?

Dr Brewda: That is quite untrue.

She now knew that the other surgeon in the theatre at the time was Dr Grabczynski, and that he had said he had done some of these operations; but she was quite sure that Dr Dering had done them all.

Mr Duncan: So when Dr Grabczynski comes here and says that he performed some of them, he is not telling the truth?

Dr Brewda: Yes.

The Judge asked whether that was not putting it a bit high. Would it not be better to say, 'He is completely mistaken'?

Dr Brewda: He is completely mistaken.

The Judge reminded Dr Brewda that Dr Grabczynski had come from Cracow and had to go back to Cracow after he had given his evidence, and that he had said in the witness box that he had performed some of these operations which, in her view, no doctor ought to perform. 'Now that I have reminded you of Dr Grabczynski's position', he asked, 'do you still say that he did not perform any of these operations?'

Dr Brewda: I am sure.

The Judge: You still say that the doctor who performed all ten operations was Dr Dering, Yes or No?

Dr Brewda: Yes.

Mr Duncan: Are you suggesting that there was anything wrong with the way in which these anaesthetics were administered?

Dr Brewda: It was the manner in which it was done, not caring very much what these poor girls were feeling. It was done with such speed and skill, so I can only speak about the manner—not from the doctor's but from the human point of view.

Mr Duncan: You used the words 'speed and skill'. Are you saying that the actual administration was done wrongly?

Dr Brewda: Probably one of them was done wrongly, because 'Marta' said she felt everything.

Mr Duncan: But nothing you saw?

Dr Brewda: It was the *manner* that was wrong. He did it with skill and speed.

Mr Duncan: But it ought to be done with speed and skill and that is the proper way?

Dr Brewda: He did it with speed and skill.

Mr Duncan: Do you criticize the way the surgeon in fact carried out the ovariectomies in these cases?

Dr Brewda: I do.

Mr Duncan: One of your criticisms is that the incision was too small?

Dr Brewda: That is right.

She explained that these operations were very deep, 'and so to do them properly you must see properly and finish the operation properly and stitch the vessels properly and put the flap on the stem. You must have some kind of field. If you do it from such a small field it cannot be done properly'.

Mr Duncan: Can you see any reason why a careless surgeon should make too small an incision?

Dr Brewda: I have explained it to you now. I cannot suggest any reason. That is what I say he did.

The Judge: What possible surgical reason could there be for an experienced gynaecological surgeon to make an incision of a size which would make the operation more difficult to perform?

Dr Brewda: I don't know the reason why. I just cannot answer, because the whole operation was wholly unnecessary. I watched these operations and saw how they were done and I came to the conclusion that they were faulty.

She had never before now been asked about the size of the incision. If she were asked something particular she would try to remember it.

Mr Duncan: I suggest that this evidence is completely wrong;

that an incision of a proper length was made; and that what you tell us you saw is quite untrue, and that everything was done in the abdominal cavity. What do you say to that?

Dr Brewda: I did not see what he was doing, but it is normal that you must take the womb a little bit outside just to put on forceps.

The Judge asked whether, when she said that Dr Dering did not cover the pedicle, it was because she had seen with her own eyes that he did not do it, or whether she had concluded from her knowledge of surgery that he could not have done it.

She had concluded from her own knowledge of surgery that he could not have done it.

The Judge: What about the stitches? Did you see how he put in the stitches, or did you conclude how he put them in?

Dr Brewda: I concluded from the manner.

Mr Duncan: Then it comes to this—there were two things: the operation took ten to twelve minutes as Dr Dering said; and you think the operation ought never to have been performed at all; and, from the combination of those two, you are convinced that the operation was improperly performed?

Dr Brewda: That is right.

The Judge: Is there anything else you rely on to say that the operation was not properly performed—the actual surgery?

Dr Brewda said that the stitching outside and putting in clips was done with such speed. She had heard what Dr Dering had said about putting on gauze and this and that, but she just could not remember that he had done that. All she knew was that she had these girls back with paper bandages on.

The Judge: So it comes to this, that the whole of your criticism —and it may be right—of the manner of performing the surgical part of the operation is based on your conclusion that it could not have been done properly, having regard to the speed with which it was done?

Dr Brewda: Yes.

After further questions, Mr Duncan said: 'You appreciate, don't you, that Dr Dering denies that he had any conversations with you, either in the theatre or in the annexe?' Dr Brewda nodded.

Mr Duncan: You were not sitting there all the time?

Dr Brewda: I was.

She repeated that she did not have an adequate supply of drugs in Block 10 to cope with the post-operative situation.

Mr Duncan: You don't suggest that that was Dr Dering's fault?

Dr Brewda: Dr Dering said it was my fault. I say it was not my fault. We did not have them.

Mr Duncan: You would agree that when patients are in the hands of competent doctors, a visit on the fifth day is the right period for the surgeon?

Dr Brewda: The custom in Poland is to visit patients every day.

Mr Duncan: Was it nobody's business to inform the surgeon that a patient had died?

Dr Brewda: If it was somebody's duty, it was, of course, mine.

Mr Duncan: When did you first tell Dr Dering that Bella, for example, had died?

Dr Brewda: I informed him when he came on the fifth day.

She had not told him before because she was not allowed to leave the block. She had sent messages asking him to come. He could walk through the camp without a warder. She could not send a written message, for they were not allowed paper or pencil.

The eight girls had remained in bed for varying times, the longest being four to five months. She did not think that any of them could have gone back to work at Birkenau very quickly.

The Judge said that he wanted to put some questions. The Court had been told that those who ran the camps regarded Jews as expendable. On the evidence that had been given, the Nazi attitude was, 'We aren't going to waste time curing those who are not going to get better, so—gas chamber'. If these girls were in bed all that time after the operations, were the Nazis making an exception of them?

Dr Brewda: It was an exceptional block. It only proves how well we hid the girls and what was happening from the Germans. We tried as much as possible not to say to anybody that they were bad.

The Judge: You managed to hide their condition from the Nazis?

Dr Brewda: Yes.

The Judge: Why did it take so long for these girls' wounds to heal up?

Dr Brewda: Because we did not have enough food and we did not have anything to help them.

The Judge: Then it was not the manner of the surgery that caused the long post-operative troubles, but the irradiation and the lack of proper nourishment?

Dr Brewda: I think everything together. If no one had operated on them, they would be like other irradiated girls in my block who just did not need such a long time to recover.

The Judge: I do regard this as important. The jury have to decide this important problem of what is Dr Dering's responsibility in doing this operation. I am asking you a purely medical thing. These girls took a long time to get better. You have given us three reasons: (1) that they were operated; (2) that they were irradiated; and (3) under-nourishment. If they had not been irradiated and not been under-nourished, and—bearing in mind your disapproval of Dr Dering's surgical work—how long would they have taken to recover?

Dr Brewda: A couple of weeks, three to four weeks.

The Judge: So the length of time was primarily due to irradiation never giving them a chance because the tissues had been damaged, and the poor nourishment, and bad conditions?

Dr Brewda: And the fact that they were operated on.

Lord Gardiner pointed out that the Judge was summarizing the witness's evidence.

The Judge: What went wrong with Dr Dering's surgery that made the time so long?

Dr Brewda: Because he did not take proper care.

The Judge: Then you say that all these troubles were due to the fact that Dr Dering did not sterilize. . . .

Again Lord Gardiner intervened to say that the witness had already stated that it was a combination of a number of different things.

Mr Duncan resumed his cross-examination: Are you suggesting that in 1943 Dr Dering was not a highly competent surgeon?

Dr Brewda: I am not suggesting that.

Mr Duncan changed the subject of inquiry: Had Dr Brewda looked overnight at what she had said in her statement at the time of the extradition proceedings in 1947? She said that she had not done so. Mr Duncan handled a document which, he said, was photographed.

Lord Gardiner demurred.

The Judge asked to see it. After studying it, he said that it was headed 'United Nations War Crimes Commission. Polish Delegation'. Strictly Dr Brewda ought to be shown the original; but Mr Duncan could ask questions, so long as he kept 'within the rules'.

Mr Duncan asked Dr Brewda whether she remembered making a statement in 1947. She said that she had made statements in Polish at not less than ten or twelve sessions 'for Dr Muszkat' in March, 1947. She had told the whole story as she remembered it.

Mr Duncan asked Dr Brewda to look at the document now in front of her. Again Lord Gardiner objected; Dr Brewda had said that she had made statements at ten or twelve sessions. He took it that they were oral statements in Polish. She was now being asked about what she had in front of her—a short document in English.

Mr Duncan said that he wanted the lady to read it to herself.

The Judge, (to Dr Brewda): After these ten or twelve sessions with Dr Muszkat, was something written out for you to read through and sign as being correct?

Dr Brewda: So far as I remember, Yes.

After Dr Brewda had studied the document she said that her statement had been 'pages and pages' in Polish. This was a summary of what she, like every other inmate of the camp, had said in connection with the investigation of war criminals, and she did not think all the details were accurate.

She had no recollection of saying that 'Dering was known for his harshness and for refusing every help, even to his own brother'. She did remember saying that 'of the 17,000 operations, some 16,500 were experiments on completely healthy people'. The reason for that, as she now saw it, was that Dr Dering had boasted that 'he did such lots of operations'. She did remember saying that 'all boys operated on by Dering had died'. She had thought that in 1947, because she 'had been told'. She had since changed her opinion on that. She did not remember having used a phrase about Dr Dering being 'detached to Professor Clauberg's disposal to work as a free man' at Clauberg's private maternity home; but she had thought that Dr Dering had been put on 'the list of *Reichsdeutsche* for his services in sterilizing prisoners'. That was what everyone in the camp thought when he was released. Many people during the war had got on to the list, because it made things easier.

She did not remember saying that Dr Dering 'became an S.S. man'.

The Judge: In 1947, did you suspect Dr Dering of having become an S.S. man.

Dr Brewda: No.

Mr Duncan: Do you still say that you never made statements about Dr Dering which were untrue?

Dr Brewda: I do not follow. I made statements, as did every other prisoner, before the Commission. I did not make statements which were untrue.

The cross-examination was at an end and Mr Duncan sat down.

The Judge then told the jury that they had heard questions being put to Dr Brewda on a document which they would not see because it was not in evidence. Where she had accepted that the statements in the document were accurate, those admissions were properly in evidence. Where she said that the document was not accurate the jury should put it out of their minds.

Mr Hirst, re-examining, asked Dr Brewda: You were asked a very large number of questions by Mr Duncan about what you saw or did not see in the theatre. Were you in the theatre?

Dr Brewda: I was there.

CHAPTER XVII

English Experts

OVARIECTOMY

THE next witness was Professor William Charles Wallace Nixon, M.D., F.R.C.S., F.R.C.O.G., Professor of Obstetrics and Gynaecology at the University of London, examiner for the Universities of London, Cambridge and Wales, and director of the obstetrics unit at University College Hospital.

Professor Nixon had been sitting on the front bench of the court usually occupied by solicitors to the parties when the women victims had been in the witness box and during the evidence of Dr Brewda, assiduously taking notes.

Lord Gardiner's first question was directly to the point: If an ovary is irradiated, is there any medical benefit to be obtained by its surgical removal?

Professor Nixon: None at all.

Lord Gardiner: Can its continued existence in the body cause any harm to the patient?

Professor Nixon: None at all. It ceases to function physiologically as an ovary.

Years ago it was the treatment employed to stop excessive bleeding in women around the change of life; and neither in 1943 nor now was it a possible medical view that radiation of a testicle might result in some major danger such as carcinoma or death. There was only one school of thought on that.

Lord Gardiner: If one wanted a testicle removed for research purposes, would it be any use if it were removed by an unqualified person?

A tissue required for research purposes, Professor Nixon said, would have to be removed by a competent person.

Radiation burns on the body would be obvious to a surgeon and would be a contra-indication to operation, for the effect of X-ray was to reduce blood supply to the area radiated and so increase the risk of infection and delay in healing.

Lord Gardiner: In carrying out an ovariectomy in England, is it usual or unusual, if done with a spinal anaesthetic, to strap the patient down?

Professor Nixon: It is most unusual. Such a person should be premedicated and would be quiet and tranquil, and the lower part of the body would be paralysed.

Lord Gardiner asked what a surgeon should do in performing an ovariectomy. Professor Nixon produced a model (which, he said, was about half actual size) and the model was made an exhibit.

To do an ovariectomy one had to put on clamps, cut the pedicle, remove the ovary, and tie the stump to prevent bleeding from the main arteries. Then one had to peritonealize it: that meant using a portion of the peritoneum as a flap to cover the stump. That was very important.

Lord Gardiner referred him to a passage in the cross-examination of Dr Dering in which he had said that 'as a matter of fact there is no peritoneal flap to use', and the pedicle could be covered with one broad stitch'.

Professor Nixon: I have been practising gynaecology for forty years and I have never yet not found peritoneum to use. It is always there and it is always possible to cover the pedicle with it.

An ovariectomy with a spinal anaesthetic should take, from first to last, twenty minutes to half an hour; from the cut to the closure, fifteen minutes at least. There was no virtue in speed except in the presence of haemorrhage. Where there was no such factor it was bad surgery today and had been bad surgery in the 'forties or even the 'thirties to operate with such celerity though one might get away with it.

There was always a risk in any operation, no matter how minor. If a surgeon did not wash his hands or have sterile equipment for each operation, he would—at least since the days of Lister and other pioneers—be committing an act amounting almost to criminal negligence. It was inconceivable that any surgeon would neglect such basic principles of surgical technique. It was also notorious that after a spinal anaesthetic there was a greater risk of post-operative haemorrhage, for when the patient came round the blood pressure went up again, so one had to be doubly careful about tying off the blood vessels.

He agreed with Dr Dering that the wound after an ovariectomy should have healed within seven to eight days, and that the patient should be out of bed in seven to ten days. If a wound took weeks to heal and there was a stench, it would indicate gross sepsis, and might be the result of insufficient care over asepsis during operation.

Lord Gardiner: Could the wounds after such an operation break down within five days?

Professor Nixon: That is usually the time in which they do break down. If the patient had constant backache after an ovariectomy with a spinal anaesthetic that could be directly attributable to the way in which the anaesthetic had been given.

'I HAVE EXAMINED EIGHT OF THEM'

Lord Gardiner: Have you examined the women patients?

Professor Nixon: I have examined eight of them.

There was a stir in court.

He gave his detailed findings: The first girl to be operated on had a scar which showed reasonably good healing with no indication of infection. The second had a marked deficiency—a gap of only skin thickness between the outer and innermost layer covering the abdominal cavity, indicating rupture in the middle because it had not healed. The actual length of the incision in that case was 'three-fingertips'. No. 8 had a very short incision—about an inch. In the next, the length was 'three-fingertips', and she had a deficiency in the middle of the scar, showing bad healing. She also had evidence of radiation, because the whole of her skin was deeply pigmented.

The Judge: Twenty-one years after?

Professor Nixon: Yes.

In the case of No. 4, the scar was only one inch, and the wound literally only paper-thin. She had been the worst in that group. 'Paper-thin' meant that all the layers of tissue below the skin had gone and 'one could almost put one's fingers on to the spine'.

Lord Gardiner observed that that had been the woman who was unable to complete her evidence.

The next case had a slightly longer scar—one and a half inches—with very poor healing. In the seventh case the scar was the longest of all, equivalent to four fingertips; but again with poor healing.

Lord Gardiner: And the last—'Marta'?

Professor Nixon: 'Marta' had two scars and had obviously had two operations. I don't know which was done first, but there was a transverse scar much longer than in any of the other cases, in all of which the one scar was vertical. 'Marta's' vertical scar was about two-fingertips length and there was a deficiency of tissue indicating infection. The transverse scar had healed better.

Lord Gardiner: Is the length of the incision any indication whether or not the pedicle was covered by the peritoneal flap?

Professor Nixon: I should say it was directly related to the amount of surgery which could be done deep down. It is anatomically impossible to do the necessary tying off and peritonealizing in such an incision. The surgery would have been 'blind'—just clamping the pedicle and removing the ovary, without any surgical finesse. In the case of two-fingertip and three-fingertip incisions it would have been impossible to operate competently.

Lord Gardiner: How do these scars compare with those you would expect to find, not in Auschwitz, but in England, after radiation?

Professor Nixon: Well, I have practised surgery in China, Africa, and the Middle East; and I have never in all my surgical life seen such scars as I saw last week when I examined the patients—such scarring, such deficiency, such pigmentation!

Lord Gardiner: How far was it possible to tell from the scars that the wounds had been properly stitched?

Professor Nixon: First of all, there was the deficiency of the abdominal wall I have mentioned. Then I could see where the stitches had come apart and the actual skin surface had not healed, so that whatever was used—I believe it was metal clips—had come apart, and it had opened up within a few days of the operation.

Lord Gardiner asked the Judge whether he might put to this witness a question on surgical ethics, in view of his experience and standing.

'THE DOUBLE EFFECT'

The Judge said that there were two moral problems here. First, the question of what a doctor should do if he was in fear of his own life or of very serious injury. Secondly, what a doctor should do in a situation where he knew that if he did not do a particular operation it would be done by someone without skill.

Lord Gardiner (to Professor Nixon): Whatever the risk to himself might be, would a surgeon, as a matter of medical ethics, be justified in carrying out an operation which he knew was not required for any legitimate medical purpose, against the will of the patient?

Professor Nixon: It would be completely contrary to my practice or that of my colleagues anywhere in Europe. For the last 2,400 years we have subscribed to the oath of Hippocrates who, by his example, showed the world what responsibility medical men carry. Most of us subscribe to the Hippocratic oath that "I will use treatment to help my patient according to my ability and judgment, but never with a view to injury or a wrong-doing' and 'I will abstain from abusing the bodies of men and women, either free or slave'.

A person who submitted himself to an experiment must be in such legal, medical, and physical state as to be able to exercise the power of choice. No prisoner was ever in that state; and therefore as a medical man, he would refrain from doing any experiment, particularly on a prisoner.

The Judge asked Professor Nixon whether he was familiar with the moral theologian's theory of 'the double effect'. What should a person do if asked to do an act which had both an evil and a good effect? In terms of this case, Dr Grabczynski had told the court that he had decided to do these operations himself because, if he did not do them, some untrained orderly would. His view seemed to be that the evil effect was going to result anyway, but that if he did the job he would minimize the evil effect. Could Professor Nixon help the jury on what he understood to be the medical ethics of such a situation?

Professor Nixon: I have never found myself in such a situation, and I hope I never shall. If I had to perform such a mutilating operation unnecessarily, the guilt would remain with me for the rest of my life and I just wonder whether I would be able to live up to such a situation.

The Judge: One aspect of this matter gives me great comfort, and that is that the jury have to take the law from me but they do not have to take my view on the moral problems!

Cross-examined by Mr Duncan, Professor Nixon said that he appreciated the circumstances in which operations in Auschwitz were performed, and also that Dr Dering was a prisoner.

Mr Duncan: Is it absolutely right to suggest that irradiation cannot be dangerous to the organs on which it is performed?

Professor Nixon: I suppose you are referring to ovaries and testicles?

Mr Duncan: No. Organs generally. Is there not always a risk that irradiation may produce malignant results?

Professor Nixon said that there was a distinction between radiation by X-ray and by radium inserted locally. He had never known of cancer developing after external radiation of the ovaries. The main damage to the patients he had seen in this case was superficial, to the skin and the tissues underneath.

Mr Duncan: Though you might take one view, it would not be surprising would it, that another doctor should take the view that it would be undesirable to leave radiated organs in the body? It would not be an outrageous view, would it?

Professor Nixon: It takes many kinds of people to make a world. But I still say that the damage here was essentially to the tissues, and not to the ovaries or testicles.

The Judge, after asking about the development of knowledge on radiation over the past sixty years, asked: 'If in 1943 a little group of prisoner-doctors had been sitting on their bunks at Auschwitz and one of them had said: "You know, there may be a grave risk of cancer through one of these gross doses of X-ray", would you have said: "Don't talk such nonsense"?'

Professor Nixon: It would depend on my experience of radiology. Are you visualizing them as doctors?

The Judge: Yes, just ordinary doctors, in 1943.

Professor Nixon: I think even in 1943 I would have considered such a suggestion was nonsense.

Mr Duncan: If a woman has had her ovaries exposed to radiation some months before, and she is going to—not ought to but is going to—have her ovary removed, is it not in her interest to have it done by a competent surgeon?

Professor Nixon: I agree.

Asked about the scars he had examined, Professor Nixon said that he had been brought up on the dictum: 'The bigger the scar, the bigger the surgeon, the smaller the wound, the smaller the surgeon'. To do an ovariectomy properly required a four-fingertip incision at least. All obstetric surgeons would, he thought, share that view, unless they were so conceited as to boast of their celerity. Adequate surgery could not be done through a two, or two-and-a half fingertip incision. He agreed that there were national variations in speed of operation; and, perhaps, surgeons in Britain were more respectful about the adequacy of their field of operation.

The Judge: If a German surgeon, seemingly of experience, did an ovariectomy in ten or twelve minutes, and those were the only facts you knew, what conclusion would you come to about the way he had done it?

Professor Nixon: I would conclude that he could not really do the proper repair of the trauma he had inflicted by his surgery in ten minutes—in other words, he could not have done the operation properly.

He told Mr Duncan that it would be impossible through a one-inch incision to do other than operate 'blind'.

Mr Duncan: Does that depend in any way on the nationality of the surgeon?

Professor Nixon: I would not have thought it had any association with his nationality. It is just crude, bad surgery!

THE MOMENT OF LAUGHTER

Sir Brian Wellingham Windeyer, F.R.C.S., said that he was a Fellow of the Faculty of Radiology, had been Professor of Radiology in the University of London since 1942, and was Dean of the Middlesex Hospital Medical School.

He did not think it possible that in 1943 anyone could reasonably have thought that testes or ovaries could become malignant after radiation.

Cross-examined by Mr Duncan, he said that there was a good deal of misapprehension about radiation hazards. Any discussion among the doctors at Auschwitz in 1943 about the possibility of radiated organs becoming malignant would have been unjustified. The effect of gross over-dosage would be damage to the skin which would not have healed. If the doses had been so serious as to damage the ovaries there could have been no question of operation. Even the doses at Auschwitz would be known 'within limits'.

After further questions Mr Duncan held up a Blue Book to Sir Brian: Do you know this book?

Sir Brian: If you will look at the first page . . .

There was a burst of laughter in court—almost the only spontaneous outburst during the whole hearing, as Mr Duncan went on: 'You wrote it, didn't you?'

The Judge directed that as Sir Brian had admitted writing the Blue Book [*The Hazards to Man of Nuclear Radiation.* H.M. Stationery Office] it was evidence and must be marked as an exhibit.

Mr Duncan put further questions to Sir Brian based on paragraphs in the publication about radiation and cancer; but he adhered to the opinion that there was no evidence to suggest that this type of radiation could or did produce cancer, though it was possible that to a Polish medical prisoner of war in 1943 the effect of unskilled irradiation on the organs might not have been very well known.

CHAPTER XVIII

La Protestante: Dr Hautval

'AMIE DES JUIFS'

THE case for the defence had reached its last witness, Dr Adelaide Hautval, a woman with grey hair and a face devoid of artificial aids, with fine bone structure, and a calm expression. She said she lived near Paris, and had been born in 1906 in Alsace-Lorraine, her father being a French Protestant pastor. She had never belonged to any political party. She had studied medicine at Strasbourg and qualified in 1934. Afterwards she worked in psychiatric clinics in Strasbourg and Switzerland.

When the Germans occupied France, she found herself in the unoccupied zone with her home in the occupied zone. She had heard that her mother was ill and applied for a pass, which was refused; when she heard that her mother had died she tried to cross from one zone to the other, and was arrested by the Germans, in 1942. They had taken her to the prison at Bourges where there were a number of Jewish prisoners. She had protested to the Gestapo about the way the Jews in France were being treated as inferior beings, not being allowed to travel in first-class carriages or on the underground. The Germans had said: 'Because you defend them you can share their lot'.

She had been kept in prison and made to stitch a yellow star on her clothes and wear a band with the words 'Friend of Jews' [*amie des juifs*]. Then in January 1943, she had been sent in a convoy of 230 non-Jewish Frenchwomen to Birkenau, arriving there on the 27th. She was sent as a doctor to a block with about 150 German anti-social or political prisoners, none of them Jewish. She fell ill, and had a rash all over her arms, and a bad foot. After she had been at Birkenau a few weeks Dr Eduard Wirths, the S.S. officer, came to see her and asked whether she wanted to practise gynaecology. She asked him the nature of the work but 'he did not want to answer'. She was suspicious, for she had already heard about the sterilization experiments at Auschwitz: 'In any case, thinking that we might leave the camp one day I wanted to know what kind of experiments'.

Lord Gardiner: What did you tell Dr Wirths?

Dr Hautval: I accepted.

She had been tattooed with a number, 31802. She still had it. When she arrived at Block 10 there were about 100 French and Greek women there—all Jewish; later, convoys brought in more French, Belgian and Dutch Jewesses. One convoy brought typhus, and she hid the women with typhus on the top floor and looked after them as best she could.

Dr Wirths and his brother had told her about experimenting with a colposcope, examining the neck of the uterus to detect pre-cancerous states. She had been astonished at the number of cases she discovered; but when she did the examinations again the results were not the same.

'Since I already had doubts on the subject of these experiments, one evening I saw Dr Dering at the entrance to Block 10. I had heard that he was a gynaecologist. I asked him what did he think about it, and he answered me, to confirm what I thought could be a dangerous thing. I saw Dr Wirths again. I told him that I had repeated my examinations and that the results were not the same. I said that my bones had become open again and that I could not work.'

Lord Gardiner: Were you in any way punished for that?

Dr Hautval: No.

'WERE YOU SHOT?'

Dr Hautval said she had also had a conversation with Dr Eduard Wirths, who said that she was to help Clauberg with his work. 'Dr Wirths asked me my opinion on sterilization and I answered that I was absolutely opposed to it.'

Lord Gardiner: What did he say?

Dr Hautval: He was surprised that a doctor practising psychiatry could find bad a method which was a selection to preserve the race. I answered that it was arguable, and also that it necessarily brought abuse. He talked to me about the Jewish question and I answered that we had no right to dispose of the life and destiny of others.

Lord Gardiner asked, in his calmest voice: Did you ever take part in any of Clauberg's experiments?

Dr Hautval: No.

Without any change of voice, Lord Gardiner immediately asked: As a result, were you shot?

There was a pause, an intensification of the quietness in court. The significance of the question took a few moments to sink in. Then there was a burst of comprehending laughter from the crowded courtroom as Dr Hautval, with a Gallic shrug and spread of the hands, and a smile, answered quite simply: *Non.*

Lord Gardiner: Were you punished in any way?

Dr Hautval: No. Not in any way.

After she had refused to do experiments for Dr Wirths, Dr Samuel had asked her 'brusquely' to give an anaesthetic for an operation for ovariectomy on a Greek girl aged about seventeen. She did not react immediately, and she gave a general anaesthetic, with evipan. Dr Samuel took about half an hour over the operation. After giving that one anaesthetic she told Dr Samuel that she would take no further part.

Lord Gardiner: What happened after you refused?

Dr Hautval: He denounced me to Dr Wirths. Dr Wirths called me to him to ask whether it was true that I refused. I said it was true. He asked why, and I said it was contrary to my conception as a doctor.

Lord Gardiner: What did he say to that?

Dr Hautval: He asked me: 'Cannot you see that these people are different from you?' and I answered him that there were several other people different from me, starting with him! [This answer was later described by the Judge as a 'devastating reply' which, he expected, 'would live in the jury's memory for many years'.]

Lord Gardiner: I shall not ask you again whether you were shot. Did Dr Wirths say anything further?

Dr Hautval: He said nothing. I remained in the block until the beginning of August, looking after patients. Then I was taken back to Birkenau where I was advised to keep myself in hiding for a few weeks.

Lord Gardiner: Were you ever in fact punished at all?

Dr Hautval: Never.

Lord Gardiner glanced briefly at the jury, and, after a few questions about Dr Hautval's later history, sat down.

Mr Duncan cross-examined Dr Hautval. She agreed that her illness at Birkenau was an infection attributable to the living conditions in the camp and was often fatal. When Dr Wirths came to see her about doing gynaecology, she had become suspicious because 'in that moment when I asked him he never gave me any explanation' and she had already heard about Clauberg's experiments in sterilization.

Mr Duncan: He, of course, was an S.S. officer?

Dr Hautval: Yes; he was dressed in S.S. uniform. I accepted to go.

Mr Duncan: I suppose you were somewhat afraid of Wirths?

She considered for a moment, and then said reflectively: No, I don't think so, because I could have refused.

She had discovered quite soon that the women in Block 10 were raw material for experiments.

Mr Duncan: And that is why you hid some of those with typhus on the top floor?—because you thought that if you did not, they would probably be sent to the gas chamber?

Dr Hautval: Exactly.

Mr Duncan: You knew, of course, that if you were found doing that you would get into serious trouble?

Dr Hautval: It was an attitude that we all felt in the camp, and it was nothing special.

Mr Duncan: It was an everyday occurrence for people to be punished, was it not?

Dr Hautval: Yes. It was sufficient to smoke a cigarette.

Mr Duncan: So wholly vile was the treatment that you yourself might have been sent to the gas chambers if you had been found out?

Dr Hautval: Everything was possible.

Mr Duncan: Did you know that Dr Dering had hidden patients in this way?

Dr Hautval: I did not know.

In answer to further questions, she agreed that she was not a surgeon but a psychiatrist. Dr Wirths had known that.

Mr Duncan questioned her about the operation by Dr Samuel

for which she had given the anaesthetic: 'Did you know at the time that it was one of the experimental operations?'

Dr Hautval: Unfortunately, yes.

Mr Duncan: And because you knew he was working under Dr Wirths' orders you did not refuse to do it?

Dr Hautval: It was not for that reason. It was because I could not react quickly enough, and in that moment I was a little afraid of the consequences. I had just refused to take part in the other experiments and it was difficult for me, taken so suddenly, to refuse this one too.

Mr Duncan: When you did the first operation was the evipan in short supply?

The Judge intervened: You keep saying, Mr Duncan, that she 'did' the thing. She was merely the anaesthetist.

Mr Duncan apologized. He asked: Did you form the view that Dr Samuel was old and incompetent?

Dr Hautval said that Dr Samuel was about seventy. He was a Jew and profoundly aware of the dangerous circumstances in which he found himself. She thought that he had at first been a very competent doctor and was amazed that her opinion of him was so different from that of Dr Lorska and Dr Brewda. She thought that the anxiety under which Dr Samuel lived had brought on senility and upset his judgment. She knew that eventually he was sent to the gas chambers.

Mr Duncan: Unhappily there was nothing very unusual about that, was there?

Dr Hautval: For a doctor it was unusual.

Mr Duncan: You were a doctor. Apart from what you have told us, were you ever punished either in Birkenau or at Auschwitz?

Dr Hautval: No, I was never punished. I refused afterwards to carry out experiments for Dr Mengele and they said, 'We cannot force her to do what she does not want to do'.

Mr Duncan asked who 'Dr Mengele' was. Dr Hautval said that he was a doctor at Birkenau who 'made selections with unheard-of cruelty' and carried out experiments 'of the worst kind' on Jewish twins.

When she first went back to Birkenau an S.S. doctor had advised her to 'let the grass grow'. 'The idea was that I should not show myself too much so that I would not arouse their fury.' She did not actually hide; but she did not work as a doctor.

Lord Gardiner re-examining, asked Dr Hautval whether she had come quite voluntarily to give evidence for the defendants.

Dr Hautval: Yes.

'That', said Lord Gardiner, 'is the case for the defendants.'

PART V: EVIDENCE CONCLUDED

CHAPTER XIX

Dr Dering Replies

MR DUNCAN made formal application for leave to recall Dr Dering, and leave was granted. Once again in the witness box, Dr Dering said that he did not remember any operation when a needle broke and did not recollect the patient [the first man] who had given evidence to that effect. Although the register recorded him as giving the anaesthetic on the occasion when the man had said there were curses in Polish, he did not recall them. German had to be spoken in the presence of German officers, and they either spoke German or kept silent, so that there was often complete silence in the theatre. There had been no occasion when he had given a second spinal injection; it must be either successful or unsuccessful. He had never given premedication; that would be given in the wards.

He denied that he had ever been present at semen tests. 'To my recollection it was done only in Block 10 or in laboratory where laboratory technician used to take immediately microscopic glass and examine semen to establish either that spermatozoa are alive or dead, mobile or immobile. If it was done far away from laboratory it would take several minutes to get to laboratory and that test would be improper. Therefore I did not see, and I was not present at any semen test.'

He did not remember a protest in Greek and could not recall the patient [the fifth man]. He did not understand Greek. Somebody might have used the word '*Ruhig*' but he did not remember any such occasion. He had never used the expression: 'Dog, you will die', and did not remember the patient [the third man], and he had never heard anyone else using any such expression in the theatre.

He entirely agreed with Professor Nixon that in normal circumstances a long incision was normal for ovariectomy. The reason for the small incision was that the girls were undernourished, with radiated skin, no proper washing facilities, and 'all suffering from scabies'. Though this operation was technically difficult for the surgeon when done 'through this small hole', it had been in the interest of the patients to do it through a small abdominal incision. With all respect to Professor Nixon, he had produced a model to demonstrate the operation, but had unfortunately not mentioned that the womb and ovaries were very soft flexible tissue. By means of an instrument he had been able to bring to the surface 'this little ovary no bigger than the tip of a finger' and, after proper ligature, cover the stump—not with the flap of peritoneum, because there was no flap—but by means of one cross stitch, quite easily, close the abdominal wall with clips, and put on a dressing and adhesive plaster. One or two of the women had admitted that there was 'such a dressing'.

Mr Duncan asked Dr Dering whether he actually remembered the operations on these ten girls. He said that he did not.

Mr Duncan: Was there any occasion when you failed to carry out the proper surgical procedure?

Dr Dering: A surgeon must do things as he was trained to do them. I cannot remember and do not admit that I would ever do differently from what I was trained to do. What is really concerned is that all these girls did not change their clothes for months—with only one wash basin; and as they suffered from scabies there was tremendous itching, and these young girls did scratch their bodies and even the wound. This was a reason for the infection. It happens to every surgeon that post-operative wounds become septic. The doctor who is looking after this kind of patient can push up the edges of the wound by means of adhesive plaster and keep the patient in bed for another ten days or a fortnight until everything is healed. As this was not done, the result was the scar and this kind of gap in the muscles.

Lord Gardiner cross-examined. Dr Dering repeated his denial of an occasion when a needle broke or there were curses in Polish, and also that he had known about or been present at the semen tests.

Lord Gardiner: So the [first] man who said you were present and that you yourself showed the stick to Schumann and said: 'That is the instrument'—he is not right?

Dr Dering: What instrument?

Lord Gardiner: The stick.

Dr Dering: So far as I know it should be done with index finger.

Lord Gardiner: And the [fifth] man who tried to get off the table—and you slapped him down? You said you could not remember so 'it is impossible' that he said something in Greek and you said '*Ruhig*'?

Dr Dering: I don't remember. It is possible that someone said '*Ruhig*'.

Lord Gardiner: And the [third] man who said that after his first operation when one testicle was removed he knew who you were when you went round the wards. Do you think that is likely?

Dr Dering: He could know my name. All prisoners knew who I was.

Lord Gardiner: And he said: 'Why do you operate on me a second time when they have operated once?'—a reasonable question in the circumstances?

Dr Dering: But I don't remember this kind of talk and especially his sentence he said in Polish.

Lord Gardiner: That you said: 'Stop barking like a dog. You are going to die anyway'?

Dr Dering: Lord Gardiner, any Slavonic language specialist will tell you that this kind of sentence could not be said by any Pole. It is not according to the spirit of Polish language. It is not a Polish sentence.

Lord Gardiner: This man was a fellow Pole?

Dr Dering: But it was not a Polish sentence. I would say it in a completely different way, if I said it.

Lord Gardiner questioned Dr Dering about the man whose evidence was heard *in camera*. Dr Dering said that he remembered the man's evidence but he did not remember him at all.

Lord Gardiner: He said he was working in the laundries across the way and constantly saw you between operations?

Dr Dering: Yes, he could have seen me.

Dr Dering said that so far as he remembered that man had had one testicle removed—presumably in the late autumn, when he himself was not operating.

Lord Gardiner: But you *did* operate after September.

Dr Dering: Very seldom, and only cases like prostate, kidneys and so on. I did not take part in any small operations.

Lord Gardiner: Do you call removal of testicles or ovaries 'small operations'?

Dr Dering: Not major operations.

Lord Gardiner: You did not take part in any such operations after September?

Dr Dering: I am sure I did not. I performed less and less operations. As I already said, the second part of the register, not in my handwriting, was written not long ago. If we had the same ink as I had. . . . The part in my handwriting is faded and this is black, fresh.

Lord Gardiner: Is there any single point where it has been shown that anything recorded in the second part is not in fact right?

Dr Dering: Not everything. A lot of things are written and my name put to them when I did not perform the operation.

Lord Gardiner: Do you remember telling the Home Office that you kept the register until 1944?

Dr Dering: Not I. Where is that register?

He agreed that if two surgeons operated the senior took responsibility.

Lord Gardiner referred him to one of his statements to the Home Office: 'You are saying there, are you not, that the register was kept by you until 1944?

Dr Dering: Yes, but the photograph showed that it was in my handwriting until August 1943, not the *end* of 1943.

As far as he remembered, he did not think that the operations on five girls were at the end of November; there was sunshine and it was warm. 'Five operations I performed, but in which month I do not remember.'

Lord Gardiner: You told Mr Duncan that you did not remember the operations.

Dr Dering: Yes, I do not remember the operations, but I remember in 1947 when I gave my evidence . . .

[Dr Dering winced.]

Lord Gardiner: Is your leg troubling you, Dr Dering?

Dr Dering: I have very bad chest, fibrositis.

The Judge: You may sit down.

[Dr Dering sat down.]

Lord Gardiner: You said in answer to Mr Duncan that you did not remember the operations?

Dr Dering: It is difficult to remember, but I knew that five ovariectomies had been performed by me, and I gave this evidence seventeen years ago and I remember doing so. I gave this evidence recently to my solicitors.

Lord Gardiner: Since 1940 these were the only ovariectomies that you performed? It is not the sort of thing one is likely to forget, is it?

Dr Dering: No. I read my evidence that I gave before, and I recollect strongly only that altogether there were eighty-five operations of this sort performed by all Polish doctors in the camp.

He did not agree with Professor Nixon that the operations must have been performed 'blind'. It was physically possible to perform them properly.

Lord Gardiner: You don't agree with Professor Nixon: and you still say that Dr Brewda was never there at all?

Dr Dering: I still say Dr Brewda was never there.

On that note the evidence, begun on 13 April, was in fact concluded. Lord Gardiner sat down, and Mr Duncan said that he had asked all that he wished to ask Dr Dering.

PART VI: ISSUES FOR THE JURY

CHAPTER XX

Closing Speech for the Defence

LORD GARDINER said that the jury had listened patiently to a story that history would describe as 'What the Christians did to the Jews in western Europe about the middle of the twentieth century'. Nowhere in all history was there a blacker picture. That was anti-Semitism, that was! Though Hitler and the German Government bore the greater share of responsibility, none of these things could have been done if hundreds and thousands of people had not been prepared to do what they knew to be wrong—even though they acted under orders.

Throughout this case there had been a grave conflict of evidence. It was not just a question of recollections. Someone obviously was not telling the truth.

As there had been much discussion on whether Dr Grabczynski would or could come back from Poland, it was right to remind the jury that he had been concerned with only one incident in the new particulars—that of the third man who alleged that Dr Dering said: 'Stop barking like a dog'. If he had been brought back from Poland, at the defendants' expense, only one question would have been put to him; and it was fair to assume that he would have replied, just as Dr Dering did on his recall, 'I have no recollection of any such incident'.

As the jury knew, the original defence had been based only on the evidence of Dr Brewda and Dr Klodzinski; but now, in addition to the register and the Home Office statements, there was the evidence of the six men and the eight women. It had never been Dr Dering's case that these witnesses had put their heads together to say something that was not true. Though their recollection differed in detail, 'the day on which you know that, whatever happens in life you will never have any children, is a day you are not likely to forget'.

It looked on the evidence as if everything in that part of the register which was not in Dr Dering's handwriting was just as reliable as that part which was. In any event, it did not matter whether Dr Dering opened the safe while the other man kept guard or vice versa. Whether Dr Dering was down in the book as principal or as assistant was irrelevant. If he was taking part in an operation in which no one should have taken part, he was taking part in it. Yet, even in the witness box, there had been no real word of regret, and his general attitude was indistinguishable from that of any anti-Semitic officer of the German officer class.

In considering whether Dr Dering was telling the truth, the jury might think that the discrepancies in his statements to the Home Office and his evidence were not irrelevant.

As to the operations on the women, here again there was as complete a conflict of evidence as one could find. One girl might have suffered from the hallucination that Dr Brewda had been there when she was not; but eight girls could not suffer independently from the same hallucination, could they? Their evidence was supported by Dr Brewda—whose evidence in chief had not been shaken at all in cross-examination. Her evidence on the matters relating to this action had not only not been shaken but it was supported by other witnesses from the camp. Of course, if there had not been the register, the question of identity would have depended entirely on Dr Brewda's evidence, for none of the girls had said that it was Dr Dering who performed the operation—but the register was there.

On the question whether the operations on the girls were properly performed, no one was attacking Dr Dering, who had given a very high testimonial to his own skill—and no one suggested that his patients usually died after operation—but in the case of these Jewish 'guinea-pigs', did he just rush into these operations, picking out ovaries and not caring what the result was? Dr Brewda had always said they were not properly done; and now the jury had heard Professor Nixon's evidence. He had examined the girls, and he called it 'bad, crude surgery'. The jury might know that it was not easy to get doctors to give evidence against doctors, so that if a surgeon of Professor Nixon's standing said that, it was likely to be right. It had been suggested, rather late in the day, that the fact that the wounds were open for so long was really due to malnutrition or irradiation; but the jury might think that was obviously wrong.

There was one odd thing about the register. Dr Brewda said that it was quite untrue that Dr Dering had showed her the register in the theatre in Block 21. He said that he did. The register up to 28 August was in his handwriting. Dr Brewda arrived at the camp in September. So they had had Dr Dering saying that, after he had handed over the keeping of the register to someone else, he showed her the register. That was odd, was it not?

If the register was reliable, this Dr Dering was the man who in fact took part in about seventy per cent of the sterilization operations in Auschwitz. That they were experimental could not be in doubt. Dr Dering had agreed that he knew that the whole object of the second part of the experiment was to find out whether the X-ray had done its work. He knew quite well that he was doing experimental operations.

The defendants' case was this man was a conscious tool in the hands of the Nazis for their policy of mass sterilization with a view to genocide. Forcibly to remove men's and women's sexual organs against their will as a help towards genocide was not an ordinary crime, but a crime against humanity. The burden of proof had shifted to Dr Dering, for if he did these things, they cried out for some justification.

What reasons had been given for it? It was said that at a meeting of doctors it had been discussed and decided that it was medically justifiable to perform the operations to save the patients' lives. The defendants said that that was not a valid and was also a dishonest excuse—it had in fact no medical basis. In 1947 he had told the Home Office: 'I called a meeting of all the doctors working in the hospital'. That was quite untrue, for the evidence about the meeting was that out of a total medical staff of fifty-eight prisoner-doctors only three others had discussed it with Dr Dering and Dr Grabczynski.

Another excuse was that 'If I had not done these operations, the prisoners would either have been sent to the gas chambers or operated on by an S.S. corporal'. Dr Schumann *might* have threatened it, but there was no evidence—although behind every young man who stood in the witness box there were fifteen shadows who might or might not have survived. Equally without support from the evidence was the statement about the S.S. corporal.

If the prisoner-doctors had refused, the whole thing would have been slowed down, and possibly abandoned. Probably the German Dr Entress would have done the operations; he did twenty anyway, as the register showed. They would never have let an untrained and unskilled S.S. corporal do it, for the organs were wanted for examination. The S.S. corporal was the biggest red herring in the case. In any event how could that be an excuse for a crime like this—that one was justified in committing a crime because some bigger criminal would otherwise commit it and that that would be worse? That could not, as a matter of right and wrong, be right.

What in the jury's view would have been likely to happen if Dr Dering had refused to carry out the orders? They might think that, on that question, the evidence of Dr Hautval was vital. She had come here voluntarily and she had enabled the jury to see what happened to Christian doctors who deliberately defied an order; but she was not punished for it at all. Dr Dering himself had refused to give a lethal injection to another prisoner, and had been threatened with some awful punishment; but the only punishment had been the rather absurd one of not being allowed to go outside the grounds in his free time for a fortnight. The jury had evidence now that there were ways of by-passing S.S. orders, and of orders being disobeyed.

Everything tended to show that the S.S. doctors recognized that there were limits beyond which Christian prisoner-doctors, as a matter of medical ethics, could not be expected to go. At that time prisoner-doctors were of great value to the Germans, who wanted the prisoner-labour. The jury might well think that Dr Dering was more important to the Germans than anyone else. After the 'Save the Doctors' order went out in 1941, there was no evidence that any Christian, or even Jewish, doctor was ever punished for declining to obey an order which would be contrary to medical ethics, still less any case of any being shot or sent to the gas chambers or hanged, other than Dr Samuel, and that was for different reasons.

From first to last, on his own evidence, Dr Dering never tried to get out of it. When he started, it was on the court order cases;

but he had also said that even if there had been no court order he would still have done it. There had been no meeting of the prisoner-doctors about that. He just decided himself; and from the first moment that Dr Schumann told him that he wanted him to remove testicles and ovaries, he started on these cases without trying to get out of them. Dr Clauberg was described in Dr Dering's own statement of claim as his 'associate'; and Dr Wirths treated him almost as 'one of them'—Dr Dering for whom there was, on his own evidence, such keen competition in Berlin.

Ultimately, of course, he did obtain his release. Maybe he would not have got that release if he had refused to do the operations on the girls. Very few people were ever released from Auschwitz; but from 1941 onwards only two prisoner-doctors were released—Dr Dering and Dr Grabczynski, the two doctors who helped the Germans by doing these operations. Was that just a coincidence? The jury should bear that in mind when they came to consider the questions to be put to them.

The gist of the paragraph had been proved to be true. Though the number of the operations had been very much exaggerated, the specific number of occasions did not really add anything.

If there were here two charges—the first, that Dr Dering carried out 'experimental' operations, and the second that he did them without an anaesthetic—the defendants said that because of the gravity of the first charge, the second did not add anything, and that if it did add something it implied that he was acting callously—and so he was. The jury, on the whole of the evidence, should find for the defendants.

If they should find 'for the plaintiff', the defendants had said throughout that the smallest coin of the realm would be the proper award; for, if what had been written was not true, it was so nearly true that a man who had done what Dr Dering admitted having done, or what the jury found him to have done, ought not to have substantial damages.

On the whole, the jury might think Dr Dering had not been unlucky. They had heard something of the appalling time which the ordinary prisoners had in the work camps and workshops, some of them for years. Dr Dering only went through that for six weeks; and after that, he was living in the sheltered atmosphere of the hospital. No doubt through his own merits he obtained a very powerful position; he was the man who had to decide every morning which twenty or thirty of the 600 or so people clamouring to get into the hospital were to be allowed in. He was one of the only two doctors released from Auschwitz to work in a private hospital and even go to the cinema.

The jury might think that a person who tended not to do anything which might cost him his release should just have lived with his conscience and not have raked it all up after twenty years, in support of a claim for damages.

What sort of damages should a man have who hoicked out the ovaries of these wretched girls without a proper anaesthetic? What excuse was there for that—and whose fault was it if they so vividly remembered to this day, and probably to the end of their lives, what happened on that occasion? Mr Duncan had told the jury that there were plenty of anaesthetics available, including those for general anaesthesia, and the only reason given by Dr Dering for not using them was that there were no anaesthetists. The register showed that ether was administered by one or other of two doctors 188 times in November 1943. What nonsense, therefore, it was to say that he had not got any anaesthetists! Why was it only when it came to Greek Jewesses that there was no anaesthetist to be found?

It was always right to put one's self in another person's place. Suppose a member of the jury were the father or mother of the girl Bella who died. How would they feel about a Nazi doctor, acting under orders and owing a duty to his German Fatherland, who killed their daughter by this experimental guinea-pig operation? Or if the parents heard that it had been done by an anti-Semitic Pole—when we had gone to war to help Poland—would that have made it better or worse? Of if they had been a young man or woman caught in France at the outbreak of war and had found themselves in an internment camp and were told that a German Nazi was going to take out their testicles or ovaries as an experiment maybe because one of their grandparents had been Jewish? They would know what to do with that German Nazi after the war. But suppose, when it came to the point, it was not a German at all, but a French doctor—or a fellow Englishman?

Would they have expected an English jury to give such a person damages? Or would not they think that it would be wise for a man who did that sort of thing to keep his mouth shut?

It would be an outrage if this man, who had done these unnecessarily cruel things, were to be awarded anything other than purely nominal damages.

CHAPTER XXI

Last Word for Dr Dering

MR COLIN DUNCAN said that Lord Gardiner had invited the jury to look at certain passages in the evidence; but they must get the whole of it. Surely they would have no difficulty about the meaning of the words to anyone reading them, 'He must be a monster'.

Then they had to say whether the words were true. The first thing the words said was that what Dr Dering did took place in Block 10. At the beginning it was conceded that that was not very important, and anyway the defendants had admitted that it took place in Block 21. But now that the jury knew what readers would not know—that Block 10 was a secret place, with its windows barred so that no one could see in or out; and that in it were kept the 'raw materials' for the Nazi manoeuvres—they might well think that there was a sinister significance attached to 'Block 10'. 'In Block 10' was not true.

Secondly, Dr Dering, with his name spelt with an 'h' was classed with 'Wirths' and 'Schumann' and 'Clauberg'. That must have struck the jury as one of the unfairest things of all—no hint that he was a Polish prisoner and himself one of the victims of Nazi brutality. It was for the jury to decide whether that made much difference.

Then came the worst of the lot—that Dr Dering 'performed 17,000 "experiments" in surgery without anaesthetics'. That raised three matters for consideration: First, the figure was '17,000' and not 1,700 or 170; secondly, 'experiments in surgery' meant at least that Dr Dering was himself experimenting by means of surgery; and thirdly, and most ghastly of all 'without anaesthetics'. It was so glib to slide over that appalling charge by saying: 'Well, without general anaesthetic'. Those two words had only one possible meaning in English. They meant that Dr Dering was practising wholesale vivisection on human beings. The sting of the viper, the defamatory imputation of the words, was, 'Dr Dering a Nazi, Dr Dering a vivisectionist, Dr Dering performing 17,000 experiments in surgery in Block 10 at Auschwitz—if that is true he must be a fiend in human guise'. The meaning of the words could not be any less grave than the words actually used. One could not say of a man, 'He has been doing operations without anaesthetics' and then say, 'That means something different'.

The defence was that the libel was true; but really there was no defence to this action, for it was absolutely untrue that Dr Dering performed 17,000 experiments in surgery without anaesthetics. The only question was: What was the proper sum to award him by way of damages?

What the defence had sought to do was to prove that Dr Dering did a number of things at Auschwitz concentration camp during the war of which Professor Nixon would not approve in Wimpole Street in 1964, and which might have surprised Hippocrates sitting under his tree 400 years before the birth of Christ.

It was also said that Dr Dering discriminated against the Jewish people; but was it not the exact reverse?

Then there had been insinuations that he was anti-Communist and a member of a non-existent Polish officers' clique and that he wore leather shoes and left Auschwitz with a suitcase. Mr Duncan was not saying these things to be facetious. On the contrary, the jury should take all those nasty insinuations into account when they came to assess the damages. If the defendants proved every single one of the particulars which they had set out, they would not be within sight of establishing that the libel was true. They had signally failed to prove those particulars, and the burden of proving them was on the defendants.

He commended Dr Dering to the jury as a palpably truthful witness, who neither hedged nor prevaricated, and who was never reluctant to make an admission against his interest. Why should he have brought this action if he were not conscious of the righteousness of his cause? It was correct that there was conflict between what he said and what some of the witnesses said; but they were dealing with events twenty years ago taking place in circumstances of unparalleled horror, when no one could be blamed for falling into error about one thing or another. What about Dr Grabczynski? He had come from Poland, and had told the court that he did exactly what Dr Dering did; but no one had libelled Dr Grabczynski nor called him a monster, nor suggested that he was part of a conspiracy to deceive the court. There was not even a suggestion that his memory was failing. The jury should accept every word of his evidence as clear, precise, and accurate; and they might also have been impressed by his manner, which was convincing without being smug.

The jury were not concerned with the interesting scientific question whether a spinal injection or an inhalant anaesthetic was the better. The only question was whether they thought that Dr Dering could reasonably have arrived at the conclusion that a spinal anaesthetic was best; and on that they had Dr Hewer's evidence.

They should remember that Dr Brewda was at Auschwitz for only four months of the time that Dr Dering was there; and also how between 1940 and 1943 he had risked his life day by day for his fellow-prisoners, most of whom were Jews; and how this doctor, of whom it was now said that he had had 'only about six weeks' of brutal treatment and then 'sheltered in the hospital', had been beaten and treated with every kind of atrocity.

The jury might have asked themselves: Where were Mr Leon Uris and William Kimber & Company Ltd.? Nobody could blame them if they had expected to see them in the witness box; but for that the jury had waited in vain. That could and should be taken into consideration when the damages were assessed.

It was not contended for Dr Dering that the defendants' witnesses were conspiring to tell lies. Every one of these unfortunate men and women had been the victims of irradiation, starved, ill-treated and humiliated; and every one of them was, quite naturally, bitter against the inhuman Nazis, the cause of their misfortunes. Who could blame them? But did it make them the best witnesses? All the details were blurred and confused. They contradicted each other—but no point was made about that.

Almost all of them had said that the spinal injections were given by a medical orderly and denied that they were given by Dr Dering. Yet he said against himself that he gave them; and so said Dr Brewda. The witnesses were not to be blamed; but it showed how careful one had to be, in picking out, like a winkle from its shell, one piece of evidence and saying that therefore the witnesses were all unreliable.

Dr Brewda, however, was in a different category; and Mr Duncan hoped he had made it perfectly clear that he was saying that she was prepared to say anything to Dr Dering's discredit, whether it was true or false. He had not minced his words about this. Her reasons might be a matter for speculation, but what was not a matter for speculation was that malice existed. At the time of the Home Office investigation in 1947 she said, knowing that what she was saying was of the utmost gravity, affecting Dr Dering's life, that all the men on whom he had operated had died. Was there a scintilla of evidence that a single one of the men died? What did the jury think of the sense of responsibility of a person prepared to state that?

She also said in 1947 that the 16,000 or 17,000 operations were 'all experimental'. Now she said that she thought that was so at that time. Fortunately the court had had more light on the state of her mind; her frame of mind was distorted. She now said that in November 1943, when she saw the operations on the girls, she had concluded that all the others about which she had been told were unnecessary, and therefore experimental. She did not think so now.

A few rather feeble pink herrings had been dragged across the trail by Lord Gardiner; but the facts were clear as daylight. Dr Dering's wrongs, like Caesar's wounds, cried out for themselves.

The criticisms against him could be summarized under four heads: first, that he did the operations at all; secondly, the way he did them; thirdly, an attempt had been made to make him the scapegoat for the subsequent state of health of the patients operated on; and fourthly, he was alleged to have been sucking up to the Nazis to 'work his passage'. Did all those nasty little things have any connection with whether 17,000 experimental operations were performed without anaesthetics?

The jury should remember that the operations were performed in Auschwitz in 1943, and not in a London hospital in 1964. There was uncontradicted evidence that it was largely due to Dr Dering that there was an aseptic operating theatre; in the early days he was virtually the only surgeon; and it was largely due to him that thousands of the unfortunates, abused, maltreated and humiliated by the Nazis, having been cared for and cured by Dr Dering, were alive today. At great risk to himself he got his fellow prisoners at night to improve conditions in the hospital. Did the jury think that he had done that to further the Führer's campaign for the 'extermination' of the Jews?

Which evidence did the jury prefer: that of the two experienced surgeons, Dr Dering and Dr Grabczynski who were actually doing the job—or that of the gravely prejudiced Dr Brewda, who drew all her adverse conclusions from the speed and expertise of the surgery performed? As to the speed, Professor Nixon had thought that fifteen to twenty minutes was a normal time. Did the jury prefer the evidence of Professor Nixon, who in 1964 drew conclusions from the present appearance of the conditions he found in the women, to that of the two surgeons? The jury should prefer the two surgeons to Professor Nixon and Dr Brewda.

A lot of gross prejudice had been introduced. The tilting of the table had been put into the pleadings to cast a slur; and how wicked it was to suggest, as had been pleaded, that the women, all of whom had been back at Birkenau after two or three months, were still languishing in bed in the summer of 1944!

The jury should draw their own conclusions from the names in the register. There was not a hint of anything against Dr Dering until 1943. There was no evidence of the suggested Polish officers' clique. That was just an attempt to denigrate the highly valuable and dangerous work which all who knew Dr Dering knew he had been doing for years at Auschwitz—as was also the matter of his clean clothes and his shoes. In those years he had been looked on as heroic, and not at a lickspittle or a time-server. It was monstrous to suggest that he had been released from Auschwitz. He left the camp as a prisoner.

Why did he do the operations? The answer was that he literally had no choice. He was satisfied that if he did not do these unpalatable operations, they would be done by inexperienced people, with disastrous results to the victims. Lord Gardiner had said that it could not be right that the victims would be sent to the gas chambers, and asked whether the jury could imagine the bodies being raked through; but the jury would remember that bodies were raked out of gas chambers in order to get gold teeth. The motives for doing the operations were mixed; and a very vital factor was that it was impossible to refuse. If doctors had refused, they, and also the patients, might have been bumped off. To operate was thought to be the best thing that could be done. When one was in Auschwitz one had no choice; and the doctors were obliged to carry out the operations. There was no limit to the imagination of what horrors would have happened to Dr Dering had he refused—and yet it was made another flogging block on which to put him.

It was said that he did not ask the patients' consent. But was that reality in the circumstances? This was not only war; it was also a brutal concentration camp.

At the end of it all, what had all these things to do with '17,000 experiments in surgery without anaesthetics'? Nothing.

The greatest damage done to Dr Dering was that he had been held up day after day with the defendants saying that this was true. The defence of justification had palpably failed. The jury had not seen the defendants giving evidence, and they had uttered not one word of regret, but had sought to justify the brandishing of Dr Dering as a Nazi and vivisectionist.

The jury would not want to lose their heads; but if they had to consider damages, this case called for a very, very substantial award.

CHAPTER XXII

The Judge Sums Up

THE JUDGE began his summing up soon after noon on the seventeenth day of the trial.

'Members of the jury', he said, 'You and I have sat in this court now for three and a half weeks and we have had to listen to evidence revealing one, and it is only one, facet of what future generations will probably come to describe as the greatest crime that has ever been committed. I have been a student of history all my life, and I cannot think of any crime that begins to compare with the crime of Auschwitz. But it is important that we should remind ourselves why we are here. We are not here acting as a war crimes tribunal, nor are we conducting an inquiry about what went on in Auschwitz. We are here to try a civil case according to the law of England.'

The first task was to decide what these words meant, the test being what the ordinary level-headed average citizen, who knew Dr Dering, or knew of him, would think they meant. Here there was a danger that the jury might read into the words meanings which they would not have read three and a half weeks ago. They now knew who 'Dr Wirths' and 'Dr Schumann' and 'Professor Clauberg' were, and what they were doing in Block 10. The average reader of *Exodus*, in 1959 or up to the time this case began, would have little or no idea of the names of those who ran the camp. It was important to remember that many people in Seven Sisters Road where Dr Dering practised or in Ealing where he lived might have taken this book out of the library and read this passage without connecting it with Dr Dering in any way. It could not mean anything to them unless they connected the name 'Dehring' with the name 'Dering' and knew that Dr Dering had been in Auschwitz. Also the jury must consider the words in their context.

Mr Duncan and Lord Gardiner had both suggested meanings for the words. Mr Duncan said that the sting of the libel was that

'Our Dr Dering is one of the Nazi fiends, and he must be a monster; and that that was one sting and one sting only; and that the defendants had not even begun to prove it. Lord Gardiner said they had two stings; the first relating to 'experiments in surgery', and the second relating to those experiments being done 'without anaesthetic'.

The question of one sting or two stings was important, because the defendants were relying on section 5[1] of the Defamation Act, 1952—an Act passed to mitigate some of the more rigorous rules relating to libel. Lord Gardiner said that that was exactly the situation here; that as they had established the truth of the first sting about the 'experiments', the fact that they had not proved the second sting about 'no anaesthetic' did not take the matter any further. Everything depended on whether the words contained two charges or one charge; that depended on their meaning; and that meaning was for the jury to decide.

Those were the signposts which led to the evidence—the meaning of the words; the sting of the words; and who had to prove that the sting existed in fact.

The defendants had sought to establish by the evidence three propositions of fact: (1) that Dr Dering performed 130 operations on men and women, mostly young, which were an essential part of a vast series of experiments on Jewish prisoners being carried out by Nazi doctors for the specific purpose of wiping out for ever, in the territories controlled by the Nazis, Jews and those of Jewish blood; (2) that Dr Dering willingly performed those operations, first, because he was an anti-Semite and, secondly, because he wanted to ingratiate himself with the Nazis in order to secure his release from Auschwitz; and (3) that he performed the operations which he did perform, with callousness and brutality.

'130 "EXPERIMENTS" IN SURGERY'

On the first proposition, it was never in dispute that the Nazis were carrying out experiments to find out a method of sterilizing Jews,

[1] Defamation Act, 1952, s. 5: 'In an action for libel . . . in respect of words containing two or more distinct charges against the plaintiff, a defence of justification shall not fail by reason only that the truth of every charge is not proved, if the words not proved to be true do not materially injure the plaintiff's reputation, having regard to the truth of the remaining charges'.

half-Jews and quarter-Jews, and that practically all the 130 operations were an essential part of those experiments. To remove ovaries and testicles, in order to submit them to laboratory examination to find out what effect irradiation had had, required a surgical operation—unless it were going to be done by a butcher; but a butchering operation might not really have been quite what the Nazis wanted because some of the scientific evidence being sought might have been destroyed. So surgery was important; and surgery was performed.

The register which had survived and had been brought to this court by the Polish Embassy had been, perhaps, the most important exhibit in this case.

There were hundreds of entries in Dr Dering's handwriting in it, and on his evidence what was in his handwriting was evidence against him. If page 112, chosen at random, was a fair sample of what was in the register, Dr Dering was doing large numbers of ordinary operations—taking out appendices, dealing with carbuncles—doing the ordinary work of a surgeon. The reason for that was that, when the Russian front opened in the summer of 1941, the Germans wanted all the doctors they could get. They were not going to waste good German doctors on prisoners; but they also did not want to have prisoners away from war work merely because they had some minor thing wrong with them, and so they set up a hospital to deal with minor disabilities.

The register showed that during the period it covered, roughly a year from February 1943 to February 1944, something like 185 of these experimental operations were performed, and that Dr Dering either carried out or assisted in 130 of them. There were forty-six cases in Dr Dering's handwriting relating to castration, sterilization, and amputation of testicles. They started off with an entry of castration which Dr Dering said was done in the presence of a German officer and pursuant to a court order.

The broad picture was that between May and the end of August 1943, Dr Dering, by his own admissions in the witness box, was taking part in a largish number of surgical operations which were part and parcel of these horrible experiments in irradiation which the German doctor, Schumann, was carrying out.

Dr Dering did not accept the accuracy of the register for any date after the end of August when he had been ordered to new duties which took him away from the theatre. He had pointed out that after that date the ink was much fresher, and he obviously felt —rightly or wrongly—that someone had been tampering with the register. That did not appear to be the view of Dr Grabczynski, who was prepared to accept entries in it relating to him as accurate.

The matter did not end with the register. A number of young men, victims of these operations, had been called, who bore on their bodies and would bear for the rest of their lives the tattoo marks put on them when they went to Auschwitz, and operations on prisoners with those numbers had been established. Some of the men said that Dr Dering in fact did the operation; and Lord Gardiner asked the jury to infer from those samples so to speak, that the register, between the end of August 1943 and January 1944, had been proved accurate in so far as it implicated Dr Dering.

That was still not the end of it, for when, in 1947, Dr Dering had been arrested by the British authorities because three governments were asking for his extradition as a war criminal, and various allegations were made against him, he was asked for his comments. At first he said that he had not done any experimental operations; but at some time he did reveal to the British Government that he had carried out operations of the nature alleged, on eighty-five men and five women. That brought the number up to ninety which he admitted doing; and that was not far off the 130 which the jury were being asked to infer—but 130 was 16,870 less than the '17,000' mentioned in the book.

WILLINGLY PERFORMED?

Then came the second proposition of fact, the much more difficult problem whether he had done them willingly. The first matter in the case against him on this was that he took part in those semen tests carried out before amputation of testicles. One witness had said that Dr Dering was present—not just standing there, but suggesting the instrument, teaching the unspeakable Schumann how to do it! Dr Dering said that that just was not true. It never happened; that if these things went on they went on in some laboratory outside any part of Block 21 over which he had control; that anything that went on, went on certainly not in his presence, emphatically not with his help, and without his knowledge. That was the first of many matters on which there was a violent conflict of evidence.

The second matter was the attitude he adopted towards the victims. Not all of them said that he behaved with callousness to them; but some did. There was an example: the man who gave his evidence in closed court. Dramatic evidence it was! If he was telling the truth it was a terrible story. That young man was only sixteen when these awful things happened to him, when he had both testicles removed. The details of the two operations were in the register. Apparently Dr Dering had nothing to do with the first; but this boy of sixteen had been called out for a second operation. He said he had gone to the prisoner-leader of his block, and having got some advice, spoke to Dr Dering before the operation, saying something like, 'B says cannot you do anything for me?' and, according to him, the answer was, 'What does it matter? We will leave you something to pass water with'! That young man had given another piece of evidence which should be weighed with the rest: he said, 'In camp you saw miserable faces; but in Dr Dering you saw a face of "I'm all right, Jack! I will be O.K." ' If that was an accurate picture of Dr Dering's attitude, the defendants said, that showed that he was a willing tool.

All these poor young people, who gave evidence of horrible things being said, had had ghastly experiences. They must have been terrified. Had they got confused, or had it never happened? The jury had to decide what reliance to put on them.

It was important, because Dr Dering said that nothing of the kind happened; that it was unthinkable that he could have behaved to these unfortunate people in the way they said he had; that he had approached these operations with distaste and reluctance, but that so far as he was concerned, they were surgically straightforward and he had no recollection of any untoward incident in the ward and he had no recollection of any untoward incident in the operating room at all. It just did not happen—and if it had, he would have remembered it.

He was borne out in that respect by Dr Grabczynski who, as the register showed and as he had said, had helped Dr Dering on a number of occasions. *He* had no recollection of any distressing incidents—none at all. Had *he* got it all wrong? Mr Duncan said that he certainly had not. Let the jury think for a moment what an appalling scene it must have been with these young Greek girls—torn away from their homes in Salonika, speaking an odd language of their own, parted from their parents, their only hope of communication being through those more educated women in this Block 10 who knew some French! What were they in Block 10 for? As guinea-pigs, called out from time to time by the unspeakable Clauberg and Schumann for these inhuman tests. The jury had seen what happened in court with one of these women who was now approaching forty. If anything like that happened, could Dr Dering and Dr Grabczynski have forgotten it for one moment? So here, too, there was a dramatic conflict of evidence.

It did not end there, because Dr Mezyk, from the United States, had said that he went to see the operations from time to time and never saw any distressing scenes. Then there was Mr Langbein, a very valuable witness in trying to get a balanced view. If he had heard of these appalling goings-on, would he have said that Dr Dering 'held a good reputation' in the camp?

Thirdly, the defendants relied on Dr Dering's attitude to Dr Brewda, particularly in the theatre on the day when the ten Greek girls were operated on. Here the conflict of evidence was in its sharpest form; for though Mr Duncan had never suggested that the victims were deliberately lying, he had said quite frankly that Dr Brewda was a dishonest witness who had come here to make things as bad as possible for Dr Dering. But did that mean that she was not telling the truth? The jury had seen Dr Brewda and Dr Dering and Dr Grabczynski; they could consider not only what the witnesses said, but how they said it. Ten operations had undoubtedly been carried out. The jury had heard the evidence of eight of the subjects, and had been told that two had died. According to the register, Dr Dering did five and Dr Grabczynski five. No one could have made Dr Grabczynski come here to give evidence, for he was outside the jurisdiction of this court. But he came here and went into the witness box and said: 'If the register says I did five I did them' and 'I remember the operations on these girls'. Why should he have said that, implicating himself in the disgraceful features of this case, if it were not true? Dr Brewda said it was not true. The jury must make up their minds.

Dr Dering had asked the jury to infer from Dr Brewda's behaviour in 1947 that she was a woman ready to say anything against him. The 1947 matters were also important. Dr Brewda did apparently have a number of interviews in 1947 with the Polish Government representative, and told him what she knew of Dr Dering's activities in Auschwitz; and at the end a Polish official produced to her what she understood was a summary of what she had said 'in the Polish language' and which she signed. Mr Duncan said that what she agreed with in that statement showed that she was irresponsible. Lord Gardiner's answer was that Mr Duncan was reading a translation of notes of what she said, and also that at the time she was being asked to say not only what she knew but also what she had heard about Dr Dering.

The defendants also relied on the statements made by Dr Dering to the Home Office in 1947 and said he had told the Home Office a pack of lies and would not have done that if he had not known that he was implicated in these unspeakable medical experiments in Auschwitz. But the jury should remember that Dr Dering's mother tongue was Polish, and that what the jury had were English translations of what he wrote in Polish, and mistakes might have been made in translation. Dr Dering said he did not want to deceive the Home Office and what he had been saying then was that he was not carrying out 'experimental' operations in any ordinary sense and that he did reveal that he had in fact carried out eighty-five on men and five on girls.

Then came a very important matter—the defendants' approach to Dr Dering's explanations as to why he did the operations.

The main reason he gave to the Home Office was that he was ordered to do the operations by Schumann; that his status at that time was that of a prisoner who had to do what he was told; and that if he did not, he was likely to suffer death or at least really serious personal injury. The second reason was that if he had not done what he was told to do, somebody else would have done it—either a German doctor with less skill in surgery than he, or somebody completely unskilled; that he knew that, whatever he said, the operations would be done, and that, as he knew that these victims were going to lose their testicles or ovaries, he thought it better for them to lose them as a result of skilled surgery rather than by unskilled surgery or butchery. The third reason was that, following a discussion he had with other doctors in the camp, he came to the conclusion that there was a possibility that these irradiated ovaries and testicles might do some later damage. The fourth —based on something Schumann had said to him—was that, if all the doctors including himself had refused to do the operations, the victims might be sent to the gas chambers and their testicles or ovaries got from their dead bodies.

The evidence on both sides in relation to those reasons should be looked at, first, on the factual and then on the moral basis.

Lord Gardiner said that by late 1943, when the whole object of having doctors in the camp was to maintain the labour supply, a doctor like Dr Dering would not have been destroyed by the Germans because they could not afford to do it; and that the jury should look at what happened to other people who refused to carry out operations. There was Dr Lorska in Block 10, who somehow avoided having to do any operations, though the Nazis knew she was a doctor. She said that punishments could be avoided, and there were ways of getting out of these things. There was Dr Brewda who said she had been faced with this problem and called on to help in Block 10 with particular experiments being done there, but dodged the issue by saying she had no experience of gynaecological surgery. Then there was Dr Hautval—perhaps one of the most impressive and courageous women who had ever given evidence in the courts of this country, a most outstanding and distinguished person—and they knew what had happened to her. She had stood up to the Nazis four times, and made it quite clear at an early stage what she was prepared to do and what she was not prepared to do. As a result of the stand she made, she found herself summoned by Dr Wirths; and she gave a reply to Dr Wirths which his Lordship expected would live in the jury's memories for many years—a devastating reply; and then she had been told by an S.S. doctor to 'let the grass grow' and he said, 'I won't punish you'. Then she found herself appointed as assistant to another beastly fellow carrying out experiments on Jewish twins; and once again she refused—and this character apparently said to someone standing by, 'If she won't, she won't'. So the jury were asked to infer that if Dr Dering had stood up, nothing would have happened to him.

His case was very different. He said—rightly—that you must never forget that these events were happening in Auschwitz in 1943, and you had to look at them through the eyes of someone who was there in 1943; that it was easy in 1964, knowing how Dr Lorska and Dr Brewda and Dr Hautval had managed to avoid them, to say, 'Anybody else could have avoided doing them'—but the ordinary person was not and did not aspire to be a saint. The problem was, what would the ordinary reasonable doctor have expected to happen in 1943? Anyone who had been in Auschwitz for as long as Dr Dering and who had been connected with the underground, as it seemed to be accepted he was, must have known what was going on in the gas chambers at Birkenau. He also knew—because he saw it happening—that the Nazis were destroying people by those phenol injections. What else? Just beside Block 10 was Block 11—and not far away was Block 21. What did the jury know about Block 11? It was the execution block where they hanged and shot people—not just as an isolated thing, but mass execution two or three times a week. Those wretched guinea-pigs in Block 10 had their windows covered up so that they should not see what was going on below. But just picture the working conditions in Block 21! Dr Dering perhaps lancing someone's foot and hearing a fusillade from Block 11. And everyone said that these unfortunate victims were beaten and ill-treated for no reason at all. Considering the evidence on both sides, had it been proved that Dr Dering was not in fear of his life or serious physical pain? That was the factual side of it.

Now for the moral side. The way Lord Gardiner put it was that even if he was in fear, Dr Dering ought not to have done what he did; that there were some things in life for the doing of which fear was not an excuse; and so, if Dr Dering did them, he must not be surprised if the rest of the world thought that his repute was of no real value.

The jury had to decide how the average man could be expected to behave in those circumstances. The Judge could not give them any guidance about morals. He had no reason to think that the judicial attitude towards morals was any better than or different from that of anybody else, and he was not going to try to guide them on this moral question; but he would be failing in his duty if he did not try to give them a little help, and he would do that by examples from history.

This problem of what a man should do when he was in fear of his life or really serious injury had been discussed by moralists throughout the ages. Primitive society tended to say that it was the doing of the act which was the blameworthy thing, and those who judged disregarded intent. That had been the position in our early law on homicide and in the early days of the Church. In the third century A.D. there was a Roman Emperor called Decius, who persecuted the early Christians ruthlessly and efficiently. (It was a curious historical fact that he was born in the Roman province where Hitler was born.) Decius, like most people, was much more interested in maintaining the supply of taxpayers than the supply of lion's meat; and when the early Christians were being dragged to a forum before the Roman crowds, the choice was put to them in simple terms: if they threw incense on the flames they were allowed to go about their business; if they refused, they were sent to the lions. Lots of them decided to throw incense, and, having done so, they had to keep away from the Christian community. When the persecution ceased on Decius' death, they came back and asked to rejoin. There had been two views on that; and there had been a controversy in the Church over what was thought to be a difficult problem; and eventually the apostates had been allowed to rejoin.

Those two views had gone on through history. Most ideas in philosophy sprang from Aristotle, who first said that it was intention that governed the quality of an act. That view had been discussed among the Greek and Roman philosophers and the early Christians; and it was St Augustine who pointed out that intention was an essential part of all the Christian scene. From that time it had always been accepted that intention was relevant in considering the quality of an act; and our law had taken the same point of view. In relation to some acts you could plead that you did them in fear of your life or of grievous harm. After the Jacobite rebellion you could say that you had been made to fight for the Germans, the French, or the Poles, because you were in fear of your life. In the last war a man who broadcast for the Germans was deemed entitled to say that he did it under fear.

But we had always said that fear was no excuse for murder; and probably the English judges would say that it was no excuse for doing really serious injury. Lord Gardiner was undoubtedly right when he said that people must make a stand at some time. There did come a point when you had to say, 'I will die rather than do this'. The defendants said that that was what Dr Dering should have been prepared to do, if the facts were as he said.

Mr Duncan said that the facts had not really got to that stage, and that in 1943 at Auschwitz Dr Dering, having consulted the other doctors, was really taking the practical course. This question of moral values and attitude was only relevant, of course, if Dr Dering was blameworthy.

The second reason which Dr Dering gave should be examined in exactly the same way, by looking at the facts first, and then examining the morals. On the facts the register showed that on a number of occasions the German doctors took off peoples' testicles; and Lord Gardiner said that if Dr Dering had not done it, the Germans would have done it themselves and that the suggestion that an S.S. corporal would have done it was fantastic; that, except for the two girls who died, the victims had all gone back to work; and that the Nazis wanted them for work and would not have treated them in a way that might lead to their death.

Dr Dering said that the Nazi mind did not work like that; and Dr Grabczynski bore him out on that, saying, 'I performed what I did because I felt that if I did not it was bound to be done, and by a more unskilled person than I'. Would Dr Grabczynski have come here from Poland and said what he did if it were not true?

The problem of morals was difficult and the Judge was glad that the jury, and not he, had to decide it. They had to decide whether any blame attached to Dr Dering and whether he operated for the reasons he gave.

If he was right about consulting with his colleagues he must have been worried; and if someone suggested that the apprehended danger from radiation was right, and it did not take much to persuade him that it was all right to operate, was he to be blamed?

It was for the jury to decide, too, whether they believed Dr Dering when he said that one reason why he operated was because if he had not, there was a danger that the victims would end up in the gas chambers.

The first of the reasons why it was said that Dr Dering was performing these operations willingly was said to be anti-Semitism. That allegation was based on what had been said about him in a document prepared by a very eminent member of the Bar acting on his behalf in 1947. It was said that he manifested his anti-

Semitism by the way he conducted these operations; that ordinary precautions were never taken because the patients were Jews and Jewesses who to him were of no value. Dr Dering said that that just was not true; that in Auschwitz they were all prisoners, and, as a doctor, he did his best for all. The jury might think that if he saved anybody—unless he went out of his way to pick Gentiles—the likelihood was that he did save Jews, for at least sixty per cent of the prisoners there were Jewish. And again, there was the evidence of Mr Langbein that he had 'a good reputation'.

The second of the reasons indicating willingness, that Dr Dering was ingratiating himself with the Germans, was based on the fact that he was 'released' from the camp, in the sense that he was taken off, still bearing his prisoner's status and answerable to the Gestapo. Just before he was released he had taken part in the ten terrible operations; and the jury were asked to infer that he had 'worked his passage'—like the dog who had done his job in the hunting field and got his piece of sugar. They would have to make up their minds whether it had been proved that he willingly performed these operations.

CALLOUSLY AND BRUTALLY?

The third proposition of fact, relied on as proving the sting of the libel, was that Dr Dering had carried out these operations with callousness and brutality. On that, the defendants said that if he were really a man troubled in his conscience and doing what he did, unwillingly, for the reasons he gave, one would have expected him to show some compassion towards these young men and women—telling the young men who were going to have one testicle removed that perhaps it would not make all that difference to their lives, and telling the young girls that they would feel nothing and it would soon be over; but that it had not even been suggested that he did any such thing, and he had never said that he gave them a word of comfort; and, as for the young women, he called on them once after the operations, and that was all.

Dr Dering on the other hand said that you should not look at it like that. He was the surgeon-in-charge; he was working from morning to night doing what he could for the suffering prisoners and operating virtually on his own; that the burden of everything fell on him; and that he had adopted towards these patients the ordinary surgeon's attitude, leaving it to others, who were to his knowledge skilled, to prepare them and to look after them afterwards; and that he had done his surgical job with reluctance, but as best and as quickly as he could, consistently with proper surgical practice. The jury should make up their mind between those two views. Obviously it was an important part of this case.

Lastly, the question of how he conducted the operations might be important in considering who was to be believed. The defendants had not sought to prove that *no* anaesthetics were administered. There was not a shred of evidence to support that. But what they said was that he performed experiments in surgery without *adequate* anaesthetic, and in a brutal way. Was Mr Duncan right in saying that these words meant that 'Dr Dering was carrying out vivisections on human beings', when the evidence was that he gave a spinal anaesthetic which was widely used on the Continent before the war by surgeons operating below the navel? Mr Duncan said that that was why he had told the jury that there was no defence to this claim.

Lord Gardiner, on the other hand, submitted that this question of 'no anaesthetic' had to be considered in relation to the main charge of carrying out ' "experiments" in surgery', and that if the jury concluded that he did that, it did not add much, if anything, to the sting of the libel to say that he did them 'without anaesthetics'. It was said that he anaesthetized them in the area on which he was operating and that saved them *some* pain, but that he did nothing to anaesthetize their minds, which must have been suffering agony.

The evidence to support this allegation of brutality and callousness was, presumably, that he chose a spinal anaesthetic because it did nothing for the mind. If that were right, the jury could imagine the agony of mind of these young men and women must have gone through—'to have your testicle removed when you are sixteen—to have your ovaries removed if you are a young girl'. What, said Lord Gardiner, did Dr Dering do to relieve that agony of mind? Nothing. Why did he do it?

From the surgeon's point of view there were advantages in using a spinal anaesthetic; and Dr Dering's explanation was that no skilled anaesthetists were available, and that a general anaesthetic administered by an unskilled person might have serious medical *sequelae*. The defendants said that that was just not true, because there *were* doctors available, and why not call one of them in? They pointed out that the register showed numerous occasions on which general anaesthetics had been given. So the jury were asked to infer that for some reason of his own Dr Dering did not give a general anaesthetic. The jury should remember that we were not now concerned with operations carried out in St Bartholomew's or in a Wimpole Street nursing home in 1964, but with Auschwitz in 1943. Maybe Dr Dering had made a wrong choice and it would have been better to give these victims a general anaesthetic. But were the jury to blame him if, in the stress of Auschwitz, he made a wrong choice?

Then it was said that he gave the spinal anaesthetic in a way that must have caused pain and distress to his patients; that it was given in the annexe with the young girls having their heads pushed downwards by two young orderlies; and that they had to be half-dragged into the theatre. Did that happen? Dr Dering said it did not. Dr Grabczynski said it took place in the theatre.

Then it was said that Dr Dering did not take the ordinary precaution taken by most doctors of giving a small injection first, to deaden the area through which the main injection would have to be given. On that, there was a direct conflict between Dr Hewer, the consultant to St Bartholomew's Hospital, and Dr Ebsworth of University College Hospital. With that difference of medical opinion, perhaps the jury would not think it right to blame Dr Dering for not administering the small initial anaesthetic.

But both Dr Ebsworth and Dr Hewer were agreed that if a spinal anaesthetic were going to be used for an ovariectomy or amputation of a testicle, it would be good medical practice to give premedication beforehand; and it was suggested that not one single one of these young men or girls had any form of premedication, the object of which was to ensure that the patient by the time of the operation was mentally indifferent to what was going on. Dr Dering said that so far as he knew, that was the condition of the patients because it was 'routine'; that the surgeon did not do it; but that he had given orders that it should be carried out in the wards and had no reason to think it was not done. Again there was a great divergence of evidence. Would not an experienced doctor appreciate whether it had been given or not? And what would he think if he found the patient screaming, struggling, protesting? Would not that indicate that something must have gone wrong in the ward? Dr Dering said nothing untoward happened. Dr Grabczynski, in so far as he helped, agreed.

The jury should contrast what was said on behalf of Dr Dering with what the victims said. All except one remembered vividly one or more aspects of the operation. Some had been able to tell what they said to Dr Dering and what Dr Dering said to them, and to give a description of seeing something reflected in the theatre table lamp.

It did not end there, for Dr Klodzinski had said that he had gone into the theatre on one occasion to watch Dr Dering removing a testicle, and had found queuing up outside a number of young Jewish men to whom he spoke. Could they have had premedication if that was true? How came it that, for an operation of this kind, men were queuing up for their turn? Some of the jury might remember in their early Army days having to queue up for injections, but that was about as near as we could get in modern England to queuing up for an operation. *This* was an operation for testicle removal. If it did happen, what did the jury think of the surgeon who allowed that?

Dr Dering had said that he had to do these operations because the Germans said he had to: but he had never suggested that the Germans told him how to do them, or that he was to make the young men queue up, or that he was not to give any morphia beforehand, or that they interfered with his surgical method. So the jury had to ask themselves what was the truth, and then decide how far the defendants had substantiated the allegation that these operations were carried out with callousness and brutality.

The most astonishing thing was this: on the evidence there was no reason to think that Dr Dering was brutal to ordinary patients in the hospital. Why did he choose to be brutal to these people—the young, who had done nothing wrong, and who had been treated by the Germans as they had been? The defendants said that it was typical of the behaviour of an anti-Semite towards victims whom he regarded as a lower form of life which could be ill-treated without any moral consequence. Dr Dering said that when you looked at it like that, it just did not make sense that he should pick on these particular patients and treat them in a brutal way.

MODE OF PERFORMANCE

The actual surgery was a matter of technical knowledge. Basically the issue was between the recollections of Dr Dering and Dr Grabczynski on the one hand, and Dr Brewda on the other, for they were the only people present at the operations on the girls who had any idea of the surgical problems involved.

One thing the jury might note; and that was that, so far as the young men were concerned, there was no suggestion that Dr Dering did not operate competently. Most of them had said that they were back at work within a couple of months. The picture with regard to the young women, said the defendants, was entirely different. One might well ask why? *Why* should he have chosen to operate in an incompetent butcher-like way on the young girls and seemingly competently on the young men? Dr Dering might say that that showed that he did not operate in a butcher-like manner on the young women. Again it was for the jury to say.

The defendants said that there was a strong corroboration of Dr Brewda's evidence from Professor Nixon, so it was just as well to review the major points of the evidence, first, as to what went on in the theatre itself and, secondly, what happened after the operations.

At once you came up against a monumental conflict. Dr Brewda said she was there and saw what happened; that she watched the incision being made, saw the general manner of the surgeon, and knew how long the operations had taken. Dr Dering said bluntly, 'It is a lie because she was not there to see'. Dr Grabczynski, less passionately said, 'She may have brought the patients into the theatre or taken them out, but she was not there while they were going on'. The jury had to resolve that one.

Then Dr Brewda said that, having seen what happened, and being herself a gynaecological surgeon, she concluded that the operations were done badly, and so rapidly, and with such a small incision, that they could not have been done properly. Her broad conclusions appeared to be derived principally from the speed.

Now the question of speed was one on which the jury should

perhaps be a little chary. Dr Brewda said they had been done in ten to twelve minutes; Dr Dering agreed; Professor Nixon said that an operation of this kind by a skilled surgeon would take fifteen to twenty minutes. That was only three minutes' difference —and no one had been there with a stop watch. The jury had heard that there were different schools of surgery, some continental surgeons operating faster than British surgeons. Was the evidence about the speed of operation all that reliable? But there it was.

The jury should, however, also remember what Professor Nixon had told the court, and remember who he was. He had, in 1964, examined eight of the ten girls operated on, and it was right to recall something of what he had said. Some of the girls still had signs of irradiation burns. He had looked at the scars and measured them in terms of his fingertips. He was asked how these scars compared with those he would expect to find in England after irradiation and his answer was, 'I have practised surgery in China, Africa and the Middle East and I have never seen such scars as I saw last week in all my surgical life'. On the length of the incision he said, 'It would have been absolutely impossible with a one-inch incision to get down deep without doing the operation "blind" '. When he was asked if his answer depended on the nationality of the surgeon, he replied, 'I would not have thought it had any association with that at all. It is just crude, bad surgery'.

Of course, it was said that the proper thing was to judge these operations by the surgical standards of Auschwitz in 1943 and not by University College Hospital standards in 1964. The jury should bear that in mind. Professor Nixon had also said that if the proper surgical process was not carried out there was a danger of internal haemorrhage—and that was exactly what happened.

Why should Dr Dering have performed the operations on these girls so crudely? The jury might like to consider this suggestion. According to Dr Brewda, 'Schumann sent for me to come over to Block 21'. Was there any significance to be attached to that fact? In the ordinary way Dr Schumann could not have had much interest in the reaction of patients; but he was there to get these pathological specimens for his laboratory and, apparently, was present part of the time. If he was faced in the theatre with screaming, struggling girls, it must have been rather difficult to get on with the job of getting the pathological material. Sometimes even men like Schumann could not stomach young girls screaming. Did he send for Dr Brewda to get a bit of quiet in the theatre? Was that why she was there? The first girl, so far as one could see now, did not have any post-operative complications. The others did. Was there a possibility that what happened was that, quite apart from Dr Schumann not being able to stand the screaming and hysterics, Dr Dering could not either? The jury might take the view, having heard and seen Dr Dering and Dr Brewda, that there could not be anything in the suggestion because Dr Brewda just was not there anyway. But there it was.

As to the post-operative condition of the girls, the evidence was that their recovery took two to three months. The defendants did appear to have exaggerated somewhat when, in their particulars, they said that some were there until the autumn of 1944. But to have been in bed for two to three months was bad enough. What happened? The girls, with one exception, said that they had considerable trouble over the healing of their wounds. All the girls, and Dr Brewda, and Dr Lorska, said that Bella died on the night of the operation. What did happen to Bella? Did she die? The jury might think it likely that she did. Why did she die? Dr Brewda said that it was an internal haemorrhage, and Professor Nixon said he would think that that was so. What had caused the internal haemorrhage? Dr Brewda thought that it was because the stump had not been covered properly, and Professor Nixon was inclined to agree. Anyway, she died. The jury must ask themselves why. This was not a very complicated operation. She did not die of infection; so if Bella did die, what was the cause?

That was not the end of the matter, because according to some of the girls and Dr Brewda, another girl called Buena died two or three days later. Did she? The particulars said that a third girl had died. That had been utterly inaccurate, for, by the grace of God, eight of these unfortunate ten girls were still living today. But the jury might think that two deaths out of ten was appallingly high.

Then the picture these girls gave was of actual pain, illness, fever, suffering in the wound—and one girl's evidence of seeing Dr Dering when he came to look at them and who described her reaction when she saw Dr Dering near her bed talking to Dr Brewda, and making with his hands a sort of discarding gesture.

How reliable was the scene painted by the girls and Dr Brewda?

Dr Dering said that it just did not begin to be reliable. He said that the operations on these girls were just ordinary simple operations; that the girls went off to Block 10; he was not worried about them and there was no reason why he should be. He knew that there were doctors who would give them proper attention and that they had proper dressings on their wounds; and that there was no reason for not adopting the ordinary practice of turning up five days after; and that that was exactly what happened. When after five days he went to Block 10, he said, 'I was surrounded by several—at least six—nice young pleasant girls who were very friendly—including Dr Brewda herself—and they just joked with me. I looked at the patients. No fever. No dirty wounds. What should I do more? I was satisfied and I left'. He also said that nobody had died and that he saw 'all operated cases'. The defendants said that could not be true because, on any view, Bella had died. Again this was something on which there was a great conflict, and on which they must decide how far Dr Dering was reliable and Dr Brewda or the girls wrong.

The jury must decide what the facts were and then consider whether they justified the sting of the libel. If they did, the jury should return a verdict for the defendants.

If the jury found that the defendants had failed to prove justification, the next problem was what damage had been done to Dr Dering's reputation. In that connection the jury should consider the circumstances of publication, in the hard-back edition—not the paper-back edition—of a novel. They should put out of their minds that it was said that this novel had been made into a film. The damage to reputation could go on, depending on the conduct of the trial, right up to the moment when the jury retired.

It was sometimes said that, if a jury took the defendants' conduct into consideration the damages they awarded were 'exemplary' damages with a punitive element, 'This amount out of your pocket may teach you not to do it again'.

If they did conclude that, in this case, there ought to be exemplary damages, they must still keep control on common sense.

The jury had to make up their minds whether this case came where Lord Gardiner said—a near miss—or where Mr Duncan said: an outrageous attack on a man who did his best. The truth must be somewhere between those limits. The jury should award a reasonable sum.

The Judge said that he could do no more for them. It was for them. It was for them to do what was fair, just and reasonable. They should take as long as they liked. It was a very difficult problem.

'Members of the jury, will you now retire and consider your verdict.'

The Judge had forgotten something, and Lord Gardiner rose to his feet.

'May I remind your Lordship,' said Lord Gardiner, 'to direct the jury as to the specific questions?'

The Judge immediately supplied the omission. He told the jury: You will, first of all find whether the verdict is for the plaintiff or the defendants; if for the plaintiff, how much?

The summing up occupied a little under five hours.

CHAPTER XXIII

Verdict

THE jury retired with their burden of documents and the register at 11.55 a.m.[1]

At 2.28 p.m. the bell from the distant jury room buzzed in court. The jury filed back into the two narrow benches at 2.30 p.m. The Associate asked which of the jury was the foreman, and a middle-aged man in the centre of the front row stood up and said, 'I am'.

The Associate: Are you all agreed on your verdict?

The Foreman: We are.

The Associate: Do you find for the plaintiff or for the defendants?

The crowded court was suddenly silent.

The Foreman: For the plaintiff.

The Associate: What sum do you award the plaintiff against the defendants?

The Foreman: One Ha'penny.

There was a gasp, and sudden movement everywhere in the court and in the Press box.

The Associate: And that is the verdict of you all?

The Foreman: Yes.

[1] The Judge immediately began the next action in his list (a week-long jury trial for libel about the business methods of a mail order company and its managing director, to whom a different jury awarded £15,000 damages against a newspaper), which was interrupted for the final stages of *Dering* v. *Uris and Others*.

CHAPTER XXIV

Judgment and Costs

THE author and publishers had a verdict against them, and 'costs normally follow the event'.

Immediately, and surprisingly, Lord Gardiner for the defendants was on his feet. 'The plaintiff', he said, 'will have judgment for a halfpenny. The costs are within your Lordship's discretion.' He added that the usual practice was that, in exercising that discretion, 'all the circumstances should be considered'; and, in cases like this, where a jury awarded contemptuous damages, the customary exercise of the judicial discretion was to deprive the plaintiff of his costs, and it was not unusual to award the defendants their costs.[1] In addition, the £500 which the printers had paid Dr Dering on 2 May 1963 had to be taken into consideration, and, in accordance with Order 82 rule 4 of the Rules of the Supreme Court[2], that sum had to be deducted from the sum awarded to Dr Dering. Quite apart from that, there was the sum of forty shillings paid into court by the publishers on 19 March 1964 which Dr Dering had not elected to take out before the trial. That was 39s. 11½d. more than the jury had awarded. Accordingly, judgment should, in any event, be entered for the defendants, with costs.

Mr Neill, for Dr Dering, questioned Lord Gardiner's interpretation of the rule. It did not mean that the £500 was to be 'set off' against the award of the jury, but did mean that the amount for which the plaintiff could execute judgment was diminished by the £500. It followed that Dr Dering was entitled to the award of ½d. damages made by the jury; but he could obviously not execute for any sum in excess of the £500 recovered from the printers. Although the publishers had paid forty shillings into court before trial, the author had paid nothing into court. Mr Uris had a verdict against him; and even if, under the ordinary rules, Dr Dering

[1] Fraser on Libel, page 197. [2] See Appendix, page 282n.

had to pay the publishers' costs after the date of payment in, that rule did not apply to Mr Uris. He could not take advantage in a roundabout way of the fact that a sum of money had been paid in by the publishers. Judgment should be entered for Dr Dering, with costs against Mr Uris.

The Judge: How do I enter judgment for the plaintiff for the sum of ½d. less £500?

Mr Neill submitted that the judgment which now had to be considered was as against the author and publishers only. Dr Dering had already recovered judgment against the printers for £500.

The Judge said that this was all highly technical. What had Mr Neill to say about the way the judicial discretion should be exercised?

Mr Neill said that it was not really technical. The difficulty here had been created by Mr Uris who had not taken the same step as the publishers. The judicial discretion should be exercised by making 'no order as to costs'. A more penal order than that against Dr Dering would not be justified.

Lord Gardiner submitted that Order 82 rule 4 was designed expressly to cover such a case as this. There could not be judgment for the plaintiff if ½d. had to be set off against £500. Judgment could not be entered for the plaintiff for 'Nothing'.

The Judge: 'Having heard Lord Gardiner and Mr Neill, I have come to the conclusion that, on the proper construction of the rules, I should enter judgment for the plaintiff for the sum of ½d., and, in the exercise of my discretion, having considered the nature of the case and the conduct of the parties, justice will be done by each party paying its own costs. The sum of 39s. 11½d. in court will be paid out to the second defendants' solicitors.'

There was a stir of consternation. Lord Gardiner was on his feet again. That order could not, on any view, be right, he submitted—for the publishers it would mean paying their own costs after the date of payment in. The author and publishers were joint tortfeasors. Before Order 82 rule 4 came into force a plaintiff could not effectively settle with one joint tortfeasor in libel because that ended the cause of action. The new rule was made entirely in the interest of a plaintiff, so that he could settle with one such defendant, take the money out, and then go on against any other. If the money received was a fair assessment of the damage caused by the joint publication, but the plaintiff thought it was not sufficient, he went on and took the risk of not getting his costs.

The Judge: Let us deal with it by stages. I have made up my mind that there should be judgment for the plaintiff for ½d. I have also made up my mind that, on the basis of what I have said, Mr Uris ought to pay his own costs. I am concerned about the publishers.

Lord Gardiner again said that this was a joint publication, and Dr Dering could at any time have taken out of court a sum very much larger than the sum he had been awarded.

The Judge said that costs followed the event unless there were some quite outstanding circumstances.

Lord Gardiner: —up to the date of payment in. But after that the defendants are entitled to their costs, because the plaintiff could then have obtained all and more than the jury awarded him.

The Judge: But he could still have gone on against Mr Uris.

Lord Gardiner: Then he would have had to deduct £502.

The Judge: It is a bit of a tangle!

Further procedural argument followed; and, at its conclusion, the Judge gave judgment for Dr Dering for the sum of one halfpenny, ordered that Mr Uris and the publishers should have the costs of the action after 19 March 1964, that Dr Dering should have no costs up to that date, and gave his reasons for making that order.[1]

Mr Neill asked for leave to appeal against the order for costs. [Costs being a discretionary matter, leave to appeal was necessary.]

The Judge: No, I do not give leave.

The jury had meanwhile sat glumly in the jury box. They had no further part to play, and were waiting only for the customary expression of thanks and indication from the Bench that they would not be required to serve on a jury for a specified number of years,[2] and their formal release. The formalities were omitted. During the Judge's temporary retirement from court, while the documents in the case were cleared from the benches, the representative from the Polish Embassy recovered the register, and counsel moved out of their rows, the jury left the box where they had sat patiently for nearly eighteen days, and went about their daily business.

[1] See Appendix, pages 282–5.

[2] The jurors were, in fact, discharged from further jury service for five years.

APPENDIX

I. DIARY OF THE TRIAL

Day 1. 13 April 1964. Monday. Case opened by Mr Duncan. Dr Dering begins giving evidence-in-chief.

Day 2. 14 April. Tuesday. Dr Dering's evidence-in-chief concluded. Cross-examination begins.

Day 3. 15 April. Wednesday. Dr Dering's cross-examination continued.

Day 4. 16 April. Thursday. Dr Dering's cross-examination concluded. His re-examination. Dr Hewer's evidence. Evidence of three Polish witnesses.

Day 5. 17 April. Friday. Dr Grabczynski.

Day 6. 20 April. Monday. Dr Mezyk. Lord Gardiner opens case for defence. The first woman. The second woman.

Day 7. 21 April. Tuesday. The first man. Herr Langbein. Dr Klodzinski. The third woman gives evidence-in-chief and her cross-examination begins.

Day 8. 22 April. Wednesday. The third woman breaks down. Dr Ebsworth. The fourth woman. The fifth woman. The sixth woman.

Day 9. 23 April. Thursday. The Judge addresses the 'Gentlemen of the Press'. Two telegrams from Poland. Legal argument and ruling on the supplementary particulars of justification in absence of jury. The seventh woman, 'Marta'. The second man. The eighth woman's evidence-in-chief begins.

Day 10. 24 April. Friday. The eighth woman's evidence concluded. Discussion on Judeo-Spanish. The third man. The fourth man. The fifth man. Dr Lorska gives evidence-in-chief and her cross-examination begins. Judge tells jury to take *Exodus* home over week-end and read paragraph complained of in its context of sixteen pages.

Day 11. 27 April. Monday. Dr Lorska's evidence concluded. Dr Brewda's evidence-in-chief begins. Interruption for evidence from the sixth man *in camera*. Dr Brewda's cross-examination begins.

Day 12. 28 April. Tuesday. Dr Brewda's evidence concluded.

Day 13. 29 April. Wednesday. Professor Nixon. Sir Brian Windeyer. Dr Hautval. Dr Dering begins evidence in rebuttal.
Day 14. 30 April. Thursday. Legal discussion in absence of jury.
Day 15. 1 May. Friday. Court sits at 2 p.m. Dr Dering's evidence in rebuttal concluded.
Day 16. 4 May. Monday. Lord Gardiner's final speech. Mr Duncan begins final speech.
Day 17. 5 May. Tuesday. Mr Duncan's final speech concluded. Judge begins summing up.
Day 18. Judge completes summing up. Jury retire at 11.55 a.m. Jury return with verdict at 2.30 p.m. Decision on judgment and costs.

2. WRIT

1962.—D.—No. 1281

IN THE HIGH COURT OF JUSTICE
QUEEN'S BENCH DIVISION

BETWEEN

WLADYSLAW ALEXANDER DERING	Plaintiff
and	
LEON URIS	First Defendant
WILLIAM KIMBER AND COMPANY LIMITED	Second Defendants
PURNELL & SONS LIMITED	Third Defendants

ELIZABETH THE SECOND by the Grace of God, of the United Kingdom of Great Britain and Northern Ireland and of Our other Realms and Territories Queen, Head of the Commonwealth, Defender of the Faith, To
Leon Uris of 575 Madison Avenue, New York, United States of America
William Kimber & Co. Limited of 46 Wilton Place, S.W.1 in the County of London
and Purnell & Sons Limited of 1 Portpool Lane, W.C.1, in the County of London
WE COMMAND YOU, That within eight days after the service of this Writ on you, inclusive of the day of such service, you do cause an

appearance to be entered for you in an action at the suit of Wladyslaw Alexander Dering
And take notice, that in default of your so doing, the Plaintiff may proceed therein, and Judgment may be given in your absence.

Witness, REGINALD EDWARD BARON DILHORNE, Lord High Chancellor of Great Britain, the 22nd day of June, in the year of Our Lord One thousand nine hundred and sixty-two.
THE PLAINTIFF'S CLAIM is for damages for libel contained in page 155 of a book entitled 'Exodus' written by the First-named Defendant, published by the Second-named Defendants, and printed by the Third-named Defendants.
This Writ was issued by Wright & Bull whose address for service is 25 Old Buildings, Lincolns Inn, W.C.1, in the County of London, Solicitors for the said Plaintiff, who resides at 4 Hamilton Road, Ealing, W.5, in the County of Middlesex.

3. STATEMENT OF CLAIM

1. The Plaintiff is a registered medical practitioner who is in partnership as a general practitioner in England.
2. The first-named Defendant is the author, the second-named Defendants are the publishers and the third-named Defendants are the printers of a book entitled 'Exodus' which was first published in 1959 and has had a wide circulation throughout the United Kingdom.
3. On page 155 of the said book the first-named Defendant falsely and maliciously wrote and caused to be published, the second-named Defendants falsely and maliciously published, and the third-named Defendants falsely and maliciously printed and published of and concerning the Plaintiff and of and concerning him and his said profession the following words: 'Here in Block X, Dr Wirthe used women as guinea-pigs and Dr Schumann sterilized by castration and X-ray and Caluberg removed ovaries and Dr Dehring performed seventeen thousand "experiments" in surgery without anaesthetic'. The Plaintiff will refer at the trial to the whole of the said book for its full term and effect.
4. The Plaintiff will contend that the said words in relation to Dr Dehring referred to him, since at the time referred to in the said words, the Plaintiff was a prisoner-doctor at Auschwitz and the

said Dr Wirthe, Dr Schumann and Caluberg were among his associates.

5. By reason of the publication of the said words the Plaintiff has been gravely injured in his character, credit and reputation and in the way of his said profession and has been brought into public scandal, odium and contempt.

AND the Plaintiff claims against the Defendants and each of them:—DAMAGES.

P. COLIN DUNCAN

Delivered . . . this 21st day of December, 1962 . . .

4. DEFENCE OF THE AUTHOR [AND PUBLISHERS]

1. Paragraphs 1 and 2 of the Statement of Claim are admitted.
2. It is admitted that on page 155 of the said book the First Named Defendant [the Second Named Defendants] published the words complained of in paragraph 3 of the Statement of Claim, and it is admitted that the said words are defamatory of the Plaintiff.
3. The said words are true in substance and in fact, subject to the exceptions particularized hereunder. Particulars of Justification exceeding 3 folios will be delivered separately.

PARTICULARS OF EXCEPTIONS

(1) This Defendant [These Defendants], while alleging that the Plaintiff performed a very large number of 'experimental' operations on both men and women, does not seek to support the precise figure of 17,000.

(2) This Defendant [These Defendants], while alleging that the Plaintiff performed the said operations under only a spinal anaesthetic (in itself causing great pain and administered contrary to the normal pre-war practice in Germany where such spinal injections were preceded by a preliminary relatively painless spinal injection in the proposed track of the main injection), so that the subject was conscious throughout, does not allege that the operations were performed entirely without anaesthetic.

(3) It is alleged that the said operations took place in the operating theatre in Block 21 and not Block 10 at Auschwitz Concentration Camp.

(4) This Defendant [These Defendants] will, if necessary, rely on section 5 of the Defamation Act, 1952.

(5) Paragraph 5 of the Statement of Claim is denied.

DAVID C-H. HIRST

Delivered this 22nd day of February 1963 by Kaufman & Seigal, of 72 New Cavendish Street, London, W.1, Solicitors for the First Defendant [13th day of December 1962, by Rubinstein Nash & Co., of 5/6 Raymond Buildings, Gray's Inn, London, W.C.1, Solicitors for the Second Defendants].

5. [AMENDED] PARTICULARS OF JUSTIFICATION, and FURTHER AND BETTER PARTICULARS OF DEFENCE [OF EXCEPTIONS]

These are summarized in the text, page 18 to page 21.

6. 'THE TIMES' 3 MAY 1963

LAW REPORT, May 2.

HIGH COURT OF JUSTICE: QUEEN'S BENCH DIVISION
PRINTERS APOLOGISE
DERING v. URIS AND OTHERS
Before MR. JUSTICE SALMON

The settlement was announced of an action so far as it was brought against Purnell & Sons Ltd., in this libel action by Dr Wladyslaw Alexander Dering, practising in Finsbury Park, against Mr Leon Uris, the author, William Kimber & Co. Ltd., the publishers, and Purnell & Sons Ltd., the printers of the book *Exodus*, arising out of a passage in that book.

Mr Colin Duncan, Q.C. appeared for the plaintiff; Mr James Evans for Purnell & Sons Ltd.

Mr DUNCAN said that the plaintiff was a registered medical practitioner in partnership as a general practitioner in England.

The three defendants were the author, the publishers, and the printers of a well-known book entitled *Exodus* which was first published in 1959 and had a wide circulation throughout the United Kingdom. In that book, it was stated that during the last war Dr

Dering 'performed seventeen thousand "experiments" in surgery without anaesthetic' at a German concentration camp. The third defendants had stated that, at the time when *Exodus* was first published, they were unaware of the plaintiff's existence or that the allegation complained of was capable of being understood to refer to him. Their attention having been drawn to the matter, they had not sought to substantiate the allegation. In these circumstances the plaintiff had accepted the retraction and apology offered him by the third defendants for having printed such a damaging and distressing allegation.

With regard to the first and second defendants, the plaintiff's action would, of course, continue. The third defendants were here by their counsel today to make public their retraction and apology. In addition, they had agreed not to print any further copies of the book save with the omission of the offending passage and to pay the plaintiff a substantial sum by way of damages and an agreed sum in respect of the expense to which he had been put in this matter. When counsel for the third defendants had addressed the Court, his Lordship would be asked for leave for the record to be withdrawn so far as the third defendants were concerned.

Mr EVANS said that on behalf of the third defendants he endorsed everything that had been said. The third defendants welcomed this opportunity to withdraw the allegation complained of and to express their sincere apologies to the plaintiff for having printed it.

Mr DUNCAN asked that the record be withdrawn so far as the third defendants were concerned and that the plaintiff's costs of this application and of making the statement be taxed as agreed, and paid by the third defendants.

The record was withdrawn so far as the third defendants were concerned.

Solicitors.—Messrs. Wright & Bull; Messrs. Oswald Hickson, Collier & Co.

7. [QUEEN'S BENCH DIVISION]

DERING *v.* URIS AND OTHERS

1964
Apr. 23

LAWTON J.

[1962 D. 1281]

Libel and Slander—Justification—Particulars—Further and better particulars—Plaintiff's case closed—Whether supplementary particulars deliverable.

Practice—Pleadings—Defence—Particulars—Application—Admission of supplementary particulars.

In an action for libel, in which the defence was justification, particulars had been delivered, and the plaintiff and his witnesses had given evidence, particulars relevant to justification previously unknown to the defendants became available to them from witnesses who had recently come from overseas for the purpose of giving evidence. The detail of the fresh particulars had, accordingly, not been put to the plaintiff or *X.*, one of his witnesses, who had returned overseas. The defendants, undertaking to pay the costs of recalling *X.*, if the plaintiff was so advised, applied for leave to deliver supplementary particulars of justification.

Held that, taking a commonsense view of such detail, and bearing in mind the difficulties, and being fair to the plaintiff, no injustice would follow, and, accordingly, the application was granted and leave given for the supplementary particulars to be delivered.

APPLICATION.

The facts sufficiently appear from the judgment.

Colin Duncan Q.C. and *Brian Neill* for the plaintiff.

Lord Gardiner Q.C., *David Hirst* and *Louis Blom-Cooper* for the author and publishers.

The following cases were cited in argument: *Lewis* v. *Daily Telegraph Ltd.*[1]; *Scott* v. *Sampson*[2]; *Hobbs* v. *Tinling*[3]; and *Speidel* v. *Plato Films Ltd*[4].

LAWTON J. reviewed the circumstances leading up to the application,[5] referred to the submissions, and continued: I have considered the draft supplementary particulars of justification, and I have borne in mind the submissions made to me. I have come to the conclusion that all the matters are relevant to the plea of justification. They all tend to show the circumstances in which the operations were performed, the manner of performing, the frame of mind of the plaintiff when he did perform them, and the desirability or otherwise of having a general anaesthetic for the performance of these operations.

It seems to me that one must take a commonsense view of detail of this kind, bearing in mind the difficulties, and being fair to the

[1] [1964] A.C. 234, H.L. (E.) [2] [1882] 8 Q.B.D. 491.
[3] [1929] 2 K.B. 1. [4] [1961] A.C. 1090, H.L.
[5] See pages 30–32.

1964
Apr. 23

LAWTON J.

plaintiff. It is an unusual case—unusual circumstances. It seems to me that I am justified, in all the circumstances, in taking what in a libel action may be a somewhat unusual course.

In order that there shall be no embarrassment to the plaintiff I have made it a condition that Lord Gardiner should give an undertaking that the defendants will pay the costs of bringing Dr Grabczynski back to this country to deal with these matters if Mr Duncan so advises the plaintiff. Lord Gardiner has given that undertaking to the court. In the circumstances, taking a broad view of it, I am satisfied that no injustice will follow. Accordingly I allow the supplementary particulars of justification to be delivered.

Order accordingly.
Plaintiff's costs of the application in any event.

Solicitors: *Wright & Bull, Kaufman & Seigal, Rubinstein Nash & Co.*

L.N.W.

8. [QUEEN'S BENCH DIVISION]

DERING *v.* URIS AND OTHERS.*

1964

Apr. 13, 14, 15, 16, 17, 20, 21, 22, 23, 24, 27, 28, 29, 30; *May* 1, 4, 5, 6.

[1962 D. 1281.]

Libel and Slander—Payment into court—Joint defendants—Payment of £500 damages by one of three defendants accepted by plaintiff—Payment into court of £2 by second defendant not accepted by plaintiff—No payment into court by third defendant—Plaintiff awarded ½d. *damages by jury—Whether plaintiff entitled to judgment—Costs—R.S.C., Ord.* 82, *r.* 4 (2).

Costs—Payment into court—Joint defendants—Libel—Payment of £2 by one of two active defendants—Record withdrawn against third defendant—Plaintiff awarded ½d. *damages—Whether both active defendants entitled to recover costs.*

In an action for libel against the author, the publishers and the printers of a novel, the record against the printers was withdrawn following a retraction and apology in open court and payment of £500 and costs to the plaintiff, but the author and publishers pleaded justification in identical defences, and the action against them was continued. Some weeks before the trial the publishers alone paid £2 into court. After a trial occupying 18 days the jury awarded the plaintiff ½d. damages. The author and publishers contended that, having regard to the payment of £500 and the payment in of £2, they were entitled to judgment under R.S.C., Ord. 82, r. 4 (2),[1] and to the costs of the action. On the plaintiff contending, inter alia,

[1] R.S.C., Ord. 82, r. 4 (2): " Where in an action for libel " ... against several defendants " sued jointly the plaintiff . . . " accepts money paid into court " by any of those defendants in

1964

DERING *v.* URIS.

that R.S.C., Ord. 82, r. 4 (2), related solely to execution and asking that judgment be entered for the plaintiff:—

Held, that R.S.C., Ord. 82, r. 4 (2), related only to execution so that a plaintiff who had accepted a sum of money from one defendant was unable to levy execution in respect of an award against another defendant and recover more than the sum awarded after deducting the sum accepted; and that, accordingly, the plaintiff having accepted £500 and having been awarded ½d. was unable to levy execution against the author and publishers in respect of the ½d., but that judgment should be entered for the plaintiff for ½d.

Held, further, that, since the object of the rule relating to payment into court was to discourage a plaintiff from continuing an action after he had been offered fair compensation in all the circumstances of the case, and the plaintiff in this case had been paid £500 and offered £2 and was awarded ½d., the broad justice between the parties, and the proper order in respect of costs was that the author and publishers should have the costs of the action after the date of payment in, and that the plaintiff should be awarded no costs up to the date of payment in.

[Reported by L. NORMAN WILLIAMS, Esq., Barrister-at-Law.]

ACTION.

On June 22, 1962, the plaintiff, Wladyslaw Alexander Dering, began an action for damages for libel in respect of a statement in a novel entitled "Exodus" written by Leon Uris ("the author"), published by William Kimber & Co. Ltd. ("the publishers"). and printed by Purnell & Sons Ltd. ("the printers"), each of whom were defendants named in the writ. The record against the printers was withdrawn following, on May 2, 1963, a statement in open court (before Salmon J.) of retraction and apology by the printers and payment by them of £500 damages and costs to the plaintiff. The author and publishers, in identical defences, pleaded justification, of which particulars and amended particulars were delivered, and the action against them proceeded to trial. On March 19, 1964, the publishers paid the sum of £2 into court. The author did not pay anything into court. The trial began before Lawton J. and a jury on April 13, 1964, and occupied 18 days. During the course of the trial, on April 23, 1964, the author and publishers applied for and were granted leave to deliver supplementary particulars of justification in respect of detailed evidence relevant to the plea of justification which came to their knowledge only after the arrival in this country of non-English

---

" satisfaction of his cause of " action against that defendant, " . . . the action shall be stayed " as against that defendant " only, but the sum paid into " court shall be set off against " any damages awarded to the " plaintiff against any other " defendant against whom the " action is continued."

1964

DERING
v.
URIS.

speaking witnesses who had been brought from various countries overseas for the purpose of giving evidence at the trial. On May 6, 1964, the jury awarded the plaintiff ½d. damages. Thereupon the author and publishers contended that, under R.S.C. Ord. 82 r. 4 (2) they were entitled to judgment, and sought an order in their favour for the costs of the action. This report is limited to the ruling on judgment and costs.

Colin Duncan Q.C. and *Brian Neill* for the plaintiff.
Lord Gardiner Q.C., *David Hirst* and *Louis Blom-Cooper* for the author and publishers.

No cases were cited in argument.

LAWTON J. I am now presented with a difficult problem, to make the order on the jury's verdict. In the ordinary way the problem would have been a simple one, the jury having found for the plaintiff but awarding him only ½d. damages. Had there not been complications by payments into court and the operation of R.S.C. Ord. 82, r. 4, I should have felt bound to enter judgment for the plaintiff, and to make no order as to costs.

The matter has been complicated in my judgment by the fact that two distinct payments have been made on behalf of the defendants. The printers, some time ago, made a payment to the plaintiff of £500. The publishers paid the sum of £2 into court. The author paid nothing into court.

Lord Gardiner has drawn my attention to the wording of R.S.C. Ord. 82, r. 4 (2), and the final words of that subparagraph are: ". . . but the sum paid into court shall be set off against any "damages awarded to the plaintiff against any other defendant "against whom the action is continued." He submits to me that that entitles the defendants in this case to judgment. Mr. Neill, on the other hand, says "No. All that that means is that, when it "comes to execution, the plaintiff cannot recover more than the "sum awarded, less the sum which he has accepted." It seems to me that on the construction of the rule that is right, and therefore the form of the order ought to be judgment for the sum of ½d. for the plaintiff, but execution cannot be levied against the defendants in respect of that ½d. because of what he has accepted.

Now comes the difficult problem of costs. The publishers have paid into court the sum of £2, which is 39s. 11½d. more than the plaintiff has recovered. That payment in was made some time ago. Lord Gardiner says on behalf of the publishers that, clearly, under the ordinary rules they are entitled to their costs after the date of payment in. On the other hand, Mr. Neill has pointed out that the author paid nothing into court. It is virtually impossible for a taxing master in an action such as this to divide up the costs between the author and the publishers. If I made any such order it would lead to further trouble between the parties.

I have got to look at this matter in the broad justice of the case, and the broad justice of the case, as I see it, is that the plaintiff some time ago got considerably more than the jury have awarded him. As the object of the payment into court rule is to discourage plaintiffs going on after they have been offered fair compensation in all the circumstances of the case it seems to me that in the exercise of my discretion, taking into consideration the policy of the rules, the proper order here, doing broad justice to the parties, is to say that there shall be judgment for the sum of ½d. for the plaintiff, that the author and publishers who have fought this action shall have the costs of the action after the date of payment in, and the plaintiff should have no costs up to the date of payment in.

Judgment for the plaintiff for ½d.
Costs to author and publishers after date of payment in.
Application for leave to appeal refused.

Solicitors: *Wright & Bull; Kaufman & Seigal; Rubinstein Nash & Co.*

9. NOTES ON GERMAN DOCTORS REFERRED TO IN EVIDENCE

BLANKENBURG, Dr Werner: Became head, at Hitler's Chancery, Berlin, of 'Euthanasia', and supplied staff for Auschwitz. On 29 April 1944 reported to Himmler that the work of 'Dr Horst Schumann on the influence of X-rays on human genital glands' for which Himmler had provided 'adequate material at Auschwitz' in achieving castration of males 'requires an effort which does not pay, as I have convinced myself operative castration requires not more than six to seven minutes and therefore can be performed more reliably and quicker than castration by X-rays'. [Trials of War Criminals: Nuremburg. Vol I. The Medical Cases, page 723.] Disappeared, and was not brought to trial.

CLAUBERG, Dr Carl: Born 1898. Chief physician of gynaecological clinic of the miners' hospital at Koenigshuette, Upper Silesia. On 30 May 1942 complained to Himmler of difficulties in procuring female concentration camp inmates for 'experiments' in the 'negative population policy', and asked that facilities at Auschwitz should be provided for experiments in sterilization without operation, to include 'occasional special billeting for five to ten women . . . corresponding to the conditions of sick rooms' and 'special X-ray apparatus'. Reported to Himmler on 7 June 1943: 'The method I contrived to achieve the sterilization of the female organs without operation is as good as perfected. It can be performed by a single injection made through the entrance of the uterus in the course of the customary gynaecological examination known to every surgeon'. Imprisoned by the Soviet authorities in 1945, he was returned to the German Federal authorities in 1955. On complaints from survivors was held during criminal investigation, and died while awaiting trial in 1957. [Trials of War Criminals: Nuremburg. Vol. I. The Medical Cases.]

ENTRESS, Dr Friedrich: Born 1914. S.S. Officer (*Hauptsturmfuehrer*). Camp doctor at Auschwitz from December 1941 to October 1943. Moved to Mauthausen as garrison doctor (*Standortarzt*). Condemned to death in May 1947 by United States Military Tribunal, and executed.

MENGELE, Dr Josef: Born 1911. S.S. Officer (*Hauptsturmfuehrer*). Volunteered to work in Auschwitz in 1943, and conducted 'experiments', particularly on Jewish twins. After the war escaped to live in Argentina. In June 1959 the German Federal authorities issued a warrant for his arrest, and applied for his extradition from Argentina; he fled from that country. Stripped of his degrees of Dr. Phil. and Dr. Med. by the Universities of Munich and Frankfurt-am-Main.

ROHDE, Dr Werner: Born 1904. S.S. Officer. Dentist 1929, doctor 1943, when he went to Auschwitz. Transferred to Struthof-Natzweiler Concentration Camp in Alsace on 1 July 1944, as garrison doctor (*Standortarzt*) with rank of Lieutenant (*Untersturmfuehrer*). In May 1946 arraigned with nine others before British Military Court for the trial of war criminals at Wuppertal for being directly concerned in the killing by injection, without any evidence of a court order, of four women, two British, one French, and one unidentified, captured by the Germans while working with Special Operations Executive in July 1944. Rohde pleaded: 'I obeyed my orders'. The Judge Advocate General (A. A. H. Marlowe, Q.C.), summing up, said: 'The one, you may think, who could have got out of it . . . was Rohde, apart from actual disobedience, because, as far as a doctor is concerned, there are a thousand and one ways of escaping a duty of this kind'. Only

Rohde was sentenced to death by hanging. [War Crimes Trials: The Natzweiler Trial (1949).]

SCHUMANN, Dr Horst: Born 1906. *Luftwaffe* medical officer. Conducted 'experiments' on possibility of castration of males and sterilization of females by X-ray at Auschwitz. Lived in German Federal Republic until after 1950 without criminal proceedings being instituted against him. Since that date has practised in various African States. Efforts to obtain his extradition were not successful. Deprived of his doctorate.

WIRTHS, Dr Eduard: Born 1909. S.S. Officer (*Sturmbannfuehrer*), and garrison doctor (*Standortarzt*) from September 1942 until Auschwitz camp was evacuated in 1945. Gave himself up to the British authorities in the summer of 1945, and committed suicide while in prison in September 1945.

INDEX